Critical Systems Thinking

Critical Systems Thinking

A Practitioner's Guide

Michael C. Jackson
University of Hull, Hull, UK

Library of Congress Cataloging-in-Publication Data Applied for:
Hardback ISBN: 9781394203574

Cover Design: Wiley
Cover Image: © Getty Images; © 4x6/Getty Images (Isolated businesswoman rear view)

Set in 9.5/12.5pt STIXTwoText by Straive, Pondicherry, India

SKY10074298_050324

Dedication

To my grandchildren –

Freddie, Henry, and Isaac.

In the hope that *Critical Systems Thinking* can help make the world a better place.

Hence people deny that Anaxagoras, Thales, and the wise of that sort are prudent ... and they assert that such men know things that are extraordinary, wondrous, difficult, and daimonic – yet useless too, because they do not investigate the human goods. But prudence [phronesis] is concerned with the human things and with those about which it is possible to deliberate. For we assert this to be the work of the prudent person especially – deliberating well – and nobody deliberates about things that cannot be otherwise, or about so many things as are without some end, an end, moreover, that is a good attainable through action. He who is a good deliberator simply is skilled in aiming, in accord with calculation, at what is best for a human being in things attainable through action.

(Aristotle, c. 340 BCE, *Nicomachean Ethics*, book 6, translated by R.C. Bartlett and S.D. Collins, University of Chicago Press, 2011)

Contents

Preface

I concluded the preface to my previous book with the statement: 'But it is definitely my last book'. I probably did the same in earlier books – I do not dare to look. Writing a book asks a lot of those close to you as you need to go 'missing' for an extended period. It is exhausting for the writer. There are other things you could be doing. So, what is the excuse for this new book?

I felt there was unfinished business. My previous book, *Critical Systems Thinking and the Management of Complexity* (Wiley, 2019), is a comprehensive overview of applied Systems Thinking (ST), demonstrating how Critical Systems Thinking (CST) could bring order to that diverse field and suggesting how best to use systems approaches in practice. I remain pleased with it, and it has been well received. The book is, however, 700 pages long and contains much (necessary for its purpose) historical and theoretical exposition. It sets a challenge to readers. Though it is one, I am assured, that is worth the effort. My only regret is that I did not manage to present a clear enough account of Critical Systems Practice (CSP) towards the end of that book. It is all there, and you cannot tie everything down, but that account could be better structured. This new book, *Critical Systems Thinking: A Practitioner's Guide*, seeks to address both these points. It is more accessible, shorter and dwells on history and theory only if essential. The book is designed to provide the most intelligible and direct account of how best to use CST in practice. To my mind, it complements the earlier book nicely.

I felt some frustration. It continues to amaze me that, in a world beset by many complex problems, there is so little recognition of what ST has to offer. From the 1940s to the 1970s, ST led the development of exciting new ideas. This was the era of the formation of the Society for General Systems Research, the Macy conferences on cybernetics, and the Gaither lectures at Berkeley. Systems practice helped transform the postwar Japanese economy (the Deming Management Method); put a man on the moon (Systems Engineering); was involved in such ambitious social experiments as the Norwegian Industrial Democracy Project (Sociotechnical Systems Thinking) and supporting the Allende government in Chile (the Viable

System Model); and was influential in the birth of the environmental movement (System Dynamics and 'limits to growth'). Today, it is rarely taught in universities and while there has been a resurgence of interest in ST, this is not accompanied by a knowledge of its history, the lessons it can impart, or the breadth and diversity of the systems tradition. I have been working on this for 45 years. I have written numerous books and articles and used ST at work and in consultancy. I have done my apprenticeship and earned my stripes. I have tried to do justice to the approach, but it seems that one more attempt is necessary.

I felt that introducing two new 'frameworks' could help me express what CST was about more clearly. The first of these I owe to Zhichang Zhu, who led me on a journey from 'paradigms to pragmatism', which at times was difficult for me. I had heard people say what a revelation and liberation it was to abandon the 'spectator theory of knowledge', seeking accurate representations of an underlying 'reality', and embrace the philosophy of pragmatism, in which theories are seen as instruments to guide action. I now know that this is the case. ST has strong pragmatist roots. I believe that, in this book, I have explained it better by paying homage to and enhancing those roots.

The second 'framework' I owe to Cathy Hobbs, who insisted that I provide greater clarity on the phases of CSP and that a mnemonic would help. We came up with *EPIC*, and Cathy supplied the first version of the diagram I use to explain *EPIC*. It is difficult to capture how exactly systems practice should proceed because it needs to be innovative and flexible in response to the exigencies of the situation in which it is employed. The invention of the mnemonic prompted me to spell out what I thought could be achieved. *EPIC* is, of course, a label used with tongue firmly in cheek. It is meant to reinforce my insistence that CSP is an 'ideal type' of good systems practice. The concept of an 'ideal type' comes from the sociologist Max Weber. I adjust its meaning to make it relevant to practice and not just theory development. I see CSP as an abstract model of good systems practice, derived from research and experience. It cannot and is not supposed to be enacted in pure form in the real world. Its use will be different in every application. Nevertheless, it is essential to guide good systems practice, to reflect on what is occurring during an intervention and adjust as necessary, and to evaluate what has been achieved.

I felt a little unfulfilled. My previous books have been structured as accounts and reflections on the work of others, from which I sought to develop new ideas of my own. That is fine; you need to know a field thoroughly to make a useful contribution. Too much of what goes under the label ST, now that it is becoming popular again, shows little appreciation of what has gone before. It does not build on what has already been achieved or seek to learn from previous mistakes. At best, it ends up reinventing the wheel. That said, I remembered Russ Ackoff insisting that one day I should stop standing on the shoulders of giants and write a book where my own ideas controlled the narrative from beginning to end. In almost all cases, you should do what Russ advises, and I have attempted to do so. I hope he would approve.

I felt I might be abandoning some aspirations too early. In 1814, Wordsworth wrote about 'The French Revolution as It Appeared to Enthusiasts at Its Commencement': 'Bliss was it in that dawn to be alive, But to be young was very heaven!' I am a child of the 1960s and have always felt about that period in the same way. Revolution was in the air; minds were expanding; wars were opposed; imperialism was called out; global and class inequalities were challenged; movements for women's, black and LGBT+ rights were underway; and environmental awareness grew. The music certainly seemed better. Of course, there were issues, but some things did change. Not enough, though. I was talking to John Mingers and suggested we had made some small contribution to management science. He pointed out how trivial that was compared to the ambitions we held in the 1960s. He was right, but what do you say? I could only respond: 'Better carry on then'.

I felt that I should continue to 'rage against the dying of the light'. This is hard to escape when you have had cancer for 12 years, another major liver operation in 2021, and you are on a monthly drug regime. I am, incidentally, very lucky. I can still enjoy beer and walking. Hull Kingston Rovers are getting closer to the success that us fans, and especially the owner, Neil Hudgell, deserve. Hull City are improving. Yorkshire County Cricket Club could do with some ST. My everyday life remains largely unaffected, thanks to the NHS, modern medicine, and a skilled surgeon, Professor Peter Lodge. I really should not go 'gentle'.

In the acknowledgements in previous books, I have referred to many individuals, and I continue to owe them all a huge debt. Here I acknowledge, in addition, some organisations responsible for flying the flag for ST in the United Kingdom. The Open University Systems Group celebrated 50 years of teaching ST in 2021. It has been preeminent in spreading systems expertise through its teaching and the 'systems thinking in practice' (STiP) approach. Systems and Complexity in Organisation (SCiO) has gained government recognition as the professional body for systems thinkers. It was instrumental in launching the 'Systems Thinking Practitioner Apprenticeship', which has spread the teaching of ST to a wider range of universities and opened opportunities for in-work systems training. Of course, I must mention the Centre for Systems Studies at the University of Hull, which celebrated its 30th anniversary in 2022. It pioneered CST and, I would claim, continues to make significant intellectual advancements in the field leading to improved forms of systems practice. Its previous directors deserve a mention: (me), Bob Flood, Gerald Midgley, Jennifer Wilby, Yasmin Merali and Amanda Gregory. Under its current sole director, Amanda Gregory, it is undergoing a significant renaissance. I also wish to acknowledge three 'communities' that I have been involved with recently, which have helped me learn more about ST. I have a lecture series in my name at the University of Hull, kindly sponsored by Dr. Andrew and Mrs. Valerie Chen. I must prepare by reading the works of the guest lecturers so I can ask sensible questions. I have, as is obvious in this book, learned much from Andrea Wulf, Fritjof Capra, Debra Hammond, Peter Senge, Carlo Rovelli, Dave Snowden and Charles Foster. I worked with a community of systems thinkers to help prepare a report for the Alliance for Health Policy and Systems Research. This project has not yet come to fruition, but I am conscious that our many exchanges have infiltrated my thinking and this book. I therefore thank Cathy Hobbs, Patrick Hoverstadt, Martin Reynolds, Luis Sambo, Anne Stephens and Bob Williams. The third 'community' consists of Paul Barnett and the facilitators, guest presenters and participants on the first two cohorts of the 'Critical Systems Thinking and Management of Complexity' executive programme that I delivered with the Enlightened Enterprise Academy. Our discussions helped me immensely in refining my thinking for the book. You are all entitled to a free copy.

Sincere thanks to Laura Kenny for some insightful, as well as careful, copyediting. And Brett Kurzman, Becky Cowan and Vishal Paduchuru, as well as Hafiza Tasneem, the Wiley team who believed in the book and brought it to fruition.

Finally, to my dog Mollie, faithful friend of nearly 19 years, who died in 2023. She lived long enough to look at her own memorial stone, inserted into a drystone wall on the way to Beverley Westwood, where we walked most days. To my children, Christopher and Richard, who live happy and (almost) independent lives with their partners Tess and Dannie, and who have given Pauline and me, to date, three wonderful grandchildren. And, of course, to my fantastic wife, Pauline. Without her nothing that I do that is good would be possible. She has suffered most from me going 'missing' to write this book.

Michael C. Jackson
Beverley and Runswick Bay, January 2024

Acronyms

These acronyms are frequently used in the text and are not always spelled out:

CSH   Critical Systems Heuristics
CSL   Critical Systems Leadership
CSP   Critical Systems Practice
CST   Critical Systems Thinking
EPIC   *Explore, Produce, Intervene, Check*
GEMs   Gender equality, Environments and Marginalized voices Framework
IP   Interactive Planning
SAST   Strategic Assumption Surfacing and Testing
SD   System Dynamics
SE   Systems Engineering
SOSM   System of Systems Methodologies
SSM   Soft Systems Methodology
ST   Systems Thinking
STS   Sociotechnical Systems Thinking
VM   The Vanguard Method
VSM   The Viable System Model

All other acronyms are clearly spelled out close to where they occur.

Introduction

The source of our power lies in the extraordinary technological capital we have succeeded in accumulating and in propagating, and the all-pervasive analytic or positivistic methodologies which by shaping our minds as well as our sensibilities, have enabled us to do what we have done. Yet our achievement has, in some unforeseen (perhaps unforeseeable) manner, failed to satisfy those other requirements that would have permitted us to evolve in ways that, for want of a better word, we shall henceforth call 'balanced'.

(Özbekan, 1970)

This book seeks to help people take decisions to improve situations that are of concern to them. It does not seek to provide solutions but to provide guidance on taking better decisions, particularly in the face of complexity and uncertainty. In philosophy, the study of human action and conduct is called *praxeology*. This is often understood in the narrow sense of calculating the optimal means of achieving known ends. Humans have become very good at this and, as Özbekan said, have 'accumulated and propagated' 'extraordinary technological capital' in support. The danger, recognised by him, is that the 'analytic or positivistic methodologies' that have enabled us to develop these powerful technologies have shaped our thinking to the extent that we are increasingly their servants rather than their masters. A way of trying to protect against this is to broaden the study of human conduct to embrace Aristotle's notion of *prudence* (*phronesis*), which certainly involves some calculation but in relation to the broader purpose of investigating and pursuing 'the human goods' i.e., what is best for humankind. This requires, in Aristotle's terms, 'good deliberation'. Critical Systems Practice (CSP) is about how to carry out 'good deliberation', giving due attention to human requirements other than those that can be met by employing linear, mechanistic, means-end logic. Perhaps we can then evolve in a more 'balanced' way.

In developing this argument, I needed some 'catch-all' concepts. I use *Systems Thinking* (ST) to refer to all the various strands of thought and practice that make use of systems philosophies, theories, perspectives, methodologies, models, methods, concepts and ideas to understand and intervene in the world. This tradition of thought embraces, for me, Cybernetics and Complexity Theory as well as, for example, General Systems Theory, Systems Engineering, System Dynamics and Soft Systems Methodology. I am aware of the differences; indeed, my point is that they are all good at different things. But it helps to have a generic term. This goes for *Systems Approaches* too. To avoid endless lists, I use this concept to refer to all the various systems philosophies, theories, methodologies, etc., employed by those in the broad ST tradition.

The book has three parts. The first traces the emergence of Critical Systems Thinking (CST) and has three chapters. Chapter 1 outlines the achievements and limitations of the scientific method, suggesting that increasing awareness of these limitations and their consequences for humanity and the environment points to the need for ST as a complementary approach, especially in the realm of human affairs. Chapter 2 sets out the challenges this poses to ST and two ways in which it has tried to meet them. The first of these, the pursuit of general systems laws, flounders, because higher levels of complexity give rise to 'emergent properties' which cannot be explained with theories appropriate to lower levels of complexity. ST has been more successful in following a second route – developing a range of systems methodologies that engage with different aspects of complexity in different ways. However, this has led to fragmentation. Chapter 3 shows how CST has sought to restore order to a field in which different systems approaches came to be seen as competing. It does so by pointing to the strengths and weaknesses of the different approaches (systemic critique) and suggesting that they could be used in combination (systemic pluralism) to achieve wide-ranging systemic improvement. Systemic pragmatism provides the rationale and justification for CST.

Part 2 looks at how CST can be translated into practical action through the *EPIC* stages (*Explore, Produce, Intervene, Check*) of CSP. Chapter 4 provides an introductory overview, explains the role of *EPIC* as an 'ideal type' of systems practice and links CSP to some related approaches. Chapter 5 details the multiperspectival *Explore* phase and how it employs five insightful 'systemic perspectives' – mechanical, interrelationships, organismic, purposeful and societal/environmental – to surface the most important issues that need attending to in a situation of interest. Justification is provided for the choice of these five perspectives. Chapter 6 considers how best to *Produce* an intervention strategy to manage those issues. This rests upon an understanding of what different systems methodologies do well. Five types of systems methodology are identified: engineering, system dynamics, living, soft and emancipatory. Each type is related to one of the 'systemic perspectives' and prioritises the concerns it highlights. Example methodologies are described, and their mode of operation is clarified using case studies. Chapter 7 discusses *Intervene*, the third stage of CSP, considering how best to conduct a flexible multimethodological intervention in accordance with agreement on which systems methodologies, models and methods are best suited to addressing the issues of concern. Chapter 8 looks at *Check*. *EPIC* should be seen as an iterative process which continually identifies and manages new issues as they come to the fore. Nevertheless, attention must be given to evaluating progress both during an intervention and as it comes to an end. *Check* considers the best way of doing this from a CSP perspective.

Part 3 contains Chapter 9. This explains Critical Systems Leadership as an approach that can best take advantage of the current upsurge in interest in ST and overcome the barriers to successful implementation deriving from the way ST is presented and perceived and from various cultural and societal constraints.

The book is a 'practitioner's guide', and the busy reader can be excused for going straight to Parts 2 and 3, which explain CSP and how to succeed in applying it, but that would be a pity. CST has the broad purpose of enhancing 'good deliberation' in ways that will allow us to evolve in a more 'balanced way' and improve the world in which we live. CSP needs to be understood as a means of realising that ambition.

The structure of the book is summarised in the Table below.
The Structure of the Book.

Introduction	
Part 1: The Emergence of Critical Systems Thinking	Chapter 1: The Scientific Method
	Chapter 2: Systems Thinking
	Chapter 3: Critical Systems Thinking
Part 2: Critical Systems Practice	Chapter 4: Critical Systems Practice: An Overview
	Chapter 5: Critical Systems Practice 1 – *Explore* the Situation of Interest
	Chapter 6: Critical Systems Practice 2 – *Produce* an Intervention Strategy
	Chapter 7: Critical Systems Practice 3 – *Intervene* Flexibly
	Chapter 8: Critical Systems Practice 4 – *Check* on Progress
Part 3: Towards a Systems Thinking World	Chapter 9: Critical Systems Leadership: Overcoming the Implementation Barriers
Conclusion	

Reference

Özbekan, H. (1970). *The Predicament of Mankind, a Quest for Structured Responses to Growing World-Wide Complexities and Uncertainties: A Proposal to the Club of Rome*. University of Pennsylvania.

Part 1

The Emergence of Critical Systems Thinking

The most striking indication of the pathology of our species is the contrast between its unique technological achievements and its equally unique incompetence in the conduct of its social affairs.
(Koestler, A., 1979, *Janus: A Summing Up*. Pan Books)

Critical Systems Thinking: A Practitioner's Guide, First Edition. Michael C. Jackson.
© 2024 John Wiley & Sons, Inc. Published 2024 by John Wiley & Sons, Inc.

1

The Scientific Method

Inquire of ancient Wisdom; go, demand
Of mighty Nature, if 'twas ever meant
That we should pry far off yet be unraised;
That we should pore, and dwindle as we pore,
Viewing all objects unremittingly
In disconnection dead and spiritless;
And still dividing, and dividing still,
Break down all grandeur ...

(Wordsworth, 1814)

1.1 Introduction

This chapter outlines the achievements and limitations of the scientific method, beginning with a brief discussion of early Systems Thinking (ST) and how it was pushed to the margins of reputable thought by the success of the Scientific Revolution. The Scientific Revolution began in the sixteenth century with Copernicus's heliocentric account of the cosmos and was consolidated in the early seventeenth century with the establishment of the scientific method based upon mechanism and reductionism. Newton's *Principia*, published in 1687, marked its apotheosis. This was a revolution that encompassed remarkable developments in mathematics, physics, astronomy, chemistry and biology. It inspired the agricultural and industrial revolutions of the eighteenth century which transformed the world in which we live. The chapter goes on to discuss some of the limitations of the mode of thought underpinning the Scientific Revolution. Recognition of these limitations, and their consequences for humanity and the environment on which we depend, has led to a positive reassessment of the value of ST as a complementary approach to the traditional scientific method.

Critical Systems Thinking: A Practitioner's Guide, First Edition. Michael C. Jackson.
© 2024 John Wiley & Sons, Inc. Published 2024 by John Wiley & Sons, Inc.

1.2   Early Systems Thinking

ST has existed for millennia and emerged amongst peoples in all continents.

Indigenous communities, living in close interrelationship with the land and dependent on knowledge sharing for community well-being, produced the first ST. Yunkaporta provided an Aboriginal perspective:

> There are no isolated variables – every element must be considered in relation to the other elements and the context. Areas of knowledge are integrated, not separated. The relationship between the knower and other knowers, places and senior knowledge-keepers is paramount. It facilitates shared memory and sustainable knowledge systems. An observer does not try to be objective, but is integrated within a sentient system that is observing itself. (Yunkaporta, 2019, pp. 169–170)

Many Eastern philosophies evince a systems orientation. The Daoist *I Ching*, with its emphasis on dynamic changes of relationship between interconnected variables, is frequently cited as the oldest systems book. The Greeks introduced systems ideas into the Western tradition of thought. The pre-Socratic philosopher Heraclitus, with his theory of the unity of opposites, is often acknowledged as an influence by later systems thinkers. Aristotle was the first to articulate the systems mantra that 'the whole is more than the sum of its parts'. He went on to reason that the parts only obtain their meaning in terms of the purpose of the whole. For example, the parts of the body make sense because of the way they function to support the existence of the whole organism. Plato anticipated cybernetics, an important strand in contemporary ST, when he drew an analogy between the 'steersman' (*kybernetes*) of a vessel and of the ship of state.

Systems ideas continued to be prominent in later Western thought, for example, in the works of Kant and Hegel and the philosophical traditions of phenomenology and pragmatism. In the twentieth century, however, the influence of the Vienna Circle turned philosophy into a form of logical analysis designed to clear away ambiguity and confusion so that science could make better observations and decide what was and was not the truth. *Language, Truth and Logic* (1936), A.J. Ayer's manifesto of logical positivism, declared that discussions on metaphysical questions – about the nature of reality, existence, consciousness, for example – were nonsensical because they did not lead to hypotheses that were subject to empirical verification. In this tradition, arguments about ethical issues equated to nothing more than shouts of approval or disapproval. At Oxford University, according to Cumhaill and Wiseman (2023), it took four women, inspired by the later work of Wittgenstein, to bring philosophy back to life. Elizabeth Anscombe, Philippa Foot, Mary Midgley and Iris Murdoch were 'metaphysical animals' who saw philosophy as relevant to the whole of human life, not just to humans as calculating machines. Philosophy had to accept humans as part of the natural world, help them navigate their lives together in a particular historical period, suggest alternative ways of going on and re-engage with the language of morality.

It is important to consider why, given its provenance, ST went out of favour and has had so little influence and impact on the development of the modern world.

1.3   The Ascendancy of the Scientific Method

The human mind can engage with the world in a multiplicity of ways. Charles Foster's (2021) exploration of 40,000 years of human consciousness demonstrated this by examining what has been lost as the Upper Palaeolithic period transitioned into the Neolithic and Enlightenment worlds. Neolithic people began the 'divorce proceedings' between humans and nature by learning 'to draw lines'. They started to see themselves as distinct from the natural world and to try to control it. But in seeking to tame nature, they also enslaved themselves. As Foster put it. 'Thoughts as well as sheep were corralled'. People had to stay in settlements throughout the year to respond to the constant demands imposed by husbandry. With larger settlements came politics and hierarchy, and the rich Palaeolithic culture was reduced to the 'priest-curated stories of Stonehenge'. In Foster's account, it was Enlightenment thought that completed the process of estranging us from nature and our humanity by ridding the world of enchantment, conceiving of it as a machine and humans as economic units.

The Enlightenment is closely associated with the Scientific Revolution, which led to significant advances in knowledge in many fields. The success of the Scientific Revolution depended on the efforts of Francis Bacon and Galileo who, in the early years of the seventeenth century, established a well-defined scientific method. First, a phenomenon of interest is identified and studied. Second, a hypothesis is constructed suggesting what causes this phenomenon to occur. Third, predictions are formulated about how the elements involved will behave in the future. Fourth, carefully devised experiments are conducted to test these predictions, and the results of these are measured. The experiments must be clearly described so that they can be repeated by other scientists to check if they get the same outcomes. Finally, the results are analysed, and conclusions are drawn about the veracity of the hypothesis. On this basis, it seemed, the progress of science could be guaranteed.

The philosopher Descartes provided the justification for the notions of mechanism and reductionism upon which the scientific method is based. This relies on a mind–matter dualism whereby an immaterial mind can use rational thought, as exemplified in logic and mathematics, to reach conclusions about the workings of an independent mechanistic universe in which wholes are no more than the sum of their parts. Writing in 1637, Descartes reasoned that, if he wanted to understand the world and the problems it posed, he had

> ... to divide each of the difficulties that I was examining into as many parts as might be possible and necessary in order best to solve it [and] beginning with the simplest objects and easiest to know ... to climb gradually ... as far as the knowledge of the most complex. (Descartes, 1637/1968, pp. 40–41)

Logic is used to build back up from the properties of the parts to an understanding of the whole. In this way, humans can achieve certainty about the nature of reality.

In 1687, in the *Principia*, Newton provided mechanism with its affirmation, setting out his laws of motion and theory of universal gravitation, and uniting terrestrial and celestial mechanics. The universe, set in motion and sustained by God, operated like clockwork. It followed entirely predictable rules that could be fully comprehended by humans. In the eighteenth century, scientists refined and extended Newtonian mechanics and, in 1814, the mathematician Laplace asserted that Newton's laws could in principle be used to predict everything for all time if the current position and velocity of all particles in the universe were known (Mitchell, 2009). In the nineteenth century, the problem of extending Newton's laws of motion to systems involving multiple elements was overcome with developments in statistics and probability theory. In systems of disorganised complexity, because the average behaviour of elements corresponds closely to actual behaviour, it is unnecessary to predict what each element is doing. It became possible to apply Newtonian mechanics to thermal phenomena whether exhibited by solids, liquids or gases. This gave rise to thermodynamics and its fundamental laws of conservation and dissipation of energy. The second of these demonstrates that all isolated systems move from order to disorder as useful energy is lost in the form of friction or heat. Entropy, as a measure of disorder, gradually increases. The universe runs down as useful energy is dissipated.

By the close of the nineteenth century,

> ... scientists had developed two different mathematical tools to model natural phenomena – exact, deterministic equations of motion for simple systems; and the equations of thermodynamics, based on statistical analysis of average quantities, for complex systems. (Capra and Luisi, 2014, p. 104)

Physicists could be forgiven for a degree of hubris in believing that the scientific method, enabled by these tools, could be extended to other fields. It surely would not be long before chemical, biological and even social phenomena would succumb to mechanistic explanations and be seen as nothing but complicated expressions of the laws of physics. Michelson proclaimed, in 1894, that

> ... it seems probable that most of the grand underlying principles have been firmly established and that further advances are to be sought chiefly in the rigorous application of these principles to all phenomena which come under our notice. (quoted in Mitchell, 2009, pp. ix–x)

More pithily, Lord Rutherford, a fellow physicist, is reputed to have declared that: 'All science is either physics or stamp collecting'.

The scientific method, underpinning the advances made in the sciences, enabled massive improvements in agricultural yields and industrial productivity. Agricultural societies were rapidly transformed into manufacturing economies through the invention of new machines, methods and processes, as well as through the more efficient harnessing of energy resources. Urbanisation, improvements in the prevention and treatment of infectious diseases, and declining childhood mortality led to population growth and longer life expectancy. Increased industrial productivity made consumer goods plentiful and affordable. The standard of living of the general population gradually increased. A greater range of jobs became available, educational opportunities increased and suffrage was widened. Transportation improved as new roads, canals and railways were built. Shipping lines were opened, increasing international trade. New methods of communication were invented, and the world became a smaller place. It was reasonable to assume that progress would continue. Improvements in science and technology seemed to be leading the way inexorably to richer societies which provided safer, more fulfilling lives for their citizens.

ST did not seem to be necessary. So, what is wrong with the traditional scientific method? In exploring this, we need to consider the opposition it aroused among the 'Romantics', its lack of success in fields such as the life and social sciences and debates about its appropriateness even in the physical sciences.

1.4 Romanticism and Disquiet

The success of the Scientific Revolution ensured that mechanism and reductionism came to dominate Enlightenment thinking. This provoked outrage and opposition from those philosophers, writers and poets who marched together under the banner of 'romanticism'. The Romantics questioned science's reliance on reason alone which, they felt, separated life from art, humankind from nature and individuals from society. The philosopher Immanuel Kant was an important influence. He believed that Newtonian physics could provide universal truths, but this was because it restricted itself to elucidating what the human mind was capable of discerning through the senses. What existed beyond the scope of the senses was beyond science's ken, and Kant provided a warning to those who seek to extend its scope into the biological and human domains. He saw that it was impossible to provide a mechanical account of the vitality, growth and diversity found in nature: 'Are we in a position to say: *Give me matter and I will show you how a caterpillar can be created?*' (Kant, quoted in Mensch, 2013). An organismic approach, going beyond the realm of 'blind efficient causes', seemed essential in the life sciences. When it came to the study of human behaviour, Kant faced a difficulty even more severe than he encountered with nature. According to science, humans are subject to causal determinism, but this undermines the notion of free will, on which the whole of morality depends. To rescue morality, alongside belief in God and immortality, Kant placed human freedom in the realm of the 'noumena' – things capable of being inferred but beyond the reach of scientific knowledge:

> We have in the world beings of but one kind whose causality is teleological, or directed to ends, and which at the same time are beings of such character that the law according to which they have to determine ends for themselves is represented by themselves as unconditional and not dependent on anything in nature, but as necessary in itself. The being of this kind is man, but man regarded as noumenon. (Kant, quoted in Kemp, 1968, pp. 120–121)

Wulf (2022) traced the liberating influence of Kant's thought on the 'magnificent rebels' of the 'Jena Set' of romantic thinkers. To them, imagination rather than reason was the faculty of mind most in need of cultivation. Imagination brought the external world into being. Focussing too much on reason impoverished reality, stripping it of poetry, spirituality and feeling. The polymath Johann Wolfgang von Goethe was the most influential figure in the Jena Set. It has been argued that he developed a 'way of science' completely at odds with what became the mainstream:

> ... there is the possibility that there could be a different science of nature, not contradictory but complementary to mainstream science. Both can be true, not because truth is relative, but because they reveal nature in different ways. Thus, whereas mainstream science enables us to discover the causal order in nature, Goethe's way of science enables us to discover the wholeness. (Bortoft, 1996, p. xi)

In Bortoft's view, mainstream science is a 'science of quantity', concerned only with those aspects of phenomena that can be quantified. The scientist seeks to exclude subjective experience. Thus, Newton's physics of light and colour is perfectly intelligible to someone who is colour-blind. Goethe offers an alternative 'science of quality'; his approach pays close attention to how the phenomena under investigation are experienced, addressing those things that cannot easily be measured. While mainstream science fragments the world, Goethe, coming to the study of colour through his interest in art, was interested in what gives rise to colours and how they relate to each other and our emotions. In his later work, as a 'phenomenologist of nature', he argued that to appreciate reality more comprehensively, to make it visible and understand its meaning, requires a consciousness that recognises the 'authentic wholeness' expressed in the reciprocal relationship of parts and wholes. This is difficult to obtain, and the eponymous hero of Goethe's tragic play *Faust* sells his soul to the devil in exchange for a hoped-for moment of transcendence on earth in which he can understand himself, nature and the universe as a harmonious, interconnected whole.

There is no one 'theory' of romanticism, but most commentators agree it possesses two common themes – the promotion of the power of the mind and an organismic worldview (Peckham, 1951). Fichte, Schelling and Novalis, important figures in the Jena Set, illustrated these themes. Fichte's 'ich-philosophy' put the self, as a free being, centre stage. Schelling saw the world as an interconnected whole within which humans and nature were inseparable. Novalis railed against the mechanistic worldview, which was drowning out the 'eternally creative music of the universe' and replacing it with 'the monotonous clatter of a gigantic millwheel'. In his view, a poet can gain a better understanding of the world than a scientist, and science needed to be poeticised.

Romanticism spread from Germany and became a strong current of thought in England, the United States and elsewhere. In England, there was recognition of the dangers posed by mechanistic thinking, especially to an understanding of humanity's 'oneness with nature'. Wordsworth saw such thinking as diminishing human potential and our enjoyment of nature:

> The world is too much with us; late and soon,
> Getting and spending, we lay waste our powers;
> Little we see in Nature that is ours;
> We have given our hearts away, a sordid boon!
> (Wordsworth, 1807, lines 1–4)

In the quotation heading this chapter, he identifies reductionism as the main culprit. As did Coleridge, who borrowed his concept of 'organic form' from the Jena Set. Keats declared, in harmony with Goethe, that Newton 'had destroyed all the Poetry of the rainbow, by reducing it to a prism' (quoted in Wulf, 2022). Blake, in his poem *London* (1794), saw the 'mind-forg'd manacles' of mechanism as giving rise to many of the problems associated with the industrial revolution. In *Jerusalem* (1808), he mourned that 'dark satanic mills' were plaguing England's 'green and pleasant land'. In the United States, Emerson, Thoreau and Whitman championed the romantic project, emphasising nature, transcendentalism and the self. A modern American songwriter who declared, with Whitman, that 'I contain multitudes' echoed the romantic frame of mind when he wrote:

> Yet one place where additional learning does not disentangle the mystery of the subject is music. As a matter of fact, the argument can be made that the more you study music, the less you understand it. Take two people – one studies contrapuntal music theory, the other cries when they hear a sad song. Which of the two really understands music better? (Dylan, 2022, p. 274)

1.5 The Challenge of Complexity

As Kant anticipated, traditional science, successful in astronomy, physics and chemistry, encountered difficulties when it sought to extend its scope to higher levels of complexity as found, for example, in the fields of biology and sociology. At these levels, mechanism and reductionism falter, raising questions about the universality of the scientific method. Complexity makes it difficult to place boundaries around a study and to isolate the key variables impacting what happens. Experiments are difficult to repeat because the phenomena under investigation are constantly changing and cannot be brought into the laboratory. Ethical issues become significant. At the human level, the existence of free will makes prediction difficult if not impossible. Intentions drive behaviour. In general, analysis of the parts alone cannot explain emergent properties, such as life and self-consciousness, which arise from the way the parts are organised. Aristotle's insight that a whole is more than the sum of its parts becomes pertinent. The domain of application of the scientific method is smaller than many thought, as will be apparent from a brief review of the fields of biology, ecology, psychology and sociology.

In biology, there are emergent properties at the level of the organism, such as life itself, viability, adaptation, growth and development, reproduction and regulation. These need to be explained, but that seems impossible in terms of physics and chemistry. Goethe, much influenced by Kant, argued that organisms are driven by 'vital forces' that provide them with their general form and properties as wholes. They are then further shaped by their environments (see Wulf, 2015). A less mystical account became possible with the birth of 'organismic biology' in the first half of the twentieth century. As Capra wrote:

> Vitalists assert that some nonphysical entity, force, or field, must be added to the laws of physics and chemistry to understand life. Organismic biologists maintain that the additional ingredient is the understanding of 'organization', or 'organizing relations'. (Capra, 1996, p. 25)

The best-known organismic biologist, Ludwig von Bertalanffy, argued that the failure of physics in explaining biological systems arises because it only considers systems which are 'closed' to their environments. Closed systems obey the second law of thermodynamics, which presents the universe as a machine that is gradually running down. Von Bertalanffy (1950) asserted that organisms are, by contrast, 'open systems'. They can temporarily defeat the second law of thermodynamics by living off their environments. They import matter and energy, which enables them to exist in a dynamic state, retaining their basic form while increasing their complexity through differentiation and integration. The history of biological science, since von Bertalanffy's time, can be seen as a series of pendulum swings between organismic and reductionist positions, with both seemingly having much to offer.

The most important figure in the early development of ecology, according to Wulf (2015), was Alexander von Humboldt, who was a friend of Goethe and was immersed in the philosophy of Kant. Under the influence of the Jena Set, he was able to

> ... [revolutionize] the way we see the natural world. He found connections everywhere. Nothing, not even the tiniest organism, was looked at on its own. 'In this great chain of causes and effects', Humboldt said 'no single fact can be considered in isolation'. With this insight, he invented the web of life, the concept of nature as we know it today. (Wulf, 2015, p. 5)

Even more remarkable for the time, von Humboldt recognised the connection between human activity – such as deforestation, ruthless irrigation and the 'great masses of steam and gas' – and the state of the natural environment. Based on his thinking, ecology sought from its beginnings to grasp interconnectivity and emergence. It was born by taking a systems approach. Twentieth-century ecology has continued in this vein with the formulation of the concept of an 'ecosystem'. The Gaia hypothesis, which postulates that the Earth itself is a living system, has also gained currency.

The Gestalt psychologists, writing in the early twentieth century, challenged the mechanistic, stimulus-response approach that dominated their field. They emphasised the importance of mind in bringing order to the chaotic reality with which it is confronted. The German word *gestalt*, meaning shape or form, refers to the patterns employed by the mind to make sense of what is perceived. For example, we see patterns of dots before the individual dots themselves. In Koffka's words, it is apparent that 'the whole is something else than the sum of its parts' (quoted in Ramage and Shipp 2009, p. 260).

Auguste Comte, writing in the early nineteenth century, called for a new science of society which he initially called 'social physics'. The scientific method was to be used to seek out general laws governing behaviour in the social world. When that failed to bring the results expected, Spencer and Durkheim took sociology in an 'organismic' direction towards what became the dominant theory: 'structural-functionalism'.

Alternative types of sociology were, however, waiting in the wings and came to the fore in the 1960s and 1970s. 'Interpretive social theory' questions the society-makes-person bias of structural-functionalism. It starts from the study of individual perception and action convinced, by Dilthey's 'hermeneutics' and Schutz's 'phenomenological' approach, of the importance of subjective meaning. The 'sociology of radical change' challenges the conservative bias of structural-functionalism, portraying society as characterised by inequalities that give rise to conflict between different groups which can, in turn, lead to change. It builds on the work of Marx and the Frankfurt School. Marx was concerned, in his early work, with the alienation of 'men' in capitalist society. Later, he argued that the contradictions that exist within capitalism will produce a revolution, led by the exploited working class, and a communist society. The most influential thinker still working in the Frankfurt School tradition is Jurgen Habermas. Whereas Marx based his early critique of capitalist society on alienated labour, Habermas (1979) emphasised the alienation that results from 'distorted communication'. A rational society depends on the existence of 'communicative competence', where citizens can engage in an 'ideal speech situation' to which they can contribute equally with the better argument winning the day. This, in turn, depends on the establishment of certain social conditions. In particular, the 'public sphere' must be re-energised as an arena where democratic discussions can take place and genuine agreements can be reached. For Habermas, the Enlightenment project can be brought to fruition by eradicating distorted communication and promoting communicative competence. He has had to rigorously defend his position against such theorists as Derrida questioning the transparency of language; Foucault emphasising the intertwining of power and knowledge; and Luhmann who, from a systems theoretical perspective, sees society in terms of function systems (economy, politics, law, education, science, mass media, etc.), each constructing the world according to their own self-producing communicative networks (Habermas, 1987). The sociology of radical change was originally focused on class as the primary source of inequality in society but has, over time, come to recognise other forms of disadvantage, developing critiques of inequality based on gender, race and sexual orientation.

1.6   Science and the Scientific Method in the Spotlight

Two revolutionary developments in twentieth-century physics – general relativity and quantum mechanics – have led natural scientists themselves to set aside the Newtonian worldview. According to Rovelli (2016), Newton's *Principia* describes a mechanical universe in which objects travel eternally on precise trajectories, determined by gravity, in geometrically immutable space. In Einstein's theory of general relativity, space-time and matter/energy are inextricably linked. He offered an account of the universe as an organic entity, more interconnected and dynamic than anything previously envisaged. The other revolutionary development, quantum mechanics, describes a world completely at odds with Newton's deterministic vision. Electrons jump from one interaction to another, and it is impossible to be certain when they will reappear. Indeed, they only seem to come into existence when interacting with other systems, for example, measuring instruments. Furthermore, the interactions do not have to be local. Particles are 'entangled' such that a change in one can impact another even across vast distances. Physics, in uncovering greater complexity in the universe, has itself had to embrace a more systemic perspective – highlighting interactions, indeterminacy, relationships and emergence (Rovelli and Jackson, 2022).

These revolutionary developments inevitably provoked reflection on the nature of the scientific method itself. It was obvious that Einstein had not come up with general relativity by following its prescriptions. Rather, the theory seemed to emerge almost fully formed, as a brand-new way of seeing the world, from some incredibly imaginative thought experiments. Popper concluded that the progress of science depends on bold conjectures rather than repeated observations. The latter can have little impact because they must be interpreted in terms of the existing theory (Chalmers, 1982). In a word, they are theory-dependent. Kuhn (1970) developed Popper's argument further in his highly influential account of the structure of Scientific Revolutions. He argued that scientists, during periods of 'normal' science, embrace a single paradigm, exploring its possibilities and finding it hard to see contradictory evidence. As serious anomalies accumulate, however, a period of uncertainty arises. Even then, it requires the appearance of a rival paradigm before scientists begin to abandon their existing theories and view the world in a different way. Science enters a 'revolutionary' phase as the scientific community shifts its thinking. The new paradigm is elevated to dominant status and becomes the basis for a new period of normal science.

The traditional account of science sees progress as cumulative. Kuhn's work suggests something very different. It also points to the impact of external factors. Because, for Kuhn, paradigms are 'incommensurable', each revealing reality to us in a different way, there are no logical grounds for choosing one over another. Fully embracing a new paradigm is akin to a religious conversion. Shifts in paradigm, therefore, do not happen for purely scientific reasons. A scientist may sense that working in a fresh paradigm will enable career advancement. A scientific community might come to believe that embracing the new will bring greater political influence and economic rewards.

The argument that scientific progress is a messy business is confirmed by historical studies showing the influence of other modes of thinking, including the occult, on its development. Alchemy was particularly important. This arcane practice encouraged the search for the philosophers' stone, promoted variously as capable of turning base metal into gold, prolonging life and bringing enlightenment. Newton left behind over a million words on the subject. White's biography painted him as 'the last sorcerer' and came to the unequivocal conclusion that

> ... based upon the evidence available ... the influence of Newton's researches in alchemy was the key to his world-changing discoveries in science. His alchemical work and his science were inextricably linked. (White, 1997, p. 5)

Strathern, charting the history of chemistry, quoted the nineteenth-century German chemist Justus Liebig on the significant role played by alchemy in the search for the elements:

> The finest imagination in the world could not have conceived of a better idea than the philosophers' stone to inspire the minds and faculties of men. Without it, chemistry would not be what it is today. In order to discover that no such thing as the philosophers' stone existed, it was necessary to ransack and analyse every substance known on earth. And in precisely this lay its miraculous influence. (quoted in Strathern, 2014, p. 59)

Today, for all the reasons enumerated, there is much less faith in the scientific method as the sole means of securing knowledge and hardly anyone claims that science is close to understanding everything, even in its favoured domains of physics, cosmology and chemistry. A more modest view of the capability of science prevails. The highly respected physicist, Carlo Rovelli, summarised this when he wrote:

> Science is not a Depository of Truth, it is based on the awareness that *there are no* Depositories of Truth. The best way to learn is to interact with the world while seeking to understand it, readjusting our mental schemes to what we encounter and find ... Every vision is partial. There is no way of

seeing reality that is not dependent on a perspective – no point of view that is absolute and universal. (Rovelli, 2021, pp. 117 and 166)

There is a further set of issues putting the scientific method under the spotlight. Science and its associated technologies have yielded many undoubted benefits, but its hegemony has also brought unintended consequences. Providing one succinct example, Schumacher wrote:

Modern man does not experience himself as a part of nature but as an outside force destined to dominate and conquer it. He even talks of a battle with nature, forgetting that if he won the battle, he would find himself on the losing side. (Schumacher, 1973, p. 3)

The scientific, industrial and information revolutions have arguably generated most of the intractable issues that we face today – climate change, environmental and species degradation, pollution, overexploitation of natural resources, food and water shortages, inequality, exclusion, mass migration, the dangers of global recession, the possibility of pandemics, nuclear proliferation, terrorism and the threat posed by artificial intelligence. Furthermore, the scientific method struggles to deal with the problems it has created because they are 'wicked problems' involving many interconnectivities and stakeholders. Increasingly, we are confronted by 'black swan' events (Taleb, 2007) that endanger our well-being and possibly our long-term survival as a species.

1.7 Conclusion

Foster's (2021) attempt to delve into the Upper Palaeolithic mind led him to argue that over-reliance on Descartes's and Newton's thinking has led us to create a world wholly unsuitable to the full expression of our human nature, one where we are cut off from 'constant ecstatic contact with earth, heaven, trees and gods'. He is not alone. Gregg contemplated the benefits and costs of the extensive use of human reason in his book *If Nietzsche Were a Narwhal*:

Is our exceptional ability to understand and manipulate the physical properties of the universe something that is *inherently* good? ... It is the greatest of paradoxes that we should have an exceptional mind that seems hell-bent on destroying itself. (Gregg, 2023, pp. 193 and 206; italics in the original)

McGilchrist (see Spencer, 2022) argued that humans can engage with the world in different ways depending on whether they emphasise left-brain or right-brain thinking. The former prioritises order, control, rationality and precision, picks things apart and tends to prefer the map to the territory. The latter prioritises change, freedom, empathy and reflection, sees the whole and values experience. Over recent centuries, the emissary has become the master and has remade the world 'in the mechanistic image favoured by the left hemisphere'.

Of course, Foster does not advocate a return to an Upper Palaeolithic existence, Gregg the abandonment of human reason, or McGilchrist left-brain lobotomies. Science, in its place, continues to be essential. Rather, the problem is that the Enlightenment had two sides, and we have prioritised one at the expense of the other (Jacob, 2006; Gare, 2008, 2023; Israel, 2010). The first, 'moderate' side promoted the scientific method and rested on the certainty provided by Descartes's philosophy and Newton's confirmation that there was order in the natural world. It sought increased control over nature and, encouraged by the political philosophies of Hobbes and Locke, over people. This side was conservative and emphasised the gradual improvement of existing institutions. The second side, the 'Radical Enlightenment', had its origins in the humanism, scepticism, freedom, relative tolerance and rediscovery of democracy that epitomised the Renaissance. This was the world in which Giordano Bruno promoted 'nature enthusiasm' and republicanism and could contemplate the possibility of life on other worlds. It allowed Montaigne and Shakespeare to flourish.

The Radical Enlightenment was born during the Renaissance, but its time was not long. Montaigne, in his *Essais* (see Bakewell, 2010), ruminated on whether, in some respects, the minds of other animals made them superior to humans. Fifty years later, Descartes was certain that animals were machines and that the screams emanating from the live dogs he dissected were the equivalent of metal screeching. Toulmin (1990) saw the pursuit and embrace of certainty as emanating from the horrors of the Thirty Years' War when apparently irreconcilable religious differences tore the European continent apart. The moderate Enlightenment triumphed.

Although pushed into the background, the Radical Enlightenment was never fully suppressed. For Israel (2010), it was a 'revolution of the mind' that resurfaced in the philosophy of Spinoza (a systems thinker *par excellence*) and, as taken forward by d'Holbach, Diderot, Helvetius and others, assumed a broader social and political significance, promoting greater democracy, challenging existing institutions, favouring greater equality and opposing colonialism. For Gare (2008, 2023), the standard-bearers of the Radical Enlightenment were Kant, Hegel and Schelling. Their emphasis was on the freedom of people to exercise imagination and create their own destinies in societies which they themselves could build. For Schelling, humans were intimately linked with nature, enabling it to be conscious of itself. The inheritors of this mode of thinking, Gare argued, were process philosophers such as the pragmatists and Whitehead. It is the project of the Radical Enlightenment that Habermas wanted to see reinvigorated. Science will continue to play a significant role in creating a better world. However, without ST it becomes blind and can potentially lead the human species to destruction. Science does not define reality. As Cassirer argued, it should be seen as just one symbolic form among several 'autonomous, irreducible modes of world formation' (Skidelsky, 2008). It needs to be complemented with systems approaches that give equal weight to interrelationships, organismic thinking, the imagination, fair and equal societies, and our natural environment.

References

Ayer, A.J. (1936). *Language, Truth and Logic*. Victor Gollancz.

Bakewell, S. (2010). *How to Live: A life of Montaigne*. Chatto & Windus.

von Bertalanffy, L. (1950). The theory of open systems in physics and biology. In: *Systems Thinking* (ed. F.E. Emery, 1969), pp. 70–85. Penguin.

Blake, W. (1794). London. In: *The Complete Poems* (ed. A. Ostriker, 1977). Penguin Classics.

Blake, W. (1808). Jerusalem. In: *The Complete Poems* (ed. A. Ostriker, 1977). Penguin Classics.

Bortoft, H. (1996). *The Wholeness of Nature: Goethe's Way of Science*. Floris Books.

Capra, F. (1996). *The Web of Life: A New Synthesis of Mind and Matter*. Harper Collins.

Capra, F. and Luisi, P.I. (2014). *The Systems View of Life: A Unifying Vision*. Cambridge University Press.

Chalmers, A.F. (1982). *What is This Thing Called Science?* 2e. Open University Press.

Cumhaill, C.M. and Wiseman, R. (2023) *Metaphysical Animals: How Four Women Brought Philosophy Back to Life*. Penguin Random House.

Descartes, R. (1968). *Discourse on Method and the Meditations*. Penguin.

Dylan, B. (2022). *The Philosophy of Modern Song*. Simon & Schuster.

Foster, C. (2021). *Being a Human*. Profile Books Ltd.

Gare, A. (2008). Reviving the radical enlightenment; process philosophy and the struggle for democracy. In: *Researching with Whitehead: System and Adventure, Essays in Honor of J.B. Cobb* (eds. F. Riffert and H.-J. Sander), pp. 25–57. Verlag.

Gare, A. (2023). Was Günter Grass's rat right? Should terrestrial life welcome the end of humans? *Borderless Philosophy* 6: 32–76.

Gregg, J. (2023). *If Nietzsche Were a Narwhal: What Animal Intelligence Reveals About Human Stupidity*. Hodder & Stoughton, Kindle edn.

Habermas, J. (1979). *Communication and the Evolution of Society*. Heinemann Educational Books.

Habermas, J. (1987). *The Philosophical Discourse of Modernity*. Polity Press.

Israel, J. (2010). *A Revolution of the Mind: Radical Enlightenment and the Intellectual Origins of Modern Democracy*. Princeton University Press.

Jacob, M.C. (2006). *The Radical Enlightenment: Pantheists, Freemasons and Republicans*, 2e. Cornerstone Book Publishers.

Kemp, J. (1968). *The Philosophy of Kant*. Oxford University Press.

Kuhn, T. (1970). *The Structure of Scientific Revolutions*, 2e. University of Chicago Press.

Mensch, J. (2013). *Kant's Organicism: Epigenesis and the Development of Critical Philosophy*. University of Chicago Press.

Mitchell, M. (2009). *Complexity: A Guided Tour*. Oxford University Press.

Peckham, M. (1951). *Toward a Theory of Romanticism*. Publications of The-Modern-Language-Association-of-America LXVI (2). https://doi.org/10.2307/459586.

Ramage, M. and Shipp, K. (2009). *Systems Thinkers*. Springer.

Rovelli, C. (2016). *Seven Brief Lessons on Physics*. Penguin.

Rovelli, C. (2021). *Helgoland*. Penguin Random House.

Rovelli, C. and Jackson, M.C. (2022). Quantum mechanics and Alexander Bogdanov's worldview: a conversation. *Systems Research and Behavioral Science*. https://doi.org/10.1002/sres.2928.

Schumacher, E.F. (1973). *Small Is Beautiful: A Study of Economics as if People Mattered*. Blond & Briggs Ltd.

Skidelsky, E. (2008). *Ernst Cassirer: The Last Philosopher of Culture*. Princeton University Press.

Spencer, N. (2022). Iain McGilchrist and the battle over the left-brain, right-brain theory. *Prospect*, April, 2022 issue.

Strathern, P. (2014). *Mendeleyev's Dream: The Quest for the Elements*. Crux Publishing, Kindle edn.

Taleb, N.N. (2007). *The Black Swan: The Impact of the Highly Improbable*. Random House.

Toulmin, S. (1990). *Cosmopolis: The Hidden Agenda of Modernity*. University of Chicago Press.

White, M. (1997). *Isaac Newton: The Last Sorcerer*. Fourth Estate Limited.

Wordsworth, W. (1807). The world is too much with us. In: *Poems in Two Volumes*, Vol. 1. Longman.

Wordsworth, W. (1814). The excursion. In: *The Poetical Works of William Wordsworth*, Vol. 5 (ed. W. Knight, in 1896), pp. 957–964. Macmillan & Co.

Wulf, A. (2015). *The Invention of Nature: The Adventures of Alexander von Humboldt*. John Murray.

Wulf, A. (2022). *Magnificent Rebels: The First Romantics and the Invention of the Self*. John Murray.

Yunkaporta, T. (2019). *Sandtalk*. Text Publishing.

2

Systems Thinking

For the astronomers and the physicists the world is, in popular words, continually "running down" to a state of dead inertness when heat has been uniformly distributed through it. For the biologists and sociologists, a part of the world, at any rate (and for us a very important part) is undergoing a progressive development in which an upward trend is seen, lower states of organisation being succeeded by higher states.

(Needham, 1941)

2.1   Introduction

This chapter begins by setting out the challenge faced by Systems Thinking (ST) if it is to provide a complementary approach to that of science. In essence, it needs to find ways of addressing issues of *organised complexity*. The nature of organised complexity is explored and consideration is given to the 'wicked problems' that it produces. ST offers two ways forward in the face of organised complexity. The first seeks general systems laws that are applicable to all forms of organised complexity – whether physical, biological, human or social. This is the route favoured in Bogdanov's 'tektology', in 'general systems theory' (GST), and in cybernetics and 'complexity theory'. It has not been as productive as was hoped, because 'organisation' takes on different characteristics at higher levels of complexity. There are emergent properties at these levels, producing behaviour that is only partially explainable using the theories and models applicable at lower levels. Boulding proposed an alternative way forward which gives recognition to emergence. This involves making the best possible use of models relevant to lower levels while developing new systems approaches which take into account the

Critical Systems Thinking: A Practitioner's Guide, First Edition. Michael C. Jackson.
© 2024 John Wiley & Sons, Inc. Published 2024 by John Wiley & Sons, Inc.

emergent properties at higher levels. ST has had greater success following this second route and has developed a range of systems methodologies that offer proven ways of engaging with organised complexity.

2.2   The Challenge Confronting Systems Thinking

In 1948, Warren Weaver, Director of Natural Sciences at the Rockefeller Foundation, stated that:

> It is soberly true that science has, to date, succeeded in solving a bewildering number of relatively easy problems, whereas the hard problems, and the ones which perhaps promise most for man's future, lie ahead. (Weaver, 2003, p. 383)

Science, he argued, is successful when confronted by problems of *simplicity*. Here, it can proceed by analysis to identify a few key variables and quantify them and the relations between them. Newton's equations of motion can explain the movements of the planets. Science can also deal with problems of *disorganised complexity*. Here, the vast number of variables involved makes it possible to ignore their individual behaviour and use a combination of statistics and probability theory to make predictions based on average behaviour. The laws of motion of gases are derived from the average behaviour of molecules.

The 'hard' problems Weaver refers to are hard because they do not fall into either of these categories and so pose severe challenges to the traditional scientific method. They are complex, impossible to reduce to a few significant variables and resist quantification. They are also organised – the variables are too impacted by their interrelationships to yield to probability statistics. In short, they

> ... involve dealing simultaneously with a *sizable number of factors which are interrelated into an organic whole*. (Weaver, 2003, p. 380, italics in the original)

Consider the problem of obesity. There are numerous variables involved, including diet, environment, food production, genetics, activity, health conditions, medications, stress, and emotions. These and their interactions are hard to specify and quantify. Obesity levels, however, are not random. They vary in different countries and amongst different sections of the population. For Weaver, problems of this kind are problems of *organised complexity*. Addressing them is crucial for the future well-being of humankind because they predominate in the human, social, political, economic and environmental domains. Something more than traditional science is needed, Weaver concluded, to help decision-makers tackle problems of this type.

ST offers that 'something more', providing guidance to decision-makers in areas where science struggles, i.e., when confronted with complex, interconnected problems involving human and social phenomena (Checkland, 1981). To grasp the challenges it faces, further consideration must be given to the nature of organised complexity and the 'wicked problems' it produces.

2.3 Complexity and Wicked Problems

It has become commonplace to say that the world in which we live exhibits VUCA characteristics – volatility, uncertainty, complexity and ambiguity. Economic, social, technological, health and ecological factors have become interconnected in unprecedented ways; 'black swan' events have become frequent; and there are fewer shared values that help tame complexity by ensuring consensus. Few doubt that 'complexity', to use the umbrella term, poses the greatest challenge to leaders and decision-makers. An Organization for Economic Co-operation and Development (OECD) report began:

> Complexity is a core feature of most policy issues today; their components are interrelated in multiple, hard-to-define ways. Yet governments are ill-equipped to deal with complex problems. (OECD, 2017)

At a more local level, decision-makers, whether operating in the private, public or voluntary sectors, are plagued by interconnectivity, volatility and pluralism of perspectives and are uncertain how to act. An International Business Machines Corporation (IBM) survey of more than 1500 chief executive officers worldwide stated that:

> The world's private and public sector leaders believe that a rapid escalation of 'complexity' is the biggest challenge confronting them. They expect it to continue – indeed, to accelerate – in the coming years. (IBM, 2010)

Despite unanimity on its significance, there is no agreed definition of complexity. Cilliers (1998), however, provided a helpful and much-cited list of 10 major characteristics of complex systems, which are as follows:

1) The number of elements is large, and they interact dynamically
2) Such interactions are rich – any element affects and is affected by several others
3) The interactions are non-linear – small changes in inputs can cause very significant changes in outputs
4) Interactions are primarily but not exclusively with immediate neighbours
5) Any interaction can feed back on itself directly or after a number of intervening stages

6) The overall behaviour of the system of elements is not predicted by the behaviour of the individual elements
7) Such systems may be open, with difficult or impossible-to-define boundaries
8) There has to be a constant flow of energy to maintain the organisation of the system
9) Complex systems evolve, and their past is co-responsible for their present behaviour
10) Elements in the system may be ignorant of the behaviour of the system as a whole

An important clarification is provided by the philosopher Nicholas Rescher (2019), who makes a distinction between 'ontological' and 'cognitive' complexity. Ontological complexity is the complexity that exists in the real world. It derives from the quantity and variety of the elements of a system and the elaborateness of their interrelationships. It seems to be increasing and is inexhaustible:

> Reality is just too many-faceted for its cognitive domestication by us to be more than very partial. (Rescher, 2019, p. 126)

Cognitive complexity, by contrast, derives from the different ways in which the world is viewed. This form of complexity is also increasing. In the natural sciences, our world picture is disintegrating as new speciality disciplines and interdisciplinary syntheses come to the fore. In the social sciences, the anarchy recognised and further encouraged by postmodernism prevails, and a pluralism of world views makes agreement virtually impossible:

> With complex social systems, decision making can thus become frustrated by the fact that much of the time no concrete way of achieving a generally agreed resolution can be achieved. (Rescher, 2019, p. 201)

Rescher separates ontological and cognitive complexity for analytical purposes but, in practice, sees them as intimately related. Cognitive complexity develops as our understanding of the complexity of the world increases and, in turn, reveals greater ontological complexity. A good example of this interrelationship is provided by the growing awareness of the importance of inequality as a factor influencing which communities were most impacted by the COVID-19 pandemic. Statistics showed, to those willing to look, that the poorest, including many from Black and minority ethnic groups, were hit the hardest. This led to a search for reasons as to why this was the case. As various hypotheses were investigated, the ontological complexity unfolded further and gave rise to yet more cognitive speculation. Was it the result of genetic factors, cultural differences, lifestyle choices, jobs and working conditions or structural racism? Ontological and cognitive complexity proliferate in tandem.

Complexity, according to Rittel and Webber (1981), gives rise to 'wicked' rather than 'tame' problems. In summary, wicked problems have the following characteristics:

- They are difficult to formulate
- It is never clear when a solution has been reached
- There are no true or false solutions, only good or bad according to the perspective taken
- A 'solution' will have drawn-out consequences that need to be considered in evaluating it
- An attempted solution will change a wicked problem, so it is difficult to learn from trial and error
- There will always be untried solutions that might have been better
- All wicked problems are essentially unique
- They have multiple, interdependent causes
- There are many explanations for any wicked problem depending on the point of view
- Solutions have consequences for which the decision-makers have a responsibility

They are constituted by interacting elements of ontological and cognitive complexity:

> The planner who works with open systems is caught up in the ambiguity of their causal webs. Moreover, his would-be solutions are confounded by a still further set of dilemmas posed by the growing pluralism of the contemporary publics, whose valuations of his proposals are judged against an array of different and contradicting scales. (Rittel and Webber, 1981, p. 99)

Ackoff (1981) has memorably described such complex problem situations as 'messes'.

The conclusion reached by those who have considered 'wicked problems' is that traditional scientific approaches cannot cope. In the complex world in which we live, trying to predict the future and prepare for it is ill-conceived; the rational model of decision-making, relying on linear cause–effect relations, is not fit for purpose; and quantitative models, which treat the world as stationary, are of limited use. Maybe, we just have to 'muddle through' (Lindblom, 1959). Or perhaps ST can do better.

ST has explored two avenues in trying to help decision-makers navigate complexity and cope with wicked problems. The first seeks general systems laws that are applicable to all forms of organised complexity – whether physical, biological, human or social. The argument of this chapter is that this approach has not yielded the expected benefits because of the emergent properties that arise at higher levels of complexity. The second route, which has seen the development of a diverse range of systems methodologies addressing different aspects of complexity, has been considerably more fruitful.

2.4 The Search for General Systems Laws

According to the standard canon, the founding fathers of ST are Bogdanov, von Bertalanffy and Wiener. They were all intent on developing a transdisciplinary science of 'organised complexity'. More recently, this endeavour has been taken up in complexity theory. Overall, the results have been disappointing. Few general laws have been found, and those involved in efforts to find them have splintered into different groups as recognition has dawned that higher levels of complexity really do exhibit emergent properties.

2.4.1 Bogdanov and Tektology

Alexander Bogdanov's three-volume *Tektology* (1989), published in Russia between 1912 and 1917, sought to establish a 'universal science of organisation'. This science was to embrace all the methods of organisation that nature has worked out, systematise them and perfect those necessary for humans to assume mastery over the forces of nature and 'the socially organized elements of the universe' (Bogdanov, 2016). He had no doubt, given the countless analogies he found between the systems investigated by the specialist sciences, that the development of a monistic science, based on the concept of 'organisation', was possible. Nor did he doubt that it would be life-changing for the human species:

> There exist general methods and natural regularities according to which the most varied elements of the universe are organized into complexes. This proposition provides the basis for the great new science .... With the help of this new science, humanity will be able systematically and comprehensively to organize its creative powers, its life .... (Bogdanov, 2016, p. 247, italics in the original)

Bogdanov, for a period a leader of the Bolshevik party, fell out with Lenin, who regarded his work as 'organizational gibberish' (Lenin, quoted in Belykh, 1998), as 'unspeakable nonsense ... sterile, lifeless and scholastic' (Lenin, quoted in Stokes, 2015). A similar criticism was more moderately voiced by Plenge, a German professor, in a 1927 review of the first edition of the

German translation of *Tektology*. He saw Bogdanov's work as underestimating the complexity of certain system types and as ignoring the vast differences between them (Şenalp, 2019).

In the Soviet Union, Bogdanov's work was suppressed. In the West, it has, until quite recently, been largely ignored. We are no further on in developing a 'universal science of organisation' and, despite the many interesting analogies between system types described in *Tektology*, this is likely to remain the case. The criticisms have some merit, and it is Bogdanov's pragmatist philosophy, espoused in other works, rather than his science of tektology that has the most to offer contemporary ST (Jackson, 2022a, 2022b).

2.4.2 Von Bertalanffy and General Systems Theory

Von Bertalanffy, the organismic biologist we met in Chapter 1, first articulated the need for a 'general system theory' (GST) at the University of Chicago in 1937. A collection of essays published in 1968 is a key resource for understanding the nature and scope of his work. It is called *General System Theory* (von Bertalanffy, 1971) although, by that time, the plural 'general systems theory' was the more normal descriptor of the approach. In this collection, he compliments Weaver for recognising that the basic problem posed to modern science is 'organised complexity'. It has become apparent, he argues, that entities of an essentially new sort, 'systems', have entered scientific discourse. Systems cannot be explained in terms of traditional science because of the strong often non-linear interactions among their parts, which means 'the whole is more than the sum of its parts'. It was obvious to him that the scientific study of 'wholes' was essential across a wide range of disciplines.

In developing this study, von Bertalanffy derived insights from his biological work but believed they are relevant across disciplines because they concern the patterns of organisation common to different systems rather than the nature of their material components. There are, he believed, general systems principles that apply to complex systems of all types, whether physical, biological or social. The study of general systems was to focus on such principles as

> ... growth, regulation, hierarchical order, equifinality, progressive differentiation, progressive mechanization, progressive centralization, closed and open systems, competition, evolution toward higher organization, teleology, and goal-directedness. (Hammond, 2003, p. 119)

GST, von Bertalanffy believed, could become a logico-mathematical discipline, formal but applicable to the range of empirical sciences.

In von Bertalanffy's view, the establishment of a general science of 'wholeness' entails the rejection of reductionism in all its forms. As we saw in Chapter 1, he argued that physics is unable to explain biological phenomena because it only deals with systems closed to their environments. Organisms are 'open systems' that, through processes of exchange with their environments, can evolve towards states of increased order and complexity. In the same vein, von Bertalanffy rejected the 'robot model of man' promoted by behaviourism (von Bertalanffy, 1967). He saw people as 'active personality systems', inner- rather than outer-directed:

> Man is not a passive receiver of stimuli coming from an external world, but in a very concrete sense *creates* his universe .... (von Bertalanffy, 1971, p. 205; italics in the original)

Furthermore, people create a cultural world of symbols which themselves gain autonomy, become self-propelling and follow their own 'inner logic of development' that cannot be understood in terms of the mental processes of their creators (von Bertalanffy, 1967). The essential point, said von Bertalanffy, was that

> ... the traditional categories of mechanistic science do not suffice (or rather exclude) basic empirical aspects. It appears, therefore, that an *expansion of categories*, models and theory is needed adequately to deal with the biological, behavioral and social universes. (von Bertalanffy, 1967, p. 62; italics in the original)

Gestalt psychology had a significant influence on von Bertalanffy's psychosocial thinking. He regarded the emphasis it placed on the primacy of psychological wholes as making an important inroad into 'the mechanistic scheme'. It is natural, therefore, to find as integral to his philosophy an awareness that

> ... perception is not a reflection of 'real things' (whatever their metaphysical status), and knowledge not a simple approximation to 'truth' or 'reality'. It is an interaction between knower and known .... (von Bertalanffy, 1971, pp. xx–xxi)

Elaborating on this, von Bertalanffy espoused a 'perspective' philosophy. Perspectivism argues that all forms of knowledge can only capture certain aspects of the truth. This is because any perspective on reality is dependent on a

> ... multiplicity of factors of a biological, psychological, cultural, linguistic, etc., nature. (von Bertalanffy, 1971, p. xxi)

There is a tension, to say the least, between von Bertalanffy's call for a mathematically rigorous general system theory and his 'perspectivism' and emphasis on emergence. It must be said that very few widely accepted 'general systems laws' have been established by von Bertalanffy and those who have followed in his wake. It seems best to regard GST not as an attempt to establish universal systems principles but as an ongoing search for insightful transdisciplinary concepts that can stimulate conversations between specialist disciplines. Von Bertalanffy's biographer put it like this:

> In the case of GST, though the golden goal of a universal systems discipline may remain out of reach indefinitely, the vintage of the GST worldview may be exceedingly plentiful. (Davidson, 1983, p. 188)

2.4.3 Wiener and Cybernetics

In 1948, Norbert Wiener's book *Cybernetics* established the famous definition of the field as the science of 'control and communication in the animal and the machine'. Cybernetics is a true transdisciplinary science, Wiener argued, because it deals with general laws that govern control processes whatever the nature of the system under governance. Control, whether in the mechanical, biological or societal domains, depends on the rapid and continuous operation of the negative feedback mechanism. A sensor compares what a system is achieving to the desired goal and feeds information about the margin of error to an effector that takes corrective action. Examples are a thermostat controlling room temperature or the 'homeostatic' mechanism controlling body temperature. For control to operate, information must be communicated within the system and between the system and its environment.

Wiener believed that cybernetics constituted a significant break with Newton's clockwork representation of the universe. His concept of circular causality enabled the pursuit of a purpose to be understood without the implication that a cause subsequent in time to an effect was involved. 'Teleology' became a scientific rather than a mystical concept. The transmission of information, in the form of messages, allowed 'organisation' to arise and persist:

> Just as entropy is a measure of disorganization, the information carried by a set of messages is a measure of organization. (Wiener, 1954, p. 21)

Bateson said that this equating of information with negative entropy 'marks the greatest single shift in human thinking since the days of Plato and Aristotle' (quoted in Kline, 2015). Machines, living beings and societies are all capable of temporarily resisting the dictates of the second law of thermodynamics by building up information and becoming enclaves of increasing organisation.

The intellectual highpoint of cybernetics in the United States was the 10 'Macy conferences' set up by McCulloch to encourage transdisciplinary work and held between 1946 and 1963. These brought together, in intense and frequently bad-tempered discussions, luminaries from mathematics, engineering, biology and the social sciences. The anthropologists Gregory Bateson and Margaret Mead hoped that concepts such as circular causality, feedback and information would translate across disciplines and 'bring the rigor of the physical sciences to the social sciences' (Kline, 2015).

Cybernetics was also flourishing in the United Kingdom, inspired by a group of scientists who came together in the Ratio Club. An early pioneer was W. Ross Ashby. Ashby was a psychiatrist interested in mental illness, which he believed resulted from brains losing their capacity to adapt to their environments. To discover how this could happen, he thought he should make a machine that would model the behaviour of a normal brain with the usual ability to learn and adapt. He built his first 'homeostat', as this machine was called, in 1948; demonstrated it at the 9th Macy conference in 1952; and published a book about it, *Design for a Brain*, in the same year. It proved to be 'ultrastable' in that it could find and maintain a state of dynamic equilibrium with its environment. Wiener called it 'one of the great philosophical contributions of the present day' (quoted in Kline, 2015). The machine brought to the fore and illustrated the significance of four cybernetic concepts – the black box, requisite variety, self-organisation and emergence. Ashby developed his ideas in *An Introduction to Cybernetics* (1956), which seeks to set out a programme for the future development of cybernetics. It was highly influential in providing a 'pragmatist' orientation to British cybernetics, which we will consider further in Chapter 6, in relation to Stafford Beer's Viable System Model.

As Ramage (2009) argued, when comparing the work of Wiener and Bateson, 'cybernetics has never been a uniform discipline'. There were disagreements at the Macy conferences as to whether it was a universal science or simply a source of useful analogies that could be transferred between disciplines. Wiener thought that cybernetics could illuminate human issues but criticised the use of mathematical cybernetics in this context (Kline, 2015). A tension existed in British cybernetics, in the early days, concerning whether a machine could be an accurate scientific model of the brain or just a pragmatic attempt to explore some things a brain can do (Pickering, 2010). The most disruptive threat to the unity of the transdiscipline, however, occurred with the emergence of 'second-order cybernetics', which is associated with the Biological Computer Laboratory which operated at the University of Illinois between 1958 and 1975, with Heinz von Foerster as its director. The phrase second-order cybernetics was first used by von Foerster in 1974. He provided this explanation:

> I submit that the cybernetics of observed systems we may consider to be first order cybernetics, while second order cybernetics is the cybernetics of observing systems. (von Foerster quoted in Clemson, 1984, p. 246)

The shift in focus to the observer was underpinned by the work of the biologists Maturana and Varela and von Glasersfeld's philosophy of 'radical constructivism'. Maturana and Varela's theory of *autopoiesis*, from the Greek for 'self-making', refers to the circular processes through which organisms ensure their continuous self-maintenance. It is these internal operations, produced by and producing their organisation and structure, that determine what environmental perturbations are noticed and responded to (Maturana and Varela, 1980). Organisms create their own environments and come to know them as they become 'structurally coupled' with them. As Capra explained:

> By specifying which perturbations from the environment trigger its changes, the system 'brings forth a world', as Maturana and Varela put it. Cognition, then, is not a representation of an independently existing world, but rather a continual *bringing forth of a world* through the process of living. (Capra, 1996, p. 260; italics in the original)

Even at the human level, there can be no access to an objective external world: 'Everything said is said by an observer to another observer that could be him or herself' (Maturana, 1987). Von Glasersfeld (1984) embraced Kant's argument that our minds do not reflect some external reality but construct reality from what is provided by experience. He goes further, however, in emphasising the considerable cognitive freedom this provides to humans because of the extremely rich raw material the experiential world provides. This led von Glasersfeld to stress, again and again, the personal responsibility we all have for our words and deeds. We cannot hide behind some notion of 'objective knowledge'.

Second-order cybernetics influenced, for example, Luhmann's sociology and the field of family therapy. Nevertheless, it has progressed little since its original formulation and has 'often become bogged down in repetitive explanations of its key commitments' (Scholte and Sweeting, 2022). The obvious criticism is that while it emphasises the capacity of people to make their own history, it ignores the constraint that this is not of their own free will but 'under given and inherited circumstances with which they are directly confronted' (Marx, 1852). Recently, there have been calls for a 'third order cybernetics' taking account of social values and societal constraints (Lepskiy, 2018), while Krippendorf has put 'critical cybernetics' on the agenda, seeking (according to Scholte and Sweeting, 2022) to hold cybernetics to account for some of the consequences of its technological inventions, interrogate its blind spots and shift it to a more active and situated engagement with the world.

In the West, cybernetics had its heyday in the 1950s and 1960s with much talk in the popular press about robot brains, automated factories and the information revolution. In the Soviet Union, it was initially condemned as a 'bourgeois science' but rehabilitated in the 1960s under Khruschev and Kosygin. Cybernetics, buoyed by increases in computing power, offered the possibility of organising the Soviet economy along less-centralised lines. Ultimately, however, it was emasculated and used in the service of the authoritarian party apparatus (Gerovitch, 2004; Spufford, 2010). In China, cybernetics played a role in nuclear armament, the Great Leap Forward and population control (King, 2022). In the latter case, cyberneticians identified the 'one-child policy' as the only feedback loop that could restrict population growth. It has continued to be influential in reforms of price control, the legal system and in the Public Security Bureau.

2.4.4 Complexity Theory

Gleick (1987) argued that twentieth-century science will be remembered for general relativity, quantum mechanics and chaos/complexity theory. All require abandoning the Newtonian worldview. In describing complexity theory, we pay attention to four distinct strands – chaos theory, the study of 'complex adaptive systems', the theory of dissipative structures and the work of Snowden on 'anthro-complexity'.

Classical science seeks to discover orderly, regular patterns of behaviour, based on cause–effect relationships, from which deterministic laws can be derived. In the 1960s and 1970s, however, a small number of scientists began to explore the 'monstrosities' that haunted traditional science and to extend its scope to the erratic, discontinuous and unpredictable aspects of nature (Gleick, 1987). Two discoveries earned 'chaos theory' an important place in science. The first was called the 'butterfly effect' and showed that very small modifications to the numbers input into equations used in a model could significantly, and unpredictably, alter the outputs. This suggested that long-term prediction is impossible. The second was that there is considerable order underlying the 'chaos' that exists in nature. Chaos does not, as in everyday language, imply anarchy. Between order and complete disorder, a hidden order can appear. In this middle ground, behaviour never repeats itself but is drawn to 'strange attractors' which seem to set limits to what is possible. In meteorology, physics and chemistry, patterns can be discerned and behaviour approximated using models based on a small number of variables with fixed interactions. Unfortunately, for advocates of chaos theory, in social and ecological systems with huge numbers of elements (people in a city and species in a forest), exhibiting different and evolving characteristics and impacted by numerous internal and external changes, it is much more difficult to recognise the influence of strange attractors (Boulton et al., 2015).

In 1984, the Santa Fe Institute (SFI) opened in New Mexico and has since become the most famous centre for research into 'complex adaptive systems'. The SFI sought to develop complexity theory beyond the limitations of chaos theory. Holland (2014) argued that chaos theory is restricted to the study of 'complex physical systems', containing elements with fixed properties, while the broader research area of 'complexity theory' also embraces 'complex adaptive systems' consisting of agents that are capable of learning and adapting as they interact with other agents. The grand aim of the SFI is 'to seek to understand and unify the underlying, shared patterns in complex physical, biological, social, cultural, technological, and even possible astrobiological worlds' and to use this understanding 'to promote the well-being of humankind and of life on earth' (Santa Fe Institute, 2023). The work of the SFI is closely associated with 'agent-based modelling'.

Agent-based modelling works from the bottom-up and seeks to explain emergent behaviour at the system level in terms of the rules of interaction of the agents that constitute the system. SFI researchers have constructed such models to simulate the behaviour of, among other things, ants, bees, forest fires, the financial system and economies (for examples, see Krakauer, 2019). The approach seems to work well to provide an understanding of the self-organising capacity of social insects and the patterns that emerge in the flocking behaviour of birds. However, despite increasing model sophistication to encompass more intelligent agents and more complex agent dynamics, evidence remains lacking that these models can explain and help manage actual social, economic and ecological systems. Incorporating human beings in agent-based models necessitates reducing them to a range of behaviours which, in real life, they massively exceed, confounding any possible predictions made about them.

A more realistic appreciation of what complexity theory can offer stems from the work on 'dissipative structures' initiated by Prigogine (1997). Physical, biological, ecological and social systems, he insists, are open, replete with disorder and demonstrate irreversible change. His 'new science' of extended thermodynamics can help us understand their behaviour. But, because their evolution continues to introduce novelty, it does not help with prediction. Drawing on Prigogine's conclusions, Boulton et al. (2015) identified a modest set of 'themes' that seem relevant to the variety of complex systems that we find in the world in which we live. The world:

- is systemic and synergistic
- is multiscalar
- has variety, diversity, variation and fluctuations
- is path-dependent
- changes episodically
- possesses more than one future
- is capable of self-organising and self-regulating and, sometimes, giving rise to novel, emergent features

In general, complexity theory can elucidate a few themes and provide some metaphors that usefully translate from the harder to the softer sciences. It falls short in its attempts to demonstrate that there are either general scientific laws or analogies that can help leaders and managers understand and improve the performance of the 'complex adaptive systems' with which they must deal (Rosenhead et al., 2019). Social systems pose particular problems. As Byrne and Callaghan argue

> ... any general complexity social science has ... to allow for structures with causal powers and it has to address human agency as capable of transcending narrow rules for behaviour. (Byrne and Callaghan, 2014, loc.1372)

In attempting to overcome its limited applicability in the social domain, complexity theory has become parasitic on social theory and has splintered according to the sociological preferences of its advocates. There are now as many competing versions of complexity theory as there are competing social theories. Stacey and Mowles (2016) drew upon Hegel, Mead and Elias to shift complexity theory from its original 'functionalist' to their favoured 'interpretive' sociological position. Cilliers (1998) believed that complexity theory is best understood from a postmodern or poststructuralist perspective. Byrne and Callaghan (2014) rejected functionalist and postmodern readings and argued for a synthesis of complexity theory and Bhaskar's critical realism. As Zhu remarks, regarding Stacey's version:

> Is it not the case that, in the end, adopting or rejecting Stacey's 'responsive process perspective' amounts more to choosing between available social theories than learning from complexity theories that are still evolving. (Zhu, 2007, p. 458)

Aligning itself with so many different social theories makes complexity theory incoherent. In this form, it can hardly act as a useful guide to decision-makers.

To set the scene for discussing Dave Snowden's work, it is important to note that he is sceptical of the 'computational' complexity approach, dominant at the SFI, which believes it is possible to produce comprehensive models of human behaviour. For him, humans are very different from ants, birds and crystals, and a complexity theory seeking to be relevant to 'anthro-complexity' must take account of human characteristics, values, intentions and cultural practices. Nevertheless, Snowden insists that his version of complexity theory is a 'naturalising' approach which brings 'good science' to bear to help decision-makers navigate complexity (Cynefin, 2022). His recent work on 'estuarine mapping' (Snowden, 2022, 2023a) can be taken as an example of what he seeks to achieve. Negotiating estuaries requires a knowledge of the tides, which features of the estuary are relatively fixed (e.g., granite cliffs) and which change frequently (e.g., sandbanks), and an ability to take advantage of the available 'flows of possibility'. Snowden saw this as a useful analogy for decision-makers. Strategy must start with learning what is possible. Estuarine mapping, therefore, begins with mapping the various constraints that can hinder or help you achieve your purpose. If possible, the 'actants' and 'effects' producing the constraints are identified. The constraints are then plotted on a grid indicating the energy cost and time it would take to change any of them. Some constraints will reveal themselves as 'counterfactuals' – essentially not worth trying to change. Efforts should instead be focussed on those which are easiest to manipulate and, if changed, will have the most impact. This enables a set of micro-projects to be designed to maintain useful constraints (or 'constructors') and amend or destroy others. These small and, therefore, 'fail safe' experiments should alter the dispositional state so that it is more likely that good things will happen in terms of the general strategy. In essence, estuarine mapping is about gaining knowledge about the way things are, and are likely going, and making 'micro-nudges' that support progress in the direction of the strategy.

The question that Snowden needs to answer is just how relevant a 'naturalising' approach can be in helping decision-makers address the range of important problems they face. It is, of course, important to know what is possible – 'to identify the zone where you can act strategically' (Snowden, 2023b). There will be cognitive, organisational and environmental constraints on what can be achieved, and cognitive science, cybernetics and complexity theory can be helpful in identifying these, saving organisations from treading the path of science fiction. Snowden, however, seems to want to extend the role of science as an aid to decision-makers beyond its capacities. Apparently, the principles that apply to estuaries can be extended to provide expert guidance to decision-makers on how to operate in complex social systems. However, social systems are not estuaries. It may be interesting to think in terms of the energy costs and the time needed to change certain elements, but it is wrong to think that these can be calculated in social systems with anything like the precision possible with natural systems. Further, in concentrating minds on how science can help, Snowden risks misleading decision-makers on where they should direct their attention. Aristotle (see quote at the opening of this book) knew that Thales and Anaxagoras were important because they ruled out what was impossible. But he was more concerned with deliberating on the 'good' that is attainable through action. Whatever scientific laws apply to human and social systems, they allow for huge differences in thought and behaviour, for different values and the creation of widely divergent cultures and for varied kinds of organisational and societal structures. It is in this direction that the most important issues lie. Providing better science will not help here. There is no relevant science. As Husserl said, in 1936:

> In our vital need ... science has nothing to say to us. It excludes in principle precisely the question which man, given over in our unhappy times to the most portentous upheavals, finds the most burning: questions about

the meaning or meaninglessness of this whole human existence. Do not these questions, universal and necessary for all men, demand universal reflections and answers based on rational insight? In the final analysis they concern man as a free, self-determining being in his behaviour toward the human and extrahuman surrounding world and free in regard to his capacities for rationally shaping himself and his surrounding world. (Husserl, 1970, p. 6)

2.5   The 'Problem' of Emergence

The reason the search for general systems laws has made such little headway is due to the 'problem' of emergence and the fact it produces systems with different properties at higher levels of complexity. The idea of 'emergence' is clearly present in Aristotle's insight that a whole can be more than the sum of its parts. Emergent properties arise at the level of the whole because of the way the parts are organised and interact. They are impossible to infer by studying the parts in isolation. Water emerges from a particular structural arrangement of the elements hydrogen and oxygen and exhibits qualitatively different physical and chemical properties. The organismic biologists argued that organisms exhibit emergent properties – life and what is necessary to reproduce life – which depend on the 'organisational relations' between the parts. Consciousness, self-consciousness and free will are seen as emergent properties of complex neuronal networks. Sociologists theorise that social systems emerge from the interactions of individual actors or communications. Heylighen et al. remark:

> In fact, on closer scrutiny practically all of the properties that matter to us in everyday-life, such as beauty, life, status, intelligence … turn out to be emergent. Therefore, it is surprising that science has ignored emergence and holism for so long. (Heylighen et al., 2006, p. 6)

There is a dispute between advocates of 'weak' and 'strong' emergence. Weak emergentists argue that reductionism fails because of limitations on our investigative abilities which may just be temporary. Strong emergentists argue that complexity gives rise to new entities with a real existence in the world and with their own distinct features (Ruphy, 2016). This dispute is exemplified in the debate between Rovelli and Ellis, as reported by Ellis (2020). Rovelli, a weak emergentist, argues that, in principle, all phenomena are reducible to microphysical causation, although, in practice, it is convenient and useful to operate with higher-level concepts because of the complexity involved and the limits on our capabilities. Ellis, an advocate of strong emergentism, argues that, at high levels of complexity, new entities emerge with properties that are irreducible to their constituent parts. Further, these new entities, based on higher-level organising principles, are capable of exhibiting 'downward causation', impacting their components and changing the physical world. Microphysical factors allow for multiple outcomes, opening an immense space of possibilities for biological, ecological, social and conceptual variables to call the tune by imposing their own constraints:

> Real world causal closure is an interlevel affair, with microphysical outcomes determined by features ranging from global warming and tropical cyclones to COVID-19 policy decisions. It simply cannot occur at the microphysics level alone. Some of the effective variables which have changed human history are abstract concepts such as the invention of arithmetic, the concept of money, and the idea of a closed corporation. They have all crucially affected microphysical outcomes, as have abstract theories such as the theory of the laser and the concepts of algorithms, compilers, and the internet. (Ellis, 2020, p. 47)

Although I think Ellis gets the better of this argument, it need not concern decision-makers too much. Even weak emergentists recognise the need to take shortcuts and work with descriptions of reality beyond the microphysical level.

Furthermore, stable levels of organised complexity appear to exist in a hierarchy, with new emergent properties at each level. Smuts, writing in 1926, invented the word 'holism' to refer to 'the operative factor in the evolution of wholes ... the ultimate principle of the universe'. He argued that evolution is marked by the progressive development of ever more highly organised wholes, the earlier structures forming the basis for later 'more evolved synthetic holistic structures' (Smuts, 1986). According to Smuts, holistic structure emerges in stages:

- Definite material structure of a physico-chemical character, e.g., in a chemical compound
- Functional structure in living bodies, e.g., in a plant
- More coordinated or regulated, although mostly unconscious, central control in living bodies, e.g., in an animal
- Central control becomes conscious and culminates in 'personality', e.g., in human minds
- Human associations, where the central control becomes super-individual, e.g., in the State
- Ideal wholes, e.g., truth, beauty, goodness

(Adapted from Smuts, 1986, pp. 106–107)

For Smuts, as for Ellis, the nature of wholes transforms the concept of causality:

> In fact the physical category of "cause" undergoes a far-reaching change in its application to organisms or wholes generally. The whole appears as the real cause of the response, and not the external stimulus, which seems to play the quite minor role of a mere excitant or condition. (Smuts, 1986, p. 119)

Wholes, therefore, are the basis of 'creativeness' and of increasing self-determination and freedom.

The significance of all this for decision-makers is that they will need access to alternative ways of thinking and require disparate tools to deal with different types of organised complexity. Of the early systems thinkers, it was Kenneth Boulding who paid the most attention to the unique characteristics of systems at different levels of complexity and to specifying an 'appropriate epistemology' for each level. The argument is set out in his seminal 1956 paper *General Systems Theory – The Skeleton of Science* (1968). Boulding produced a nine-level hierarchy of levels of real-world complexity, stretching from structures and frameworks, at the simplest level, to transcendental systems at the most complex. The hierarchy is summarised in Table 2.1.

Table 2.1 A summary of Boulding's (1956) hierarchy of complexity.

1. At level 1 are structures and frameworks which exhibit static behavior and are studied by verbal or pictorial description in any discipline; an example being crystal structures

2. At level 2 are clockworks which exhibit predetermined motion and are studied by classical natural science; an example being the solar system

3. At level 3 are control mechanisms which exhibit closed-loop control and are studied by cybernetics; an example being a thermostat

4. At level 4 are open systems which exhibit structural self-maintenance and are studied by theories of metabolism; an example being a biological cell

5. At level 5 are lower organisms which have functional parts, exhibit blue-printed growth and reproduction and are studied by botany; an example being a plant

6. At level 6 are animals which have a brain to guide behaviour, are capable of learning and are studied by zoology; an example being an elephant

7. At level 7 are people who possess self-consciousness, know that they know, employ symbolic language and are studied by biology and psychology; an example being any human being

8. At level 8 are sociocultural systems which are typified by the existence of roles, communications and the transmission of values and are studied by history, sociology, anthropology and behavioural science; an example being a nation

9. At level 9 are transcendental systems, the home of 'inescapable unknowables' which no scientific discipline can capture; an example being the idea of God

Reviewing his hierarchy, Boulding notes that the characteristics of lower-level systems, such as level 3 closed-loop control, can be found at higher levels, for example, in the 'homeostatic' regulation of body temperature. Each level, however, presents emergent properties that cannot be understood simply in terms of the theoretical concepts employed successfully at lower levels, hence the need for new disciplines like biology, psychology, anthropology and sociology at more complex system levels. A key issue in understanding and predicting system behaviour at higher levels of complexity is the intervention of 'the image' into the chain of causality. In his most influential book, *The Image* (1961), he charts the growing sophistication of the images systems have of their environments and, eventually, of themselves. Simple organisms have knowledge in the form of structured images which can change with experience. At the people level, the human brain organises the information it receives into extremely rich and complex images which are massively enhanced by language. These images consist of facts, or what is believed to be true about the world, which are inextricably linked to values, standards of good and bad. Whatever is made available to a person biologically is built upon as a result of experiences including, particularly, socialisation in the family and at school. Images are generally resistant to change and ignore messages that do not conform to their internal settings. Sometimes, however, they can alter in an incremental or even revolutionary manner. Humans can talk about and share their images and, in the symbolic universe they create, reflect upon what is and what might be. This 'brings the actor into the act', capable, in part at least, of moulding the future (Boulding, 1961).

Boulding uses his hierarchy to point to gaps in our knowledge and to alert us to a potential danger – employing a level of theoretical analysis below the level of complexity of the empirical phenomenon of interest. For example, it is wrong to treat an organisation as though it is a machine or an organism, although it will share some of the characteristics of machines and organisms. But he also notes a surprising twist:

> Nevertheless as we move towards the human and societal level a curious thing happens: the fact that we have, as it were, an inside track, and that we ourselves *are* the systems which we are studying, enables us to utilize systems which we do not really understand. (Boulding, 1968, p. 9; italics in the original)

This has important implications. ST cannot just be about extending some version of the scientific method to higher levels of complexity. As Schumacher puts it:

> As soon, however, as we accept the existence of 'levels of being', we can readily understand, for instance, why the methods of physical science

cannot be applied to the study of politics or economics, or why the findings of physics – as Einstein recognized – have no philosophical implications (Schumacher, 1973, p. 75)

At the people and sociocultural levels, a very different kind of knowledge is necessary and must be sought using an approach more in tune with pragmatism and interpretive social science.

Modifications to the hierarchy have been proposed over the years, and greater sophistication is possible. Stanislaw Lem (2013), ever insightful, envisages sophisticated entities with the freedom to choose the materials from which they 'build themselves'. However, it continues to be useful as the intuitive guide that Boulding intended.

2.6 A Pluralistic Approach to the Use of Systems Thinking

The phenomenon of emergence and the stratification of 'organised complexity' limit what can be achieved by those working for the 'unity of science'. Rovelli called for physicists to be more modest:

> The separation of reality into levels is relative to our way of being in interaction with it ... There is an autonomy and independence of levels of understanding of the world that justifies the autonomy of the different areas of knowledge. In this sense, elementary physics is much less useful than physicists would like to think. (Rovelli, 2021, p. 156)

Toulmin elaborated on this theme, commenting on developments in science in the modern era:

> Instead of being varied parts of a single, comprehensive, 'unified science', the sciences now represented, rather, a confederation of enterprises, with methods and patterns of explanation to meet their own distinct problems ... the Platonist image of a single, formal type of knowledge is replaced by a picture of enterprises that are always in flux, and whose methods of inquiry are adapted – as Aristotle taught – to 'the nature of the case'. (Toulmin, 1990, p. 165)

Systems thinkers, aiming for unity based on the existence of general systems laws, have also been frustrated. However, the efforts made by general systems theorists, cyberneticians and complexity theorists have not been entirely in vain. Rather like the alchemists examining every substance on earth in pursuit of the philosophers' stone, their work has had some positive outcomes. It has brought to the fore some insightful metaphors and an array of concepts suited to systemic research and practice and unearthed a few transferable principles and laws (for example, negative feedback). Examining this work, Checkland (1981) identified 'emergence and hierarchy' and 'communication and control' as the central systems ideas. Cabrera and Cabrera (2022) argued that 'distinctions', 'systems', 'relationships' and 'perspectives' (DSRP) constitute core concepts. Hoverstadt (2022) has derived 33 putative 'systems laws and principles' that tend to cluster into three groups concerned with dynamic, structural and perceptual aspects of complexity. This hints at what is necessary. To be meaningful and impactful, systems concepts and principles need to be pulled together in a theoretically informed way to provide appropriate responses to different levels of complexity. When systems practitioners do this, employing systems ideas coherently to manage complexity and the wicked problems to which it gives rise, they are said to be using a 'systems methodology'. ST now has at its disposal a toolkit of different systems methodologies corresponding to the various levels of Boulding's hierarchy. These express varied judgements on what are the most important aspects of complexity and seek to address complexity in different ways. Newcomers are often surprised by the variety of systems methodologies, but it should be clear that this is a strength rather than a weakness of ST.

2.7 The Development of Systems Methodologies

This section provides a brief description of the development of the variety of systems methodologies, concentrating on those which rest upon strong research traditions and have a record of successful application. These methodologies will receive detailed attention in Chapter 6, where full references will be provided. Although the account is brief, readers will note a growing shift in emphasis from ontological towards cognitive complexity (Rescher, 2019). Earlier methodologies give primary attention to managing the complexity that they see as existing in the world, while the later ones give primary attention to navigating the complexity arising from the different ways the world is viewed. Also obvious is the effort made to develop methodologies appropriate to higher levels of Boulding's hierarchy, with organismic and 'soft systems' approaches establishing themselves alongside mechanical variants.

The earliest systems methodologies were developed from within the engineering tradition. Influenced by work conducted at the Bell Telephone Laboratories in the United States, Deming developed his famous 'Management Method'. This promoted a radical transformation in management thinking away from the reductionism of the classical, hierarchical model based on the thinking of Taylor and Fayol.

The adoption of this way of thinking in Japan is credited with helping to create the post-WW2 economic miracle in that country. The Deming Management Method encouraged the spread of process mapping and other techniques to many industries. John Seddon's Vanguard Method, developed in the United Kingdom, built on Deming's approach, recasting it for service organisations and enriching it with insights from intervention theory.

Systems Engineering is another product of the Bell Telephone Laboratories, emerging in the 1940s and 1950s as engineering began to extend its scope from individual components to the design of complex systems involving many interacting elements. It was widely deployed in the defence and aerospace industries. Systems Engineering was the methodology used to guide and structure the Apollo project. It became bathed in 'moonglow', and attempts were made to transfer the approach (and Systems Analysis, its sister methodology) to a wide range of issues in the human and social domains.

The 1960s witnessed the development of industrial dynamics, later known as System Dynamics, by Jay Forrester at MIT. This was inspired by his wartime experience with servomechanisms and drew on the 'same general subject area as feedback systems, servomechanisms theory, and cybernetics' (Forrester, quoted in Kline, 2015). Forrester believed in the capacity of modern computers to enhance the capacity of the human mind to grasp the interactions between the many variables that constitute complex systems. The System Dynamics methodology was used to produce the influential 'Club of Rome' report *The Limits to Growth*, which was understood as suggesting that the 'world system' was heading for a catastrophic collapse well before the year 2100. System Dynamics is *The Fifth Discipline* underpinning Senge's famous book of that name.

The 1960s also saw the emergence of systems methodologies of an organismic or 'living systems' nature. A central concern became the ability of a system to remain viable and effective in the face of a turbulent environment. Researchers at the Tavistock Institute of Human Relations in the United Kingdom took note of von Bertalanffy's 'open systems theory' to develop an approach to intervention known as Sociotechnical Systems Thinking (STS). There was significant take-up of STS in the United Kingdom, Scandinavia and elsewhere.

In a similar organismic vein, Beer (1972) reasoned that the human body, controlled by the nervous system, could act as a template to build a model of any viable system. The Viable System Model that resulted can, it is claimed, recommend specific, cybernetically justified improvements to the viability and effectiveness of systems of all types and scales. Its most famous early application was in support of the socialist government of Salvador Allende in Chile between 1971 and 1973.

The importance of human intentionality and free will was recognised in some of the earliest work on applied ST, for example, in that of Boulding and Churchman.

ST only put human purposes centre stage, however, with the development of 'soft systems methodologies' in the 1980s. These methodologies are distinguished by their efforts to address matters of cognitive complexity. Three of the most sophisticated and well-tested of the many 'softer' methodologies are Mason and Mitroff's Strategic Assumption Surfacing and Testing (based on Churchman's thinking), Ackoff's Interactive Planning and Checkland's Soft Systems Methodology. These approaches accept and respect the pluralism generated by different viewpoints and seek to manage this while capitalising on the creativity it generates. Soft systems methodologies challenge fixed beliefs, seek alignment of purposes, and organise discussion and debate in a manner which ensures enough agreement is obtained among stakeholders to enable action to be taken.

A more recent development has been the birth of 'emancipatory systems methodologies' such as Ulrich's Critical Systems Heuristics and the Gender equality, Environments and Marginalized voices framework. These methodologies seek to address issues of legitimacy, bring to the fore the voices of the disadvantaged and highlight environmental concerns. They encourage decision-makers to pay attention to the consequences their actions have for the affected. They endeavour to promote full and open participation among stakeholders and to eliminate discrimination and disadvantage. They can reveal cases of marginalisation and multiple linked oppressions, be employed to promote the interests of oppressed groups and ensure consideration is given to other species, ecological systems, the wider environment and future generations.

It should be stressed that while this has been something of a historical account, all the systems methodologies mentioned are currently flourishing. Those developed later have not displaced those developed earlier, nor should they. All have much to offer in navigating different aspects of complexity.

2.8 Conclusion

The endeavours of those seeking to discover 'general systems laws' should be acknowledged. Expecting them to come up with findings that will significantly help leaders, managers and decision-makers is, however, akin to waiting for Godot. Even the belief that there are such laws has its dangers. It can lead the powerful to attempt social engineering based on the expert knowledge they believe is available. Von Bertalanffy, when it served his interests, was able to represent his biological writings as a scientific contribution to the National Socialist worldview:

> *The organism appears no longer, as earlier in the theory of the 'cell state', as a republic of autonomous parts with the same rights, but rather like a*

> *hierarchical structure, dominated on each level by the* Führer *principle.*
> (von Bertalanffy, quoted in Pouvreau, 2009, p. 65; italics in the original)

The use made of cybernetics to bolster authoritarian regimes and practices, in the Soviet Union and China, has been noted. In the United States, to Wiener's despair, McCulloch and von Foerster were happy for cybernetics to take the shilling of the Central Intelligence Agency (CIA) and the military (see Kline, 2015).

The greatest and most significant achievement of ST has been the establishment of a range of systems methodologies which order relevant systems ideas, principles and concepts, according to the dictates of well-established worldviews – mechanistic, interrelationships, organismic, purposeful and emancipatory – to produce powerful vehicles for seeking improvement. One consequence, of course, is that ST became fragmented. Critical Systems Thinking sets itself the task of restoring some coherence. It is to this that we now turn.

References

Ackoff, R.L. (1981). *Creating the Corporate Future*. Wiley.

Ashby, W.R. (1952). *Design for a Brain*. Chapman and Hall.

Ashby, W.R. (1956). *An Introduction to Cybernetics*. Methuen.

Beer, S. (1972). *Brain of the Firm*. Allen Lane.

Belykh, A. (1998). Bogdanov's Tektology and economic theory. In: *Alexander Bogdanov and the Origins of Systems Thinking in Russia* (eds J. Biggart, P. Dudley and F. King, 1998), pp. 143–156. Ashgate.

von Bertalanffy, L. (1967). *Robots, Men and Minds*. George Braziller, Inc.

von Bertalanffy, L. (1971). *General System Theory*. Penguin.

Bogdanov, A. (1989). *Tektology: The Universal Science of Organization, book 1*. Centre for Systems Studies Press.

Bogdanov, A. (2016). *The Philosophy of Living Experience*. Haymarket Books.

Boulding, K.E. (1961). *The Image*. Ann Arbor Paperback, University of Michigan Press.

Boulding, K.E. (1968). General systems theory – the skeleton of science. In: *Modern Systems Research for the Behavioral Scientist* (ed. W. Buckley), pp. 3–10. Aldine.

Boulton, J., Allen, P. and Bowman, C. (2015). *Embracing Complexity: Strategic Perspectives for an Age of Turbulence*. Oxford University Press.

Byrne, D. and Callaghan, G. (2014). *Complexity Theory and the Social Sciences: The State of the Art*. Routledge, Kindle edn.

Cabrera, D. and Cabrera, L. (2022). DSRP theory: a primer. *Systems* 10, 26. https://doi.org/10.3390/systems10020026.

Capra, F. (1996). *The Web of Life: A New Synthesis of Mind and Matter*. Harper Collins.

Checkland, P.B. (1981). *Systems Thinking, Systems Practice*. Chichester: Wiley.

Cilliers, P. (1998). *Complexity and Postmodernism: Understanding Complex Systems*. Routledge, Kindle edn.

Clemson, B. (1984). *Cybernetics: A New Management Tool*. Abacus.

Cynefin (2022). Naturalising sense-making. https://cynefin.io (accessed 5 June 2023).

Davidson, M. (1983). *Uncommon Sense: The Life and Thought of Ludwig von Bertalanffy*. J.P. Tarcher.

Ellis, G.F.R. (2020). Physics, determinism, and the brain. Manuscript. https://arXiv:2008.12674v3.

Gerovitch, S. (2004). *From Newspeak to Cyberspeak: A History of Soviet Cybernetics*. MIT Press.

Gleick, J. (1987). *Chaos: The Making of a New Science*. Abacus.

Hammond, D. (2003). *The Science of Synthesis: Exploring the Social Implications of General Systems Theory*. University Press of Colorado.

Heylighen, F., Cilliers, P. and Gershenson, C. (2006). Complexity and philosophy. Manuscript. https://arXiv:cs/0604072.

Holland, J.H. (2014). *Complexity: A Very Short Introduction*. Oxford University Press.

Hoverstadt, P. (2022). *The Grammar of Systems: From Order to Chaos & Back*. SCiO Publications.

Husserl, E. (1970). *The Crisis of European Sciences and Transcendental Phenomenology*. Northwestern University Press.

IBM. (2010). *Capitalizing on Complexity: Insights from the Global Chief Executive Officer Study*. IBM Publishing.

Jackson, M.C. (2022a). Rebooting the systems approach by applying the thinking of Bogdanov and the pragmatists. *Systems Research and Behavioral Science*: 1–17. https://doi.org/10.10002/sres.2908.

Jackson, M.C. (2022b). Alexander Bogdanov, Stafford Beer and intimations of a post-capitalist future. *Systems Research and Behavioral Science*: 1–15. https://doi.org/10.10002/sres.2911.

King, D.L. (2022). The genealogy of Chinese Cybernetics. *Palladium: Governance Futurism*, October 17.

Kline, R.R. (2015). *The Cybernetics Moment*. John Hopkins University Press.

Krakauer, D.C. (Ed) (2019). *Worlds Hidden in Plain Sight: The Evolving Idea of Complexity at the Santa Fe Institute 1984–2019*. SFI Press.

Lem, S. (2013). *Summa Technologiae*. University of Minnesota Press.

Lepskiy, V.E. (2018). Philosophical-methodological basis for the formation of third-order cybernetics. *Russian Journal of Philosophical Sciences* 10: 7–36.

Lindblom, C.E. (1959). The science of muddling through. *Public Administration Review* 19 (2): 79–88.

Marx, K. (1852, 1973). *Surveys from Exile: The Eighteenth Brumaire of Louis Bonaparte*. Penguin.

Maturana, H.R. (1987). The biological foundations of self-consciousness and the physical domain of existence. In: *Physics of Cognitive Processes: Amalfi 1986* (ed. E.R. Caianiello), pp. 324–380. World Scientific.

Maturana, H.R. and Varela, F.J. (1980). *Autopoiesis and Cognition: The Realization of the Living*. Reidel.

Needham, J. (1941). Evolution and thermodynamics. In: *Moulds of Understanding* (ed. G. Werskey, 1976), pp. 173–199. St. Martin's Press.

OECD. (2017*). Systems Approaches to Public Sector Challenges: Working with Change*. OECD Publishing.

Pickering, A. (2010). *The Cybernetic Brain: Sketches of Another Future*. University of Chicago Press, Kindle edn.

Pouvreau, D. (2009). *The Dialectical Tragedy of the Concept of Wholeness*. ISCE Publishing.

Prigogine, I. (1997). *The End of Certainty: Time, Chaos and the New Laws of Nature*. The Free Press.

Ramage, M. (2009). Norbert and Gregory: two strands of cybernetics. *Information, Communication & Society* 12: 735–749.

Rescher, N. (2019). *Complexity: A Philosophical Overview*. Routledge.

Rittel, H.W.J. and Webber, M.M. (1981). Dilemmas in a general theory of planning. In: *Systems Thinking*, vol. 2 (ed. F.E. Emery), pp. 81–102. Penguin.

Rosenhead, J., Franco, L.A., Grint, K. and Friedland, B. (2019). Complexity theory and leadership practice: a review, a critique, and some recommendations. *The Leadership Quarterly* 30: 1–24. https://doi.org/10.1016/j.leaQUA.2019.07.002.

Rovelli, C. (2021). *Helgoland*. Allen Lane.

Ruphy, S. (2016). *Scientific Pluralism Reconsidered*. University of Pittsburgh Press.

Santa Fe Institute. (2023). Our mission. www.santafe.edu.

Scholte, T. and Sweeting, B. (2022). Possibilities for a critical cybernetics. *Systems Research and Behavioral Science* 39: 986–989.

Schumacher, E.F. (1973). *Small Is Beautiful: A Study of Economics as if People Mattered*. Blond & Briggs Ltd.

Şenalp, O. (2019). The 'emergence' of the new world view was with Tektology, not Systemology; with Alexander Bogdanov, not Ludwig von Bertalanffy. *Social Network Unionism. Posted*, 2 April 2019.

Smuts, J.C. (1986). *Holism and Evolution*. The Gestalt Journal Press.

Snowden, D. (2022). *Estuarine Mapping Strategy*. The Cynefin Co.

Snowden, D. (2023a). Estuarine mapping. Presentation for Red Team Thinking, 28 May 2023.

Snowden, D. (2023b). Estuarine framework. Cynefin, 4 December.

Spufford, F. (2010). *Red Plenty*. Faber and Faber.

Stacey, R.D. and Mowles, C. (2016). *Strategic Management and Organisational Dynamics: The Challenge of Complexity to Ways of Thinking about Organisations*, 7e. Pearson.

Stokes, K.M. (2015). *Paradigm Lost*. Routledge.

Toulmin, S. (1990). *Cosmopolis*. Macmillan.

Von Glasersfeld, E. (1984). An introduction to radical constructivism. In: *The Invented Reality* (ed. P. Watzlawick), pp. 17–40. Norton.

Weaver, W. (2003). Science and complexity. In: *Systems Thinking*, vol. 1 (ed. G. Midgley), pp. 377–385. California: Sage.

Wiener, N. (1948). *Cybernetics*. Wiley.

Wiener, N. (1954). *The Human Use of Human Beings*. Eyre and Spottiswoode.

Zhu, Z. (2007). Complexity science, systems thinking and pragmatic sensibility. *Systems Research and Behavioral Science* 24: 445–464.

3

Critical Systems Thinking

Different problem-solving methodologies, instead of being compared with one another in relation to their ability to solve the generality of problem types, should be evaluated in relation to their success in solving problems for which they are most suited. This should encourage mutual respect among the proponents of the different approaches ... then a diversity of approaches may herald, not crisis, but increased competence and effectiveness in a variety of different problem contexts.

(Jackson and Keys, 1984)

3.1 Introduction

Critical Systems Thinking (CST) is a systems approach that aims to assist decision-makers to better understand and address the complex issues they face. This chapter looks at the origins and early development of CST. A brief account of the state of Systems Thinking (ST) in the early 1980s is necessary to discern the reasons for the emergence of the approach. The development of CST is then traced up to 1991. By that time, it had become formalised around a set of three commitments, to which it has largely remained true. The first, 'systemic critique', insists that all systems approaches are partial, and this leads to their different strengths and weaknesses. The second, 'systemic pluralism', suggests that the maximum benefit can be obtained by using systems methodologies in combination during an intervention. The third, 'systemic improvement', explains what improvement means in systems terms and how it can be pursued. The case is then made for CST to embrace a fourth commitment, to 'systemic pragmatism'. It is argued that this can support the other three and take CST forward.

3.2   The Origins and Early Development of Critical Systems Thinking

In Chapter 2, we traced the emergence of systems methodologies designed to translate ST into practice. The 1950s and 1960s saw significant success using methodologies such as Systems Engineering (SE) and Systems Analysis (SA) in technical fields. However, attempts to extend the approaches to tackle a broader range of human and social issues were less successful. Hoos (1974) documented the failures that ensued when applying them to problems of information management, crime, welfare, transportation and waste management, in California in the 1960s. She concluded:

> The question we have asked in this research study is, "Are the techniques of systems analysis appropriate when we are dealing with problems which are essentially human and social?" The findings indicate that in their present condition they are not. (Hoos, 1974, p. 247)

During the 1970s, SE and SA, labelled 'hard systems' approaches, were subject to sustained criticism from other systems thinkers (Checkland, 1978; Ackoff, 1979; Churchman, 1979).

Not surprisingly, other systems methodologies came to the fore explicitly designed to extend the scope of ST. Forrester developed System Dynamics (SD) and Beer his Viable System Model (VSM). Churchman, Ackoff and Checkland formulated 'soft systems approaches', which they claimed were more attuned to the reality of social systems in which multiple perspectives proliferate and political machinations are common. The originators of the newer methodologies trumpeted the superiority of their own creations and pointed to examples of successful applications. When communication did take place between advocates of the different strands of ST, it tended to be antagonistic. Furthermore, the period of the 1960s and 1970s was one of cultural and political upheaval, and ST had its own 'radicals' who criticised soft systems approaches for taking a 'reformist' rather than an 'emancipatory' stance (Thomas and Lockett, 1979; Jackson, 1982). The plethora of warring factions led some to ask whether there was a 'Kuhnian crisis' in the field (Dando and Bennett, 1981). It was argued that the dominant paradigm, as exemplified by SE, had broken down, but no alternative had yet succeeded in mustering sufficient support to replace it.

It was into this world that CST was born. CST has been largely developed at the Centre for Systems Studies, University of Hull. The primary inspiration for taking ST in a critical direction was the work of the Frankfurt School, especially that of Habermas (1970, 1974). The Frankfurt School of social theorists was committed, as neatly summarised by Finlayson (2005), to interdisciplinarity, a dialectical understanding of the relationship between theory and society, respect for traditional methods of enquiry but only in the right context and a critique of society with a view to transforming it for the better. All these characteristics became embedded in CST.

CST was constituted from three strands of research that became intertwined. First, Mingers (1980, 1984) and Jackson (1982, 1985) built on Checkland's assertion that hard systems thinking was unable to conceptualise and manage different stakeholder perspectives because of its 'functionalist underpinnings'. They argued that soft systems thinkers were themselves constrained by adhering, explicitly or implicitly, to 'interpretive' assumptions. Interpretive social theory cannot understand structural sources of disadvantage in society, or how power operates, and so leaves soft systems approaches helpless in addressing the consequences. Mingers and Jackson called for an extensive critical appraisal based upon Habermas's work of the social theories underpinning different systems approaches and how these impacted their modes of practical engagement.

The second strand concluded that pluralism was the best way forward for ST. Jackson and Keys (1984) explored the relationships between different systems methodologies to better understand their respective strengths and weaknesses and assist practitioners in choosing an appropriate methodology for an intervention. They created the System of Systems Methodologies (SOSM), which classified methodologies according to their ability to deal with the difficulties posed by, on the one hand, increasing system and environmental complexity and, on the other, by the increasing divergence of perspectives among stakeholders. This suggested that different systems methodologies had different strengths and could be seen as complementary rather than competitive. Later, making use of Habermas's theory of different 'human interests', I argued (Jackson, 1987) that pluralism offered the best developmental strategy for ST. Hard systems thinking could serve the 'technical' interest in greater prediction and control; soft systems thinking the 'practical' interest in mutual understanding; and 'radical' systems approaches the 'emancipatory' interest. Pluralism would respect the strengths of the different versions of ST, encourage their theoretical development and suggest how they could be appropriately fitted to a variety of problem situations.

The third strand resulted from the desire to extend ST to respond to the radical change agenda. At the time of constructing the SOSM, Jackson and Keys acknowledged that relationships between stakeholders could be 'coercive', but they were not aware of any systems methodologies that responded to this possibility. The demand for an 'emancipatory systems approach' seemed to be met with Ulrich's (1983) Critical Systems Heuristics (CSH). This was an independently developed strand of ST, drawing on the works of Kant, Churchman and Habermas, which appeared to address the issues posed by coercive contexts. It was arguably capable of providing guidelines for action on behalf of disadvantaged stakeholders.

CST came to prominence in 1991 with the publication of three books – *Critical Systems Thinking: Directed Readings* (Flood and Jackson, 1991b), *Systems Methodology for the Management Sciences* (Jackson, 1991) and *Creative Problem Solving: Total Systems Intervention* (Flood and Jackson 1991a). The first was a collection of papers, accompanied by a commentary, which traced the origins and outlined the major themes of the approach. It highlighted the contributions to CST of authors such as Flood, Fuenmayor, Jackson, Mingers, Oliga and Ulrich. The second responded to the earlier call for a critique of all the major systems methodologies from the perspective of social theory, made the case for CST and sought to demonstrate that it could take the lead in enriching theory and practice in the management sciences. The third book was the first attempt to show how CST could be used in practice. Flood and Jackson offered the ambitious 'Total Systems Intervention' (TSI) meta-methodology as an attempt to show how the theory underpinning CST could be operationalised. TSI claimed to be able to organise and employ, in an appropriate manner, all the different systems methodologies according to their strengths and weaknesses in the service of a general project of improving complex organisational and societal systems. The work of Habermas provided the theoretical backdrop.

Since 1991, CST has been taken forward (citing only a selection of books) by Flood (1995, 1999), Jackson (2000, 2003, 2019), Mingers (2006, 2014), Midgley (2000), Hobbs (2019) and Chowdhury (2019), among others. Although there are differences in emphasis, CST retains a strong identity, and three shared commitments can be picked out for discussion. I call these *systemic critique, systemic pluralism* and *systemic improvement*. Agreement on an appropriate philosophy to ground these commitments has been harder to establish. I regard *systemic pragmatism* as such a philosophy and as essential to the advancement of CST. I develop the argument in its favour later in the chapter.

3.3 Systemic Critique

CST has always prioritised systemic critique. It recognised, following Churchman, that it is impossible for any systems approach to understand the whole system. In *The Design of Inquiring Systems* (1971), Churchman argued that each of five possible designs for acquiring useful knowledge (derived from Leibniz, Locke, Kant, Hegel and Singer) is insufficient, resting upon assumptions that cannot be proved using its own logic. Singer's is the most comprehensive but is still incomplete. Ulrich (1983) offered a way forward for systems thinkers. The ideal standard of whole system design could be used as a spur to reflection on the lack of comprehensiveness of any actual or proposed design. CST directs the focus onto systems approaches and methodologies and conducts a second-order critique of the assumptions they make about social reality and how to intervene successfully to improve it. Social theory and the SOSM have been used to ground the analysis. Recently, I provided a critique of ten well-established systems methodologies to show how the theoretical distinctions they employ determine what aspects of 'reality' they give precedence to in seeking to improve the human condition (Jackson, 2019). This furnishes systems practitioners with an awareness of the potential strengths and weaknesses of the approaches they have in their armoury.

Strong support for systemic critique can be derived from the works of Luhmann and Morin. In Luhmann's view, social theory must give up its quest for ontological certainty and become the study of how first-order observers observe. Such second-order observation represents a shift from ontology to epistemology. Instead of trying to uphold claims about the nature of social reality, sociologists should concentrate on how different social theories construct societal issues from the 'distinctions' they employ:

> Second-order observation is observation of an observer with a view to that which he cannot see ... we become interested in the distinctions with which the observed observer works, and in how he divides up the world, and in what he considers important (or not) in which situations. (Luhmann, 2013, p. 112)

In Morin's view, ST reveals two different responses to the diagnosis that decision-makers confront increasing complexity. He labels these responses as 'restricted complexity' and 'general complexity' (Morin, 2006). Those who follow a restricted complexity path continue to refine computational modelling techniques through which, they believe, they can explain complex systems. This is true of those in SD who build computer simulation models of real-world systems and seek to validate them scientifically. It is true of those who conduct agent-based modelling of complex adaptive systems, trying to explain the behaviour of the whole in terms of rules governing the interaction of the agents constituting the system. Morin accepts that the restricted complexity viewpoint encourages advances in formalisation, modelling and interdisciplinary working but regards it as remaining 'within the epistemology of classical science', searching for hidden laws under the surface. Morin insists on the general complexity option. General complexity

> ... asserts itself first of all as an impossibility to simplify; it arises where complex unity produces its emergences, where distinctions and clarities in identities and causalities are lost, where disorder and uncertainty disturb phenomena, where the subject/observer surprises his own face in the object of his observation, where antinomies make the course of the reasoning go astray .... (Morin, 1992, p. 386)

General complexity is 'unknowable' and so is resistant to universal truth. All attempts to model it are partial and, therefore, the fundamental problem of general complexity 'is epistemological, cognitive, paradigmatic' – concerned with the ways we seek to understand and manage the complexity (Morin, 2006). In Morin's view:

> Here we have an absolute requirement which allows us to distinguish between a more simple mode of thinking – where one believes one possesses the truth – and complex knowing which demands a self-observing (and I would add, self-criticizing) turn on the part of the observer – conceiver. (Morin, 2008, p. 92)

Complex knowing asks us to make the fundamental distinctions employed by theories as clear as possible. It also points out that our actions will likely have unpredictable consequences. More humility is in order.

Systemic critique is a positive manoeuvre because it enables systems practitioners to capitalise on the strengths of existing systems methodologies while also calling attention to their limitations. It provides CST with the capacity to use such systems approaches as SE, SD, the VSM, soft systems approaches, CSH and others together in a responsive and flexible way, to maximise the benefits they can bring. Of course, this will include taking advantage of those more attuned to restricted complexity, but only with a clear appreciation of their limitations.

3.4 Systemic Pluralism

The second commitment of CST is to systemic pluralism. In the face of complexity, decision-making is enhanced if it takes advantage of multiple perspectives, and intervention is more effective if it can make use of a range of methodologies and methods. Decision-makers need to learn how to see through different systemic lenses and use different combinations of systems methodologies to maximise the strengths and compensate for the weaknesses of each. Ruphy (2016) offered two justifications for 'scientific pluralism'. One is that the complexity of the world is such that incompatible representations are inescapable and so 'epistemically acceptable'. The other is that there are different kinds of things in the world that can only be known in different ways. Both stand in support of systemic pluralism.

CST has constructed an 'ideal type' of systemic pluralism (Jackson, 2019). The first requirement is that a 'multiperspectival' approach is adopted. A variety of insightful systemic perspectives should be employed to achieve a rich appreciation of the situation we hope to improve. These should reflect worldviews that have proven themselves useful. The learning gained needs translating into action. The second requirement is, therefore, for 'multimethodological' pluralism. This is possible because systemic critique reveals that the different systems methodologies rest upon alternative worldviews and recommend intervening in different ways. Awareness of their strengths and weaknesses informs multimethodological practice relevant to improving the situation of interest. A third requirement is that pluralism should be 'multimethod'. It should encourage flexibility in the use of the widest set of relevant methods, models, tools and techniques in any intervention. This enables practitioners to respond to the uniqueness of the situations they confront and the exigencies they throw up during an intervention. A final requirement is that pluralism operates at all stages of an intervention. This is what Pollack (2009) called a 'parallel' rather than 'serial' use of different systems approaches. It is tempting to adopt a serial approach and allocate different methodologies to the various phases of an intervention because they seem most suitable to that phase. Mingers (1992) noted that some information systems researchers advocate using Checkland's Soft Systems Methodology (SSM) at the beginning of a study to reconcile multiple perceptions, before proceeding with structured design methods. But there is no justification for such a course of action. Different perspectives, and issues arising from politics and power, cannot simply be made to disappear at the beginning of a project, never to be seen again. They will remain as a crucial backdrop in any intervention and must be attended to continuously as it progresses.

3.5 Systemic Improvement

The third commitment of CST is to achieve systemic improvement. Churchman and Ackoff, writing in 1950, saw improvement in terms of the progress of human-kind in pursuit of the 'ideal'. This ideal, as summarised by Ing (2023), has four aspects:

1) The ideal of 'plenty' (perfect production and distribution)
2) The ideal of 'truth' (perfect knowledge)
3) The ideal of 'moral good' (perfect cooperation)
4) The ideal of 'freedom' (perfect regeneration in ideal pursuit)

CST, similarly, embraces a broad conception of improvement. It derives the parameters it uses from its understanding of those things which appear essential to the survival and prosperity of the human species on this planet. Improvement is not just about increased efficiency and efficacy but also, for example, effectiveness (are we doing the right things?), mutual understanding, resilience, anti-fragility, fairness and sustainability. These are the purposes, as will become clear, which are served by the range of systems methodologies now available.

For CST, the pursuit of systemic improvement has two aspects – improvement in the actual situation in which an intervention takes place, and improvement in the means of bringing about improvement. To achieve both, it draws upon a form of study known in the social sciences as 'action research', which aims, in Rapoport's definition, to contribute

> ... *both* to the practical concerns of people in an immediate problematic situation and to the goals of social science by joint collaboration within a mutually agreed ethical framework. (Rapoport, 1970, p. 499; italics in the original)

The term 'action research' was coined around 1944 by the social psychologist Kurt Lewin, who was much influenced by Gestalt psychology. Lewin firmly believed that research in the social sciences should serve social practice: 'Research that produces nothing but books will not suffice' (Lewin, 1967). This means that any research programme set up in an organisation

> ... must be guided closely by the needs of that organization, and must help define those needs more specifically. (Lewin, 1967, p. 444)

The research must have the full cooperation of those engaged in the situation, and they will be involved in monitoring and assessing the results obtained. In Lewin's view, this does not necessarily lead to any loss in scientific rigour and so the outcomes can, at the same time, enhance knowledge in the social sciences.

Action research is well established in the systems tradition. From its beginnings, employing methodologies such as SE, the emphasis has been on meeting the requirements of 'clients' while learning from that experience how to improve future projects. Checkland developed and gradually improved SSM in a prolonged action research programme. Checkland and Holwell (1998) set out a rigorous framework for carrying out action research in ST, and this is fully considered in Chapter 8. Umpleby (2016), from a second-order cybernetics perspective, recommended action research as a means of doing 'science from within'. Boulton et al. (2015) argued that, because knowledge can only ever be local and contextual, complexity thinkers must content themselves with trying to find out 'what works' using an action research approach based on trial and error and reflection. In general, ST has a good record of bringing about improvement in the situations in which it has been used. The record of the various systems communities in developing their theories and methodologies has been less healthy. There has been a tendency to stick to favoured worldviews and methodologies whatever the evidence from the real world might be. This has contributed to the divisions and disputes in ST. Later, I hope to show how Critical Systems Practice (CSP) can take both aspects of systemic improvement to a higher level.

3.6 The Argument for Systemic Pragmatism

The world in which we live exhibits the characteristics of volatility, uncertainty, complexity and ambiguity (VUCA), stemming from increasing ontological and cognitive complexity. Mingers (2006), drawing on Habermas, saw reality as 'multi-dimensional', consisting of a 'complex interaction of substantively different elements'. Things are in constant flux, and little is predictable. Kay and King (2020) represented our world as one of 'radical uncertainty' in which we simply do not know how to act. As Zhu (forthcoming) argues, it is this world of heterogeneity, with its emergent complexities, that justifies systemic pragmatism. It took CST some time to get there.

3.6.1 From Paradigms to Pragmatism

CST's early justification for its three commitments was to present itself as a 'metaparadigm' based on Habermas's theory of human interests (Flood and Jackson, 1991a). This allowed it to stand above the paradigms and pick out appropriate methodologies according to whether the technical, practical or emancipatory interest needed support. This solution does not work because, in Luhmann's words:

> The observer does not exist somewhere high above reality. He does not hover above things and does not look down from above in order to observe what is going on. Nor is he a subject ... outside the world of objects. Instead, he is in the middle of it all .... (Luhmann, 2013, p. 101)

CST had to find a different way forward. Wendy Gregory's (1996) argument for 'discordant pluralism' and Morgan's (1983) idea of 'reflective conversation' between paradigms provided a possibility. CST offered itself as a framework enabling critique of each paradigm based on the assumptions of the others (Jackson, 2000, 2019). This sees CST as managing paradigm diversity not by aspiring to be a metaparadigm but by using the paradigms to confront one another. Critique is managed *between* the paradigms. No paradigm is allowed to escape unquestioned because it is continually challenged by alternatives. At a stroke, however, CST loses whatever justification it obtains from the theory (some overarching paradigm) underpinning its claim to metaparadigmatic status. The problem of relativism raises its head. How can CST abandon adherence to a theory that supported its pluralism and, at the same time, avoid relativism?

Zhu was particularly scathing about the endless discussions around paradigms that have dominated the history of CST. He regards the search for a theoretical foundation for CST as not only ill-conceived but also as holding back acceptance and use of the ideas by practitioners:

> Paradigm-based theorizing is not working. It fails to make a practical difference. This is certified as OR [Operational Research] workers manage to mix methodologies satisfactorily in intervention without theorists sorting out the paradigm incommensurability mess. (Zhu, 2011, p. 795)

He argues forcefully in favour of a 'pragmatist alternative' for CST that seeks justification in terms of practical effectiveness. I think this argument is correct and will develop it here.

3.6.2 What Is Pragmatism?

Pragmatism has a long history. Aristotle's championing of practical wisdom (Greek *phronesis*) – the capacity to act according to what is good or bad for people according to the circumstances – against Plato's search for knowledge of a universal, timeless kind, is in tune with one of its key concerns (Toulmin, 1990). Rescher (1977) traced its development in the 'Sceptical school' of Greek philosophy – in the works of Pyrrho, Archesilaus and Carneades. Gradually, the argument that there can be no certain knowledge transmuted into the claim that 'if a thesis is presumptively true, then it will serve the rational man with an adequate basis for practice' (Rescher, 1977). Spinoza's insistence that there are two equally valid ways of describing the universe, in terms of matter and in terms of mind, opened the way to a pragmatist acceptance of multiple truths (Rorty, 1997). Marx's argument that truth can only emerge from engagement with the world illustrates another theme of pragmatism:

> The question whether objective truth can be attributed to human thinking is not a question of theory but is a *practical* question. Man must prove the truth, i.e. the reality and power, the this-sidedness of his thinking in practice. The dispute over the reality or non-reality of thinking that is isolated from practice is a purely *scholastic* question. (Marx, 1845, p. 422; italics in the original)

The term 'pragmatism' was derived from Kant. Kant was in awe of Newton's science but believed it could supply certainty only about the physical world. In most areas of human endeavour, we must use 'pragmatic belief' to guide our actions:

> The physician must do something for a patient in danger, but he does not know the nature of his illness. He ... judges it to be a case of phthisis. Now even in his own estimation his belief is contingent only; another observer might perhaps come to a sounder conclusion. Such contingent belief, which yet forms the ground for the actual employment of means to certain actions, I entitle *pragmatic belief*. (Kant, quoted in Menand, 2002, p. 227; italics in the original)

We concentrate on the work of the American pragmatists, Peirce, James and Dewey, who made their major contributions in the late nineteenth and early twentieth centuries. They viewed the realm in which humans are forced to act based on 'pragmatic belief' as vast and hoped to make philosophy relevant again by offering guidance to help navigate it. They had their differences, and it is frequently said that there are as many pragmatisms as there are pragmatists. Nevertheless, I am encouraged that Menand (2002), Talisse and Aikin (2008) and Bacon (2012) have succeeded in writing coherent accounts of pragmatism from historical, thematic and individual (sections on the individual pragmatists) perspectives, respectively. I have been influenced by these excellent introductions in identifying five themes of the pragmatist tradition.

Pragmatists *reject the spectator theory of knowledge*, set forth by Plato and Descartes, in which the self stands aside from the world and seeks to gain an accurate representation of it. Menand summarises their alternative:

> They all believed that ideas are not 'out there' waiting to be discovered, but are tools – like forks and knives and microchips – that people devise to cope with the world in which they find themselves. (Menand, 2002, p. xi)

This led Dewey to call for the 'recovery of philosophy', rescuing it from the pointless pursuit of 'eternal wisdom' and making it relevant to everyday affairs. For him, knowledge emerges from the dynamic interaction of an organism with its environment as it seeks to achieve equilibrium in the face of 'problematic situations'. Encouraged by Darwinism, he asserted that:

> If the living, experiencing being is an intimate participant in the activities of the world to which it belongs, then knowledge is a mode of participation, valuable in the degree in which it is effective. It cannot be the idle view of an unconcerned spectator. (Dewey, 1997, p. 210)

Peirce (1997) used the term 'fallibilism' to express his view that there are *no universal truths*. Even though we must accept and act on truths 'ultimately agreed to by all who investigate', we can never be certain that they will not come crashing down. For James, there could be no final and definitive truths because reality is forever changing; it is in flux, not complete and ready-made. We will never get anything done if we wait for some absolute truth to be discovered and confirmed:

> Meanwhile we have to live today by what truth we can get today and be ready tomorrow to call it falsehood. (James, 1997a, pp. 124–125)

Dewey gave a historical account of the relationship between philosophical 'truth' and social conditions. For example, the scholastic method had relevance to the times during which it held sway (Dewey, 1997).

For Peirce, there was no reason why philosophy should begin with 'universal doubt', as Descartes advocated. If beliefs lead to 'habits of action' which have predictable consequences, then they can be regarded as true. *Beliefs can be evaluated according to their consequences.* From this follows his famous 'pragmatic maxim':

> Consider what effects, which might conceivably have practical bearings, we conceive the object of our conception to have. Then, our conception of these effects is the whole of our conception of the object. (Peirce, 1997, p. 36)

James, a psychologist, broadened the maxim to make it directly relevant to the consequences of beliefs for people's lives:

> The whole function of philosophy ought to be to find out what definite difference it will make to you and me, at definite instants of our life, if this world-formula or that world-formula be the true one. (James, 1997b, p. 96)

Noting the previous two themes, Putnam wrote:

> That one can be both fallibilistic *and* antisceptical is perhaps *the* basic insight of American Pragmatism. (Putnam, quoted in Bacon, 2012, p. 6; italics in the original)

James saw *reality as a multiverse.* A multiverse allows for multiple truths and can be explored by science and metaphysics working together. James called this position 'pluralism' – a term that, according to Menand (2002), he introduced to English-language philosophy. He explains this position using an analogy provided by the Italian pragmatist Papini. Papini argued that pragmatism

> ... lies in the midst of our theories, like a corridor in a hotel. Innumerable chambers open out of it. In one you may find a man writing an atheistic volume; in the next someone on his knees praying for faith and strength; in a third a chemist investigating a body's properties. In a fourth a system of

idealistic metaphysics is being excogitated; in a fifth the impossibility of meta-physics is being shown. But they all own the corridor, and all must pass through it if they want a practical way of getting into or out of their respective rooms. (James, 1997b, p. 98)

The corridor of pragmatism evaluates the evidence of all these endeavours in terms of what 'pays' in life.

Finally, James saw *theories as instruments of action* rather than attempts to mirror the world. They should be used to change existing realities. Truth is not fixed; indeed, we have the freedom to make ideas come true:

The truth of an idea is not a stagnant property inherent in it. Truth *happens* to an idea. It *becomes* true, is *made* true by events. Its verity *is* in fact an event, a process: the process namely of its verifying itself, its veri-*fication*. Its validity is the process of its valid-*ation*. (James, 1997a, p. 114; italics in the original)

People have a responsibility to improve the world and should employ ideas that promote purposeful action to this end – in a spirit of hopefulness, even though we cannot be certain of success. For Dewey, once the 'spectator theory of knowledge' is abandoned and the self is seen as part and parcel of events, then the possibility arises for philosophy to help us act in intelligent ways:

Philosophy recovers itself when it ceases to be a device for dealing with the problems of philosophers and becomes a method, cultivated by philoso-phers, for dealing with the problems of men. (Dewey, quoted in Menand, 2002, p. 362)

3.6.3 Towards Systemic Pragmatism

In developing systemic pragmatism, CST sees itself as building on ST's pragmatist roots rather than charting a new direction for the transdiscipline.

Bogdanov, von Bertalanffy and Wiener all lean towards pragmatism in philosophy despite the claims they otherwise make that their work offers the pos-sibility of a universal science. Bogdanov, like James, was influenced by the Austrian physicist and philosopher Ernst Mach, and all five of the pragmatist themes elaborated on above are present and correct in his writings (Jackson, 2023). For example, Bogdanov clearly regarded truth as a tool for serving human activity:

Thus, philosophical truth is a tool for living, as are all other truths. It is a tool for the *general guidance* of human practice, just as a compass and geo-graphical chart are tools for guidance on journeys. (Bogdanov, 2016, p. 13; italics in the original)

Mach's philosophy also had an impact on the Gestalt school of psychology which, in turn, influenced von Bertalanffy. As we saw in Chapter 2, von Bertalanffy advocated a 'perspective' philosophy which argues that all forms of knowledge can only capture certain aspects of the truth. He shared with Bogdanov and the pragmatists a belief in the creative role played by cognition in shaping the 'buzzing, blooming confusion' of sense-data, in James's famous phrase. Humans are in the unique position of being able to shape their own destiny. Wiener studied with Dewey for a time and read James's books with zeal. Peters and Peters argued that we should recognise his work as contributing far more than just a footnote in the historical evolution of pragmatism:

> If the pragmatist tradition is characterized by interests in epistemological short-cuts, a vision of the continuity of evolving life forms, and cosmological ambition, Norbert Wiener is a worthy pragmatist descendent in all respects. (Peters and Peters, 2016, p. 170)

James's (1997c) vision of a pluralist universe, fluid and ever-changing, hanging together loosely, provisionally and 'every which way' and exhibiting novelty, spontaneity and variety, is music to the ears of some complexity theorists. Mowles (2022) saw pragmatism, complexity science, process sociology and group analytic theory/practice as the four traditions of thought that are key to his understanding of complex social reality. Boulton et al. (2015), much influenced by Prigogine, identified pragmatism as the philosophy underpinning their version of complexity management. Pragmatists view the world as one of 'indeterminacy, uncertainty, and spontaneity'. Prigogine's work on dissipative structures confirmed that knowledge can only ever be local and contextual. Ansell and Geyer (2017) argued for a marriage of the tradition of American pragmatism and the newer approach of complexity theory and set out a framework for 'pragmatic complexity'.

Turning to the more applied areas of ST, it has been argued that Deming's work and SE are best understood in pragmatist terms (Lovitt, 1997; Carayannis and Forbes, 2001). Barton (1999) set out some direct and less-direct influences of pragmatism on applied ST, paying particular attention to SD. STS combines von Bertalanffy's ideas with the 'action research' of Lewin, who derived his methodology from Peirce and was influenced by Dewey (Adelman, 1993).

Pickering (2010) argued that British cybernetics embraced a distinctive philosophy which resembles the pragmatism of James. Ashby, Beer and others operated according to what Pickering calls a 'performative idiom'. Ashby viewed the human brain not as a cognitive organ seeking true representations of reality but as an 'embodied organ' that has evolved to help human beings find their way in a world they can never fully know. It follows that knowledge is not something fixed but always in the making, emerging from interactions between systems and forever leaving new things to be discovered. Designing an organisation according to Beer's VSM, for example, allows that organisation to co-evolve with its environment and explore the possibilities that become available.

The most obvious genealogical link from pragmatism to ST runs from James through his pupil, the pragmatist philosopher E.A. Singer, to the purposeful or soft systems thinking of Churchman and Ackoff, who discussed pragmatism at length in their 1950 book *Methods of Inquiry*. Following Britton and McCallion (1994) and Ing (2023), the influence of Singer's 'nonrelativistic' or 'experimental-ist' version of pragmatism on ST can be summarised in three points, which are as follows:

1) Problems are interrelated, and all the sciences are necessary to explore them
2) Science should be judged from an ethical point of view in terms of what scientists ought to be doing
3) Reality should be seen as an ideal end-state in which people cooperate to realise their desires – it can be approached but never attained

Churchman, Singer's PhD student, sought to apply Singer's philosophy to practical problems. His overriding concern was to produce knowledge relevant to securing improvement in the human condition. We should be driven by moral outrage: 'kids are starving in great numbers, damn it all!' (Churchman, 1982). This knowledge is difficult to obtain because everything is interrelated, and it is impossible to comprehend the 'whole system'. Systems are the products of observers, and there is always an ethical element because who is served by a system design depends on where the system's boundaries are drawn. Science is not enough. Other viewpoints, often regarded as 'enemies' of the systems approach, must have a place in any inquiry, for example, politics, morality, religion and aesthetics (Churchman, 1979b). Churchman saw social systems design as 'unfolding' the implications of partial perspectives in terms of their restricted 'boundary judgements' and 'sweeping-in' as many viewpoints as possible in a never-ending process of increasing purposefulness, carried out in the 'heroic mood'. Ackoff was Churchman's first doctoral student. He rejected the conventional scientific view that objectivity results from constructing value-free models and then verifying or falsifying them against some real-world 'out there'. For him, in social systems science, objectivity can only be approached through the interaction of groups of individuals with diverse values. It is 'value-full', not 'value-free'. Harnessing human agency is central to his 'interactive planning' approach. Rather than 'predict and prepare', people should design a desirable future and invent ways of bringing it about.

Churchman's impact on ST was widespread. Matthews (2006) argued that:

> No thinker has had a greater influence on the systems movement over the course of their intellectual life than Charles West Churchman. Under Churchman's watchful eye, the systems community has adopted many of the epistemic precepts of pragmatism whilst remaining, in the main, unaware about the content of the American pragmatic discourse .... (Matthews, 2006, p. 208)

Churchman was at the heart of the 'Berkeley Bubble' whose members shared the aspiration, as described by Nelson (2022), of 'turning deep thinking into the right action'. Between 1965 and 1981, the Gaither Lecture Series in Systems Science was convened at UC Berkeley with an impressive set of contributors, making the Bubble central to the development of ST. Churchman, though, had his reservations, stating in the final lecture of the series:

> With one exception, none of the lecturers addressed the question of the proper determination of ethical values at all, even though I believe that every one of them assumed some ethical foundation in his work. (Churchman, quoted in Tomlinson and Kiss, 1984, p. 69)

Matthews (2006) traced the impact of Churchman's thinking on Mason and Mitroff, Ulrich and Midgley. Mason and Mitroff based their Strategic Assumption Surfacing and Testing (SAST) methodology on his philosophy, emphasising the role of dialectical debate between opposing viewpoints in bringing about progress. Ulrich and Midgley took forward the critical potential present in Churchman's injunction to always question the 'boundary judgements' made in defining a system of interest. Checkland's SSM is also indebted to Churchman.

Churchman called his own approach 'social systems design', and it had a significant impact on design theory. Bela H. Banathy, a visiting professor at Berkeley, and Harold Nelson, a graduate student of Churchman's, had ongoing conversations about the integration of human values into the process of designing social systems. Nelson and Stolterman's book *The Design Way* (2012) is recognised as having established the basis for design inquiry. Design is seen as 'a third culture', distinct from the arts and sciences:

> Design is the ability to imagine that-which-does-not-yet-exist, to make it appear in concrete form as a new, purposeful addition to the real world. (Nelson and Stolterman, 2012, p. 27)

Design is richer than 'problem solving' because designers focus on achieving desirable states of reality, not just on avoiding undesirable ones. Designers need to be systems thinkers, bringing different perspectives to bear during an inquiry and moving between them to allow different images of the system of concern to be revealed.

Stokes (2015) made the case that Bogdanov's form of systemic pragmatism constitutes a 'lost paradigm' that could have provided a link between critical Marxism and the CST more recently formulated at the University of Hull. CST, as we saw, began its development with a philosophical allegiance to the work of Habermas, who was much influenced by Peirce and Dewey. Recently, I have been explicitly seeking to rebuild CST and CSP on pragmatist foundations (Jackson, 2019, 2020, 2023). It should be clear how the three 'commitments' of CST are supported by and endorse philosophical pragmatism. *Systemic critique* rejects the 'spectator theory of truth' and accepts that there are 'no universal truths'. *Systemic pluralism* takes forward the notion of 'reality as a multiverse'. *Systemic improvement* sees 'theories as instruments of action' and agrees that 'beliefs can be evaluated according to their consequences'.

By embracing pragmatism and taking it forward through CST and CSP, ST can ground itself on a robust philosophical base, realize the hopes of the original pioneers and chart a bright future for itself. A shared philosophical orientation will bring greater mutual understanding between the currently disparate strands of the systems movement and provide more unity of purpose. Pragmatism can help extend this conversation to the Eastern and Indigenous traditions (Nonaka and Zhu, 2012; Yunkaporta, 2019), and it will enable ST to engage more fully with, and have greater influence on, contemporary debates in philosophy and social theory, and about social change and the role of science. As Bernstein noted, 'the important conclusions in twentieth century philosophy can be understood as variations on pragmatic themes' (Bacon, 2012). Systems thinkers familiar with pragmatism can contribute confidently to debates stimulated by the neo-pragmatism and/or post-pragmatism of philosophers such as Quine, Sellers, Davidson and Rorty, as well as by social theorists such as Habermas, Putnam [himself strongly influenced by Churchman in his undergraduate years (Ing, 2023)], Bernstein and Misak. They will learn from these debates how to improve their thinking and practice. Schools of thought closely related to pragmatism, like those deriving from Heidegger and Wittgenstein (Bernstein, 2010), will become available to provide insight.

Finally, ST can offer devotees of pragmatism – and by inference other philosophies, theories and social change agendas – practical relevance. There are several well-researched systems methodologies and models that have proved their worth and, when used in informed combinations, can help ensure improvement in the world (Jackson, 2019). Pragmatism has become too intellectual for its own good and has not fulfilled the hopes of its founders that it would return philosophy to the task of illuminating the everyday practical concerns of men and women. It needs retooling. CST and CSP can assist pragmatism to achieve what it set out to do.

3.7   Conclusion

I think that most would agree that, over the 40 years of its existence, CST has registered three significant achievements:

1) A thorough critique of the variety of systems approaches and methodologies, pointing to their various theoretical and practical strengths and weaknesses
2) Establishing the argument for pluralism in ST. This has helped end the 'paradigm wars' that have plagued ST
3) Defining what 'improvement' means in systems terms and ensuring that issues of disadvantage, marginalisation and empowerment are to the fore

A fourth achievement is on the horizon. This is the establishment of pragmatism as the philosophy upon which ST and systems practice can be grounded and further developed. The current three commitments of CST are congruent with pragmatism and supported by it. By explicitly embracing pragmatism, ST can realise the hopes of the original pioneers and chart a bright future for itself. Accepting pragmatism as a shared philosophical position will bring greater mutual understanding, unity and clout to the systems movement.

CST has also sought to enhance the practical orientation of ST by encouraging multimethodological practice and providing guidance on how to pursue it. It has had some impact, but is not as widely known or used in practice as it could be. There is an issue concerning how best to present it to decision-makers. The challenge is to make it more user-friendly while not distorting its central premises. This challenge is taken up in the next part of this book with a full discussion of CSP and its four stages.

References

Ackoff, R.L. (1979). The future of operational research is past. *Journal of the Operational Research Society* 30: 93–104.

Adelman, C. (1993). Kurt Lewin and the origins of action research. *Educational Action Research* 1: 7–24.

Ansell, C. and Geyer, R. (2017). 'Pragmatic complexity' a new foundation for moving beyond 'evidence-based policy making'? *Policy Studies* 38: 149–167.

Bacon, M. (2012). *Pragmatism: An Introduction*. Polity Press.

Barton, J. (1999). *Pragmatism, Systems Thinking and System Dynamics*. Melbourne, unpublished manuscript.

Bernstein, R.J. (2010). *The Pragmatic Turn*. Polity.

Bogdanov, A. (2016). *The Philosophy of Living Experience*. Haymarket Books.

Boulton, J.G., Allen, P. and Bowman, C. (2015). *Embracing Complexity: Strategic Perspectives for an Age of Turbulence*. Oxford University Press.

Britton, G. and McCallion, H. (1994). An overview of the Singer/Churchman/Ackoff school of thought. *Systems Practice* 7: 487–521.

Carayannis, E. and Forbes, J. (2001). A pragmatic representation of systems engineering based on technological learning. *Technovation* 21: 197–207.

Checkland, P.B. (1978). The origins and nature of 'hard' systems thinking. *Journal of Applied Systems Analysis* 5: 99–110.

Checkland, P.B. and Holwell, S. (1998). *Information, Systems and Information Systems*. Wiley

Chowdhury, R. (2019). *Systems Thinking for Management Consultants: Introducing Holistic Flexibility*. Springer.

Churchman, C.W. (1971). *The Design of Inquiring Systems*. Basic Books.

Churchman, C.W. (1979a). Paradise regained: a hope for the future of systems design education. In: *Education in Systems Science* (ed. B.A. Bayraktar et al.), pp. 17–22. Taylor & Francis.

Churchman, C.W. (1979b). *The Systems Approach and Its Enemies*. Basic Books.

Churchman, C.W. (1982). *Thought and Wisdom*. Intersystems Publications.

Churchman, C.W. and Ackoff, R. (1950). *Methods of Inquiry: An Introduction to Philosophy and Scientific Method*. Educational Publishers.

Dando, M.R. and Bennett, P.G. (1981). A Kuhnian crisis in management science? *Journal of the Operational Research Society* 32: 91–103.

Dewey, J. (1997). Theories of knowledge. In: *Pragmatism: A Reader* (ed. L. Menand), pp. 205–218. Vintage Books.

Finlayson, J.G. (2005). *Habermas – A Very Short Introduction*. Oxford University Press.

Flood, R.L. (1995). *Solving Problem Solving*. Wiley.

Flood, R.L. (1999). *Rethinking the Fifth Discipline*. Routledge.

Flood, R.L. and Jackson, M.C. (1991a). *Creative Problem Solving: Total Systems Intervention*. Wiley.

Flood, R.L. and Jackson, M.C. (Eds) (1991b). *Critical Systems Thinking: Directed Readings*. Wiley.

Gregory, W. (1996). Discordant pluralism; a new strategy for critical systems thinking. *Systems Practice* 9: 37–60.

Habermas, J. (1970). Knowledge and Interest. In: *Sociological Theory and Philosophical Analysis* (eds D. Emmett and A. MacIntyre), pp. 36–54. Macmillan.

Habermas, J. (1974). *Theory and Practice*. London.

Hobbs, C. (2019). *Systemic Leadership for Local Governance*. Palgrave MacMillan.

Hoos, I.R. (1974). *Systems Analysis in Public Policy: A Critique*. University of California Press.

Ing, D. (2023). Nonrelativistic pragmatism and systems thinking. *Coevolving Innovations*, July 9.

Jackson, M.C. (1982). The nature of soft systems thinking: the work of Churchman, Ackoff and Checkland. *Journal of Applied Systems Analysis* 9: 17–28.

Jackson, M.C. (1985). Social systems theory and practice: the need for a critical approach. *International Journal of General Systems* 10: 135–151.

Jackson, M.C. (1987). Present positions and future prospects in management science. *Omega* 15: 455–466.

Jackson, M.C. (1991). *Systems Methodology for the Management Sciences*. Plenum.

Jackson, M.C. (2000). *Systems Approaches to Management*. Kluwer/Plenum.

Jackson, M.C. (2003). *Systems Thinking: Creative Holism for Managers*. Wiley.

Jackson, M.C. (2019). *Critical Systems Thinking and the Management of Complexity*. Wiley.

Jackson, M.C. (2020). Critical systems practice 1: *explore* – starting a multi-methodological intervention. *Systems Research and Behavioral Science* 37: 839–858.

Jackson, M.C. (2023). Rebooting the systems approach by applying the thinking of Bogdanov and the pragmatists. *Systems Research and Behavioral Science* 40: 349–365. https://doi.org/10.1002/sres.2908.

Jackson, M.C. and Keys, P. (1984). Towards a system of systems methodologies. *Journal of the Operational Research Society* 35: 473–486.

James, W. (1997a). Pragmatism's conception of truth. In: *Pragmatism: A Reader* (ed. L. Menand), pp. 112–131. Vintage Books.

James, W. (1997b). What Pragmatism Means. In: *Pragmatism: A Reader* (ed. L. Menand), pp. 93–111. Vintage Books.

James, W. (1997c). A pluralist universe. In: *Pragmatism: A Reader* (ed. L. Menand), pp. 132–135. Vintage Books.

Kay, J. and King, M. (2020). *Radical Uncertainty: Decision-Making for an Unknowable Future*. Bridge Street Press.

Lewin, K. (1967). Feedback problems of social diagnosis and action. In: *Modern Systems Research for the Behavioral Sciences* (ed. W. Buckley), pp. 441–444. Aldine.

Lovitt, M.R. (1997). The new pragmatism: going beyond Shewhart and Deming. *Quality Progress* 30: 99–105.

Luhmann, N. (2013). *Introduction to Systems Theory*. Polity Press.

Marx, K. (1845). Concerning Feuerbach. In: *Early Writings* (ed. L. Colletti), pp. 421–423. Penguin Books.

Matthews, D. (2006). Pragmatism meets systems thinking: the Legacy of C. West Churchman. In: *Rescuing the Enlightenment from Itself*, vol. 1, pp. 165–212. Springer.

Menand, L. (2002). *The Metaphysical Club*. Flamingo.

Midgley, G. (2000). *Systemic Intervention: Philosophy, Methodology, and Practice.* Kluwer/Plenum.

Mingers, J. (1980). Towards an appropriate social theory for applied systems thinking: critical theory and soft systems methodology. *Journal of Applied Systems Analysis* 7: 41–49.

Mingers, J. (1984). Subjectivism and soft systems methodology – a critique. *Journal of Applied Systems Analysis* 11: 85–104.

Mingers, J. (1992). SSM and information systems: an overview. *Systemist* 14: 82–88.

Mingers, J. (2006). *Realizing Systems Thinking: Knowledge and Action in Management.* Springer.

Mingers, J. (2014). *Systems Thinking, Critical Realism and Philosophy.* Routledge.

Morgan, G. (Ed.) (1983). *Beyond Method.* Sage.

Morin, E. (1992). *Method: Towards a Study of Humankind,* vol. 1, *The Nature of Nature.* Peter Lang Publishers. Translated from French by J.L. Roland Bélanger.

Morin, E. (2006). Restricted complexity, general complexity. Presented at the Colloquium 'Intelligence de la complexité: épistémologie et pragmatique', Cerisy-La-Salle, France, 26 June 2005. Translated from French by Carlos Gershenson.

Morin, E. (2008). *On Complexity.* Hampton Press.

Mowles, C. (2022). *Complexity: A key Idea for Business and Society.* Routledge.

Nelson, H.G. (2022). Systemic design as born from the Berkeley Bubble. *Contexts – The Journal of Systemic Design* 1. https://doi.org/10.58279/v1001

Nelson, H.G. and Stolterman, E. (2012). *The Design Way: Intentional Change in an Unpredictable World,* second edn. The MIT Press, Kindle version.

Nonaka, I. and Zhu, Z. (2012). *Pragmatic Strategy: Eastern Wisdom, Global Success.* Cambridge University Press.

Peirce, C.S. (1997). How to make our ideas clear. In: *Pragmatism: A Reader* (ed. L. Menand), pp. 26–48. Vintage Books.

Peters, J.D. and Peters, B. (2016). Norbert Wiener as pragmatist. *Empedocles: European Journal for the Philosophy of Communication* 7: 157–172.

Pickering, A. (2010). *The Cybernetic Brain: Sketches of Another Future.* University of Chicago Press.

Pollack, J. (2009). Multimethodology in series and parallel: strategic planning using hard and soft OR. *Journal of the Operational Research Society* 60: 156–167.

Rapoport, R.N. (1970). Three dilemmas in action research. *Human Relations* 23: 499–513.

Rescher, N. (1977). *Methodological Pragmatism: A Systems-Theoretic Approach to the Theory of Knowledge.* Basil Blackwell.

Rorty, R. (1997). Spinoza's Legacy. Spinoza lecture, University of Amsterdam.

Ruphy, S. (2016). *Scientific Pluralism Reconsidered.* University of Pittsburgh Press.

Stokes, K.M. (2015). *Paradigm Lost.* Routledge.

Talisse, R.B. and Aikin, S.F. (2008). *Pragmatism: A Guide for the Perplexed*. Continuum Books.

Thomas, A. and Lockett, M. (1979). Marxism and systems research: values in practical action. In: *Proceedings of the SGSR*, pp. 284–293. Society for General Systems Research.

Tomlinson, R. and Kiss, I. (Eds) (1984). *Rethinking the Process of Operational Research and Systems Analysis*. Pergamon Press.

Toulmin, S. (1990). *Cosmopolis*. Macmillan.

Ulrich, W. (1983). *Critical Heuristics of Social Planning*. Haupt.

Umpleby, S.A. (2016). Second-order cybernetics as a fundamental revolution in science. *Constructivist Foundations* 11: 455–465.

Yunkaporta, T. (2019). *Sandtalk*. Text Publishing.

Zhu, Z. (2011). After paradigm: why mixing-methodology theorizing fails and how to make it work again. *Journal of the Operational Research Society* 62: 784–798.

Zhu, Z. (forthcoming). Pragmatic ontology as a working hypothesis – enhancing philosophical propositions for critical systems thinking/practice. Systems Research and Behavioral Science.

Part 2

Critical Systems Practice

Since these four world theories were regarded by us as having about the same degree of adequacy, no one of them can be the judge of the others. Our general stand, therefore, is for **rational clarity in theory and reasonable eclecticism in practice**. *That an eclecticism should be excluded from within world theories is obvious in the interests of clarity ... But for practical application we must be mindful of the judgments of all such rationally justifiable theories. Here – each of the four highly adequate theories stands on a par. We wish in matters of serious discussion to have the benefit of all the available evidence and modes of corroboration. In practice, therefore, we shall want to be rational but reasonable, and to seek, on the matter in question, the judgment supplied from each of these relatively adequate world theories.*

(Pepper, S.C., 1942, *World Hypotheses*. University of California Press; emphasis in the original)

Critical Systems Thinking: A Practitioner's Guide, First Edition. Michael C. Jackson.
© 2024 John Wiley & Sons, Inc. Published 2024 by John Wiley & Sons, Inc.

4

Critical Systems Practice: An Overview

There is always a well-known solution to every human problem – neat, plausible, and wrong.

(H. L. Mencken, 1917)

4.1 Introduction

This chapter begins with a brief account of the emergence of Critical Systems Practice (CSP) from the original critical systems 'multimethodology' called Total Systems Intervention (TSI). It then provides a summary of contemporary CSP and its four stages – *Explore, Produce, Intervene* and *Check* – called to mind by the mnemonic *EPIC*. Next, it sets out several considerations that underpin the successful employment of CSP. These include its primary purpose, its use for both diagnosis and design and its role as an 'ideal type' of multiperspectival and multimethodological systems practice. Five approaches to inquiry and change that have similarities with CSP are outlined. Two of these – 'reflective pragmatism' and 'phronetic social science' – are from the Western tradition. Two – 'relational systems thinking' and 'trans-systemics' – reflect Indigenous systems thinking. Finally, WSR (*wuli-shili-renli*) is of Chinese origin. A conclusion sets the scene for the closer examination of the four stages of CSP in the following chapters.

4.2 The Origins of Critical Systems Practice

Once Critical Systems Thinking (CST) had been formulated as a theory and set of principles, it needed guidelines that would enable it to be applied in practice. These were initially provided in 1991 with the publication of Flood and Jackson's

Critical Systems Thinking: A Practitioner's Guide, First Edition. Michael C. Jackson.
© 2024 John Wiley & Sons, Inc. Published 2024 by John Wiley & Sons, Inc.

Creative Problem Solving: Total Systems Intervention – the first critical systems multimethodology. TSI was presented as a new approach to planning, designing, problem-solving and evaluation based on CST. It was seen as a 'metamethodology' which could organise and employ, in an appropriate manner, other systems methodologies. The aim was to put them all to work in a coherent way, according to their strengths and weaknesses, in the service of a general project of improving complex organisational and societal systems. This project embraced efficiency, effectiveness and viability; sought to promote mutual understanding; and to give attention to issues of empowerment and emancipation. The book was popular and the approach well-received. However, the damning postmodern critique of 'totalising' discourses, together with the loss of faith in the guiding 'metaparadigm' supplied by Habermas's theory of 'human interests', demanded a rethink. Flood (1999) sought to remodel systems practice as an approach to 'learning within the unknowable', responding to the lessons of chaos and complexity theory. My own work led me to develop CSP, and I have been seeking to extend and improve this approach ever since (Jackson, 2000, 2003, 2019). Both Bob Flood and I now regard TSI as the worst possible name we could have given to the critical learning process we were seeking to describe.

4.3 Contemporary Critical Systems Practice

This brief description of contemporary CSP will cover its essence, the *EPIC* framework and the four main stages.

4.3.1 Essence

Complexity is at the core of most policy and strategy issues confronting governments and organisations of all types. There are no simple ways to improve complex situations. They constitute multidimensional 'messes' which cross boundaries and where technical, economic, organisational, human, cultural, political and environmental elements interact. CSP takes this complexity seriously; it is a multiperspectival and multimethodological approach that makes use of the variety of systemic perspectives, methodologies, models and methods, aware of their different strengths and weaknesses. CSP employs them in combination to maximise their benefits. It produces a balanced evaluation of outcomes and suggests what needs doing next to ensure continuous improvement.

CSP seeks:

- To use various 'systemic perspectives' to provide an appreciation of the complexity of a situation of interest
- To provide an understanding of the strengths and weaknesses of the different systems approaches

- To take appropriate systems methodologies, models and methods and use them together in an intervention that will improve the situation of interest
- To provide a balanced evaluation of the outcomes of an intervention
- To improve the systems thinking capabilities of those who take part in an intervention

4.3.2 The *EPIC* Framework

CSP has four main stages (***EPIC***) and some sub-stages, which are as follows:

Stage 1: Explore the situation of interest
- View it from five systemic perspectives
- Identify primary and secondary issues

Stage 2: Produce an intervention strategy
- Appreciate the variety of systems approaches
- Choose appropriate systems methodologies
- Choose appropriate systems models and methods
- Structure, schedule and set objectives for the intervention

Stage 3: Intervene flexibly
- Use systems methodologies, models and methods flexibly
- Stay alert to the evolving situation (revisit Stage 1)
- Stay flexible about appropriate methodologies, models and methods (revisit Stage 2)

Stage 4: Check on progress
- Evaluate the improvements achieved
- Reflect on the learning gained about the systems approaches used
- Discuss and agree next steps

Figure 4.1 represents these stages and sub-stages diagrammatically.

4.3.3 The Four Stages

4.3.3.1 *Explore* the Situation of Interest
Let us assume that a crisis, or just a feeling that 'things could be better', has provoked a call for action. After examining the issues, those involved conclude that they are interconnected, that there is no obvious boundary to the area of interest and that any action will have wide ramifications. They are engaged with 'general complexity'. It is not easy to untangle and get to grips with such situations, because they exhibit VUCA characteristics – volatility, uncertainty, complexity and ambiguity. This is often compounded by stakeholder conflict. Complex situations of this kind are 'messes' which give rise to 'wicked problems'. Attempts to model them are always partial. No one systems approach can understand them as 'a whole'. It is

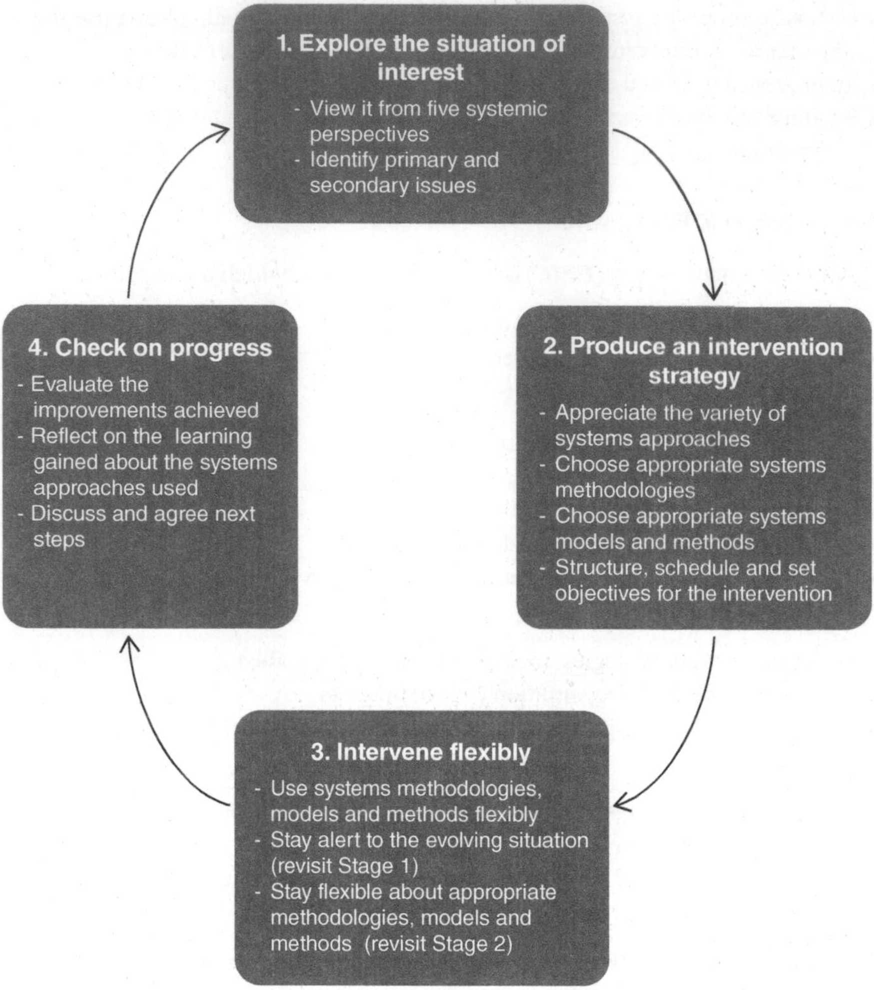

1. Explore the situation of interest
- View it from five systemic perspectives
- Identify primary and secondary issues

2. Produce an intervention strategy
- Appreciate the variety of systems approaches
- Choose appropriate systems methodologies
- Choose appropriate systems models and methods
- Structure, schedule and set objectives for the intervention

3. Intervene flexibly
- Use systems methodologies, models and methods flexibly
- Stay alert to the evolving situation (revisit Stage 1)
- Stay flexible about appropriate methodologies, models and methods (revisit Stage 2)

4. Check on progress
- Evaluate the improvements achieved
- Reflect on the learning gained about the systems approaches used
- Discuss and agree next steps

Figure 4.1 The four *EPIC* stages of Critical Systems Practice.

essential to be realistic about this and proceed to learn about the complexity by exploring it through a variety of different lenses. CSP argues that a rich appreciation of complex problem situations can be achieved by making use of the lenses provided by five well-tested and clearly formulated systemic perspectives.

View It from Five Systemic Perspectives Five systemic perspectives have demonstrated a capacity to provide significant insight into complex situations – *mechanical, interrelationships, organismic, purposeful* and *societal/environmental*. Using these enables us to make suggestions about where failings are occurring and what might improve things, as is detailed in Chapter 5. The different systemic perspectives provide breadth to the exploration of the situation of interest. For example, major projects can usefully be viewed as machines designed to achieve a purpose; as having parts that interact in unpredictable ways; as organisms evolving over time; as systems in which purposes diverge and where accommodations between stakeholders need to be reached; and as systems with negative consequences for some stakeholders and/or the environment. Each perspective will reveal new matters worthy of attention and may provide a different explanation as to why issues of concern are arising.

Identify Primary and Secondary Issues　The most important issues that emerge from the exploration of the situation of interest are called the 'primary issues'. There will be 'secondary issues' which should be kept in mind because they may assume greater importance later.

4.3.3.2 *Produce* an Intervention Strategy

Appreciate the Variety of Systems Approaches　*Systems methodologies* guide the intervention in the most appropriate way to ensure the primary issues are addressed. *Systems models* and *methods* are chosen that support the principles of the guiding methodologies and are suitable and helpful in the context.

Choose Appropriate Systems Methodologies　We need to know what each systems methodology is good at to choose appropriate ones to address the primary issues identified. One convenient way of doing this is to consider how they view the world (i.e., what systemic perspective they privilege) and, therefore, what issues they prioritise. Broadly, *engineering systems methodologies* privilege the mechanical systemic perspective; *system dynamics* privileges the interrelationships systemic perspective; *living systems methodologies* privilege the organismic systemic perspective; *soft systems methodologies* privilege the purposeful systemic perspective; and *emancipatory systems methodologies* privilege the societal/environmental systemic perspective. This awareness of the strengths of the different systems methodologies can be linked to the issues raised during the *Explore* stage and can be used to inform the choice of methodologies to address those issues.

Choose Appropriate Systems Models and Methods　Once agreement has been reached on what systems methodology, or methodologies, to employ at the start of the intervention, it is time to decide on appropriate systems models and methods. Models and methods that originate from outside the systems thinking tradition can, of course, also be considered.

Structure, Schedule and Set Objectives for the Intervention　Exploration of a complex situation usually reveals a host of issues. For example, the COVID-19 pandemic threw up materials, logistics, staffing, process, structural, cultural and inequality issues, all of which confronted decision-makers at the same time. This indicates the need to use many methodologies in parallel. However, doing this can cause confusion, lead to upheaval and extend beyond the resources available. In normal circumstances, it is better to start with one methodology (or possibly two) relevant to the greatest number of primary issues.

The intervention strategy can now be designed and scheduled. Consideration must be given to the precise objectives and specific measures of success of the scheduled intervention.

4.3.3.3 *Intervene* Flexibly
- Use systems methodologies, models and methods flexibly
- Stay alert to the evolving situation (revisit Stage 1)
- Stay flexible about appropriate methodologies, models and methods (revisit Stage 2)

The intervention can begin by following the steps indicated in the methodology or methodologies chosen to start the process. In the best-case scenario, that methodology – and associated models and methods – will resolve the primary issues. Attention can then turn to producing an appropriate intervention strategy to deal with the secondary issues. It is more likely, however, that the situation will simply change, new priorities will come to the fore and new issues surface. The key to successful intervention with CSP is to recognise changes by continuing to view the situation of interest through different systemic perspectives. This must be accompanied by a willingness to reconsider which systems methodologies, models and methods are most appropriate. Stages 1 and 2 will need to be revisited constantly during the intervention.

4.3.3.4 *Check* on Progress
Evaluate the Improvements Achieved To be consistent with the CSP view that complex situations are multidimensional, it is necessary to ensure that the concerns of all five systemic perspectives are invoked in any evaluation. The intervention may seem successful according to some measures but, viewed through alternative lenses, it might have made things worse. Evaluation, therefore, should ask questions from the mechanical systemic perspective (efficiency and efficacy); the interrelationships systemic perspective (factors taken into account and possible unintended consequences); the organismic systemic perspective (viability and resilience); the purposeful systemic perspective (effectiveness, mutual understanding and conflict resolution); and the societal/environmental systemic perspective (marginalised stakeholders, sustainability and the environment).

Reflect on the Learning Gained About the Systems Approaches Used Participants should reflect on what they have learned from the intervention. Exposure to the range of systemic perspectives and methodologies will enhance their cognitive flexibility – essential for working in a multimethodological way to address complexity. It is important that the learning is carried forward in future work. Academic researchers will want to take this reflection further and, in the action research mode, ask what has been learned about the complex problem situation itself, CSP, and the individual systems methodologies, models and methods.

Discuss and Agree Next Steps The evaluation, and the priorities of the decision-makers, will suggest what to do next. The aim of a prolonged CSP intervention is to achieve and demonstrate improvement viewed from the entire range of systemic perspectives.

4.4 Considerations on the Nature of Critical Systems Practice

Policymaking and consulting are often described as having a lifecycle that can be broken down into four stages – diagnosis of the problem, project design, implementation and evaluation of the results (Chowdhury, 2022). To the casual observer, the four stages of CSP may look no different. This provides an initial orientation as long as the ways in which CSP differs are also understood. I can find no better way of expressing the shift in overall 'problem-solving mentality' required to understand CSP than by referring to Lakoff and Johnson's comparison of the 'puzzle' and 'chemical' metaphors applied to problems. At present, they argued, we mostly conceptualise and deal with problems using the puzzle metaphor

> ... in which problems are PUZZLES for which, typically, there is a correct solution – and, once solved, they are solved forever. The PROBLEMS ARE PUZZLES metaphor characterizes our present reality. (Lakoff and Johnson, 1980, pp. 144–145; upper case in the original)

Adopting a 'chemical metaphor', they argued, would create a different reality in which problems were seen and addressed differently:

> To live by the CHEMICAL metaphor would be to accept it as a fact that no problem ever disappears forever. Rather than direct your energies toward solving your problems once and for all, you would direct your energies toward finding out what catalysts will dissolve your most pressing problems for the longest time without precipitating worse ones. The reappearance of

a problem is viewed as a natural occurrence rather than a failure on your part to find 'the right way to solve it'. (Lakoff and Johnson, 1980, p. 144; upper case in the original)

CSP sees the chemical metaphor as more appropriate in the VUCA world of general complexity and wicked problems. Primarily, CSP is designed for the big issues, for example, when governments are confronted by 'black swan' events or trying to get to grips with educational reform, transportation, an ageing population, inequality and healthcare; when companies are facing a crisis, rethinking their strategies, considering risk and addressing their social and environmental responsibilities; when local authorities are restructuring, redesigning their services, seeking to work in partnership or engage citizens; and when environmentalists are tackling pollution, climate change and reductions in species diversity. CSP is not designed for problem situations when there is agreement on what needs doing and decision-makers can use best practices or simple techniques to achieve results. However, situations of interest that initially appear 'simple' or 'complicated' often turn out 'complex' or 'chaotic' when examined more closely and/or are prodded as part of an intervention (Snowden and Boone, 2007). As Boulding (1956) pointed out, few errors are more costly than treating systems that possess a high level of complexity with methodologies and models that lack the appropriate sophistication. There is, therefore, always a strong case for running through the *Explore* stage of CSP before jumping to conclusions.

CSP can be employed by decision-makers, managers, consultants and those without formal power. It can be used for diagnosing issues in an existing system or designing a new one. In the former case, for example, it might be used to help investigate why a health system has met problems dealing with an unexpected disease outbreak. In the latter, it can be applied to plan and bring into being a new organisation, such as a recruitment agency.

Following Checkland and Scholes's (1990) terminology, CSP offers 'Mode 1' and 'Mode 2' alternatives. In Mode 1, it governs the intervention and leads it along an orderly path. In Mode 2, it ceases to dominate. In this case, the intervention is situation-driven, and CSP breaks the surface only occasionally to help reflect upon, and sometimes drive forward, what is happening in the everyday flux of events.

Two points on the structure of the approach. CSP seeks to translate the philosophy of CST into practical application. It sets out four stages that are necessary to ensure this happens (see Figure 4.1). We are dealing with these in turn, but they are interdependent. Every stage must be true to the four commitments of CST if it is to support the others appropriately. For example, *Explore* must be conducted in a manner that allows later stages to be true to

CST. It must be designed to ensure that advantage can be taken of the capabilities of the full range of systems methodologies at the *Produce* stage. No methodology should be proscribed because *Explore* itself is narrowly bounded and fails to bring to the fore issues for which that methodology is best suited.

Second, despite being presented as having four stages, CSP is decidedly non-linear when used in practice. There is constant iteration between and among the stages. As Figure 4.1 indicates, this is particularly the case during *Intervene*, where frequent re-entry into the multimethodological cycle is encouraged to track the situation of interest as it changes and to make methodological adjustments as necessary. *Check* indicates the need to occasionally catch breath and reflect, but otherwise is designed to produce outcomes that feed easily into *Explore,* provoking another cycle of CSP.

Further, in this book, I present CSP as an 'ideal type' of good systems practice which takes advantage of the best that the Western tradition of ST has to offer. The clue is in the mnemonic *EPIC*. I regard few things as 'epic' except, perhaps, if Hull Kingston Rovers win the Grand Final. An 'ideal type' can rarely be replicated in the real world. It can, nevertheless, act as a beacon, a challenge, a stimulus to reflection and a rebuke. *EPIC* describes what is necessary to put CST fully into effect to guide a systems intervention. In the chapters that follow, appropriate attention will be given to what can realistically be achieved in practice.

Finally, it should be acknowledged that CSP is a product of the Western systems tradition. In non-Western contexts, it may be more appropriate to employ a multi-perspectival and multimethodological approach with alternative roots. This is taken up in the next section.

4.5 Related Approaches

It is not surprising to find multiperspectival and multimethodological approaches, akin to CSP, offered by those who share a CST orientation, for example, Flood's (1999) 'learning within the unknowable', Midgley's (2000) 'systemic intervention', Hobbs's (2019) 'systemic leadership' and Chowdhury's (2019, 2024) 'holistic flexibility'. Here, we look further afield and outline five approaches from other traditions of thought which have similarities to CSP.

Kenneth Gergen, working from the Taos Institute, expressed regret that the prevailing metaphor of social science is still the 'mirror'. According to this metaphor, the role of social scientists is to provide knowledge of the world by accurately describing aspects of individual or social life. Gergen argued instead for a reflective, pluralist pragmatics which sees the role of the social researcher as future-forming or world-making. In this view

... reflection moves from issues of philosophic grounding to social utility ... the question then becomes one of outcomes. What does the research ultimately contribute to the world more generally? And this question is accompanied by a critical concern with politics and ideology. For whom are the outcomes useful, and in what way; who is benefited, who may be harmed; and who is absent from the discussion? We have, then, pragmatism with a social conscience. (Gergen, 2015, p. 289)

Bent Flyvbjerg (2001) similarly argued that social science should be directed to social change rather than academic input. Attempting to function as an *episteme*, producing knowledge of general propositions along the lines of the natural sciences, has led it to a dead-end. No predictive laws have been found. Instead, Flyvbjerg argues for social science as *phronesis*. This concept, in Aristotle's thought, concerns that combination of understanding and virtue that produces right action in particular circumstances. As *phronesis*, social science can properly engage in public deliberation and decision-making, contributing by asking questions such as: What are we doing? Is it desirable? Who might gain and lose? What mechanisms of power are involved? What should we do about it? Not surprisingly, Nicholas (2022) found complementarity between CST and phronetic social science. Both are in the game of 'values-directed social change', reflect on the way different models frame different realities and pay attention to the influence of power.

Turning now to Indigenous systems thinking, I have no wish to re-colonise systems of knowledge that are only just recovering from centuries of suppression. I will inevitably be translating this knowledge back into the language of the coloniser. However, I seek in the process to offer some space for it to flourish. I also offer CSP for retheorising from Indigenous standpoints so that it can be used in the service of those emerging from colonisation.

It is the possibility of peaceful co-existence between Indigenous and non-Indigenous ways of thinking and knowing, and of the benefits that can be derived from their interaction, that powers 'relational systems thinking' (Goodchild et al., 2021; Goodchild, 2022). The Western scientific method pursues knowledge analytically and seeks to exclude the observer to ensure 'objectivity'. From the Indigenous perspective, knowledge is relational. It must consider the interconnections between people, between people and non-humans, people and future generations and people and Mother Earth. Knowledge is also situational and only makes sense if we know where it comes from. The question then is:

How do you incorporate multiple ways of knowing, in a respectful way, into the practice of awareness-based systems change? (Goodchild et al., 2021, p. 81)

The Haudenosaunee 'two-row wampum belt' provides the central metaphor for what is required. The two rows symbolise the Mohawk canoe and the Dutch sailing ship. Each row represents valuable experiential knowledge which the other can learn from and exposes biases and blind spots in the other. 'Two-eyed seeing' is required to avoid the domination of one worldview over the other and to ensure that the appropriate lens, or some harmonisation of the two, is employed according to the circumstances. Equality and friendship are possible because both travel 'the river of life' together (Goodchild et al., 2021; Goodchild, 2022).

Another paper, on 'Indigenous trans-systemics' (McIntyre et al., 2023), emerged from conversations between Anishinabe and non-Indigenous scholars and directly tackled the relationship between CST and Indigenous thought. In the Anishinabe worldview, everything is connected, relationships are all-important and individuals are embedded in systems for which they take responsibility. The task is to 'turn up the volume' of the Indigenous perspective so that it can be heard above the noise created by the dominant Eurocentric approach. This can benefit Eurocentric as well as Indigenous ST. Trans-systemics calls for an acceptance that there are different ways of knowing, humility on all sides and critical reflection on the limitations of different perspectives. It asks for an expansion of the voices heard 'in studying, engaging, and transforming the systems we inhabit'. The paper recognises the value of CST but, on its reading of rather old sources, argues that it is capable only of tackling 'some of the simpler challenges'. Its origins restrict its ability to navigate 'multiple, overlapping systems and worldviews'.

As a final case, we draw on the Oriental tradition. Gu and Zhu (2000) have translated their experiences of using management science in China into a multimethodology they call WSR (*wuli-shili-renli*). WSR draws its inspiration from Chinese philosophy of a pragmatist orientation, and the similarities with CSP are evident. Zhu explained:

> WSR suggests that it is useful to see real-world projects as conditioned by a differentiable whole, i.e., the interplay among *wuli* (relations within the world), *shili* (relations between the self and the world) and *renli* (relations between the self and others). In conducting operations research (OR) and management projects, we are ideally inquiring into three domains, i.e., to investigate and model objective existence, to consider and reflect on subjective ways of seeing and doing, and to manage the working of inter-subjective human relations. We call this knowing *wuli,* sensing *shili,* and caring, *renli* ... WSR urges practitioners to bring all *wu, shi,* and *ren* elements and perspectives into a holistic consideration, and accordingly to search for appropriate methods to address various *lis* as well as their dynamic interactions. (Zhu, 2000, p. 184; italics in the original)

I could go on, but enough has been said to show that interest in pragmatic multiperspectival and multimethodological approaches is widespread and growing.

4.6 Conclusion

We are now ready to study the four stages of CSP in more detail. The following four chapters use a similar format and set out, for each stage:

- Preliminaries – essential background information
- Process – guidance on how to do it
- Example(s) – applications
- Issues – difficulties and criticisms

References

Boulding, K.E. (1956). General systems theory – the skeleton of science. *Management Science* 2: 197–208. https://doi.org/10.1287/mnsc.2.3.197.

Checkland, P.B. and Scholes, J. (1990). *Soft Systems Methodology in Action*. Wiley.

Chowdhury, R. (2019). *Systems Thinking for Management Consultants*. Springer.

Chowdhury, R. (2022). Methodological flexibility in systems thinking: musings from the standpoint of a systems consultant. *Systemic Practice and Action Research* 36: 59–86.

Chowdhury, R. (2024). *Holistic Flexibility for Systems Thinking and Practice*. Routledge.

Flood, R.L. (1999). *Rethinking the Fifth Discipline: Learning within the Unknowable*. Routledge.

Flood, R.L. and Jackson, M.C. (1991). *Creative Problem Solving: Total Systems Intervention*. Wiley.

Flyvbjerg, B. (2001). *Making Social Science Matter*. Cambridge University Press.

Gergen, K.J. (2015). From mirroring to world-making: research as future forming. *Journal for the Theory of Social Behaviour* 45: 287–310.

Goodchild, M. (2022). Relational systems thinking: the Dibaajimowin (story) of re-theorizing "systems thinking" and "complexity science". *Journal of Awareness-Based Systems Change* 1: 53–76.

Goodchild, M. (with Senge, P., Scharmer, O., et al.) (2021). Relational systems thinking: that's how change is going to come, from our Mother Earth. *Journal of Awareness-Based Systems Change* 1: 75–103.

Gu, J. and Zhu, Z. (2000). Knowing wuli, sensing shili, caring for renli: methodology of the WSR approach. *Systemic Practice and Action Research* 13: 11–20.

Hobbs, C. (2019). *Systemic Leadership for Local Governance*. Palgrave Macmillan.

Jackson, M.C. (2000). *Systems Approaches to Management*. Kluwer/Plenum.

Jackson, M.C. (2003). *Systems Thinking: Creative Holism for Managers*. Wiley.

Jackson, M.C. (2019). *Critical Systems Thinking and the Management of Complexity*. Wiley.

Lakoff, G. and Johnson, M. (1980). *Metaphors We Live By*. University of Chicago Press.

McIntyre, D.G., Cloutis, G.A. and McCarthy, D. (2023). Indigenous trans-systemics: changing the volume on systems. *Sustainability Science* 18: 1961–1975.

Midgley, G. (2000). *Systemic Intervention: Philosophy, Methodology and Practice*. Kluwer/Plenum.

Nicholas, G. (2022). Getting to practical: complementarity between critical systems thinking and phronetic social science. *Systems Research and Behavioral Science* 39: 913–922.

Snowden, D. and Boone, M.E. (2007). A leader's framework for decision making. *Harvard Business Review*, November.

Zhu, Z. (2000). WSR: a systems approach for information systems development. *Systems Research and Behavioral Science* 17: 183–203.

5

Critical Systems Practice 1 – *Explore* the Situation of Interest

> *If my mind could gain a firm footing, I would not make essays, I would make decisions; but it is always in apprenticeship and on trial.*
>
> (Montaigne, c. 1580)

5.1 Introduction

Chapter 5 details how the *Explore* stage of Critical Systems Practice (CSP) is conducted to provide the best starting point for a multimethodological intervention. *Explore* requires teasing out the multidimensional character of a situation of interest by bringing a variety of 'systemic perspectives' to bear. An analysis of multiperspectival work in philosophy, social science and Systems Thinking (ST) leads to the conclusion that five systemic perspectives are sufficient to drive an insightful investigation of this kind. The nature of these five perspectives – mechanical, interrelationships, organismic, purposeful and societal/environmental – is discussed and the process of using them in *Explore* is explained. An example is provided of how they can be employed to throw light on the difficulties faced by the UK health system in the early days of the COVID-19 pandemic. Finally, there is reflection on certain issues that arise from the nature of *Explore*. These include whether the different perspectives can be integrated, what *Explore* implies about ST and the capabilities that it demands.

5.2 *Explore* – Preliminaries

We are driven to explore the modern world with a 'general complexity' orientation that eschews universal truths. As Cassirer put it:

Critical Systems Thinking: A Practitioner's Guide, First Edition. Michael C. Jackson.
© 2024 John Wiley & Sons, Inc. Published 2024 by John Wiley & Sons, Inc.

> We are in quest for truth, for an absolute truth. But instead of finding it we find ourselves bound to the endlessly revolving wheel of our own concepts, our images, our symbols, our abstractions. (Cassirer, quoted in Skidelsky, 2008, p. 100)

Or, more prosaically:

> As one of [Montaigne's] favourite adages had it, there is no escaping our perspective: we can walk only on our own legs and sit only on our own bum. (Bakewell, 2010, p. 10)

Even so, we feel the urge to make decisions. We know that we cannot 'solve' the complex problems that arise from general complexity but perhaps we can transform, modify or improve the situations in which we find ourselves (Woermann et al., 2018). A promising way forward seems to be to proceed using multiple perspectives. Support for this comes from an unexpected source. Here is William Burroughs explaining to David Bowie his vision for his 'Final Academy':

> Its aim will be to extend awareness and alter consciousness in the direction of greater range, flexibility and effectiveness at a time when traditional disciplines have failed to come up with viable solutions ... We will be considering only non-chemical methods with the emphasis on combination, synthesis, interaction and rotation of methods now being used in the East and West. (Burroughs, quoted in Rae, 2020, loc. 2097)

Inquiry using multiple perspectives is also encouraged in more traditional disciplines. Francisco Sagasti, a management scientist (and former President of Peru), wrote:

> These wicked problems ... demand unconventional thinking, require the capacity to simultaneously view problems and conditions from different points of view ... require ... nimble minds ... even following the advice Alice received from the White Queen to believe 'six impossible things before breakfast' ... we must embrace paradox and acquire the capacity to think in contradictory ways; in short, we need *paradoxists*. (Sagasti, 2019, p. 212; italics in the original)

Tsoukas (2017), from the point of view of organisation theory, argued that we need to 'complexify' our theories beyond Newtonian-style thinking to account for organisational complexity. As Ashby taught, 'only variety can absorb variety'.

A complex 'system of picturing' is therefore required which consists of 'an open-world ontology, a performative epistemology, and a poetic praxeology'.

Explore embraces a multiperspectival approach. It believes that, if it is to honour the commitments of Critical Systems Thinking (CST), it must discover some partial truths that can open the door to a multimethodological approach in the following stages of CSP. To find these 'partial truths' requires a review of relevant work in philosophy, social science and ST.

5.2.1 Metaphors and World Hypotheses in Philosophy

Lakoff and Johnson claimed that their book, *Metaphors We Live By* (1980), offers a 'pragmatic theory' in the tradition of Pierce, James and Dewey. The authors argued for the pervasiveness of metaphor in our thinking, defining the 'essence of metaphor' as 'understanding and experiencing one kind of thing in terms of another'. In their view, metaphors should be seen not just as literary devices, employed by poets and novelists. Rather, they dominate and structure our conceptual systems, creating the reality we experience and determining how we act. New metaphors can create a new reality in which we think and act differently. If our reasoning is dominated by metaphors, Lakoff and Johnson argue, 'objectivism' is a myth. There is no one truth but:

> Metaphor is one of our most important tools for trying to comprehend partially what cannot be comprehended totally. (Lakoff and Johnson, 1980, p. 193)

Each metaphor provides a certain structured comprehension of a situation, revealing some things and suppressing others. If the result is a set of inconsistent metaphors, then so much the better since:

> To operate only in terms of a consistent set of metaphors is to hide many aspects of reality. Successfully functioning in our daily lives seems to require a constant shifting of metaphors. The use of many metaphors that are inconsistent with one another seems necessary for us if we are to comprehend the details of our daily existence. (Lakoff and Johnson, 1980, p. 221)

Often the metaphors we live by are of an objectivist orientation. These have an important role in restricted situations, even in the human sciences, but also hide many aspects of reality. In doing so they can contribute to the 'degradation' of humanity and the natural world – for example, encouraging us to see labour as a 'resource' rather than something that should be 'meaningful', and the environment as something to 'control' rather than 'interact' with.

If their analysis precludes objectivism, Lakoff and Johnson are equally opposed to 'subjectivism'. For them

> ... the system of conceptual metaphors is not arbitrary or just historically contingent; rather, it is shaped to a significant extent by the common nature of our bodies and the shared ways that we all function in the everyday world. (Lakoff and Johnson, 1980, p. 245)

We have developed structured sets of metaphors, or 'experiential gestalts', suitable for successful functioning in our physical and cultural environments. These experiential gestalts provide 'truths' which are essential for human purposes in the contexts in which they are employed. They can, of course, vary between cultures because they reflect different experiential domains, although the 'natural dimensions' of reality will impose some constraints. This is, Lakoff and Johnson state, a 'pragmatic theory' with some elements of 'realism'.

The obvious next step is to ask which experiential gestalts have been most useful in helping humans understand and find their way in the world. According to the American pragmatist philosopher Stephen Pepper:

> Men have made thousands of metaphors, but when these are turned to cognitive use for unrestricted hypotheses they melt down to a very few. (Pepper, 1942, p. 343)

Pepper's 1942 book *World Hypotheses*, based on a 'complete survey of metaphysics', argues that just four 'world hypotheses' have shown themselves to be 'adequate' when challenged to provide comprehensive accounts of the structure of the world. These are 'formism', 'mechanism', 'contextualism' and 'organicism'. He was convinced that 'these four keys will open any closet now built that is worth opening'. They have distinguished themselves as 'adequate' because they are based on 'root metaphors' which, over time, have proved more fertile in scope and precision than other metaphors. Unlike, for example, 'animism' and 'mysticism', they have generated refined knowledge in the form of cohesive theories supported by an array of observations and evidence, and they yield better predictions. *Formism* is underpinned by the root metaphor of 'similarity'. It emphasises the regularity of pure forms, structural points of balance and stability produced by natural laws. Plato's philosophy is an exemplar. *Mechanism* sees the world in Newtonian terms, as made up of objects in space and time determined in their movements by causal laws. Its root metaphor is the 'machine'. The root metaphor of *contextualism* is the 'act in its context'. This highlights continuous change, unpredictability and multiple possible interpretations. Pragmatist philosophers, such as Pierce, James and Dewey, are contextualists. *Organicism* is exemplified in

Hegel's philosophy. It is underpinned by the root metaphor of 'integration'. A process can be identified in which fragments of understanding are progressively integrated into an organic whole in which there are no contradictions.

According to Pepper none of the four world hypotheses can support a claim of absolute truth but they do represent 'successes of cognition', the 'creative discoveries of many generations', and do contain some knowledge:

> The gears grind, the lights flicker, and the lenses distort. Nevertheless, we do seem to get some idea of our world from these vehicles, and without them we should have to walk pretty much in the dark. (Pepper, 1942, p. 80)

Further, in his view, the four world hypotheses demonstrate 'equal or nearly equal adequacy'. They stand on a par, and we cannot afford to lose any of them. Having four alternative theories supplies us with considerably more information on a subject than any one alone. In a nice phrase, he states that 'four good lights cast fewer shadows than one when the sun is hid'. Each world hypothesis is of unlimited scope and the four are, therefore, mutually exclusive. We cannot allocate them to different purposes because they all have useful things to say about everything. Basically, they are irreconcilable. Here Pepper anticipates Kuhn's theory of paradigm incommensurability (Kuhn, 1970). Both agree that we cannot use 'facts' to decide between world hypotheses or paradigms because each interprets the facts according to its own assumptions. Nor is there any higher truth to legislate over the four world hypotheses. The only legitimate critics of world theories are other world theories.

5.2.2 Paradigms and Metaphors in Organisation Theory

Pepper may have been an excellent philosopher, but he was not a social scientist. Two contributions from organisation theory enable us to confirm the significance of his world hypotheses while drawing attention to other useful perspectives on social reality. Burrell and Morgan (1979) consider the 'sociological paradigms' that have dominated in organisational analysis. Morgan (1986) reviews the metaphors behind our taken-for-granted 'images of organisations'.

Burrell and Morgan's thesis is that theories about the social world can be conceived of in terms of four fundamental paradigms. It is these paradigms that govern organisational analysis. The paradigms reflect assumptions made about social science and society. Social science is either 'objective' or 'subjective'. It is pursued on the basis that society makes wo/man or wo/man makes society. Society is seen as in need of 'regulation' or 'radical change'. It is assumed that the status quo needs either supporting or challenging. Combining the objective–subjective and regulation–radical change dimensions, Burrell and Morgan produced a matrix defining the four paradigms. These are labelled 'functionalist' (objective and regulative), 'interpretive' (subjective and regulative), 'radical structuralist' (radical change and objective) and 'radical humanist' (radical change and subjective). The stark difference to Pepper's analysis is the addition of a 'radical change' dimension for understanding what happens in the social world. In seeking to get to grips with social reality, theorists have needed to pay attention to the conflict that arises when oppressed groups challenge the alienation, social constraints and structural inequalities which social systems can produce.

All four of Burrell and Morgan's sociological paradigms remain firmly on the table as ways of understanding social reality and organisations. The crucial point, for CSP, is to ensure that the perspectives of these different paradigms are fully represented at the *Explore* stage of a systems intervention. If any of these well-formulated and well-grounded paradigms are ignored, our initial grasp of the situation of interest will be too narrow.

Morgan's account of different 'images of organisation' returns us to the crucial role metaphors play in thinking. Now, however, the target is specifically organisation theory:

> I believe that by building on the use of metaphor – which is basic to our way of thinking generally – we have a means of enhancing our capacity for creative yet disciplined thought, in a way that allows us to grasp and deal with the many-sided character of organizational life. (Morgan, 1986, p. 17)

Morgan identified eight common metaphors in the literature – organisations as 'machines', 'organisms', 'brains', 'cultures', 'political systems', 'psychic prisons', 'flux and transformation' and 'instruments of domination'. Each offers a distinctive yet partial view of organisations and yields an alternative understanding of their nature. He did not regard these metaphors as incommensurable, but rather as offering different 'readings' which provide us with a richer insight into the ambiguity and complexity of organisational life. Effective managers and professionals can use metaphors to

> ... develop the knack of reading situations with various scenarios in mind, and of forging actions that seem appropriate to the readings thus obtained. (Morgan, 1986, p. 11)

They can be used to enhance creative insight and develop critical thinking. The 'psychic prisons', 'flux and transformation' and 'instruments of domination' metaphors certainly add new considerations and possibilities compared to Pepper's account of world hypotheses.

5.2.3 Multiperspectival Approaches in Systems Thinking

It is interesting to look at some precursors of *Explore* in ST itself. In 1984, Harold Linstone, another member of the Berkeley Bubble, published *Multiple Perspectives for Decision Making*, a book influenced by Churchman's *The Design of Inquiring Systems*. This sought to demonstrate how taking three different viewpoints can yield a rich appreciation of the nature of any problem situation. The Traditional or technical (T) perspective, dependent on data and model-based analysis, should be augmented by an Organisational (O) or societal perspective, and a Personal (P) or individual perspective. The T, O and P perspectives act as filters through which systems can be viewed and each yields insights that are not attainable with the others. Linstone argued that these different perspectives are most powerfully employed when they are clearly differentiated from one another but are used together to interrogate the same complex problem. One should not expect consistency in the findings – two perspectives may reinforce one another but may equally cancel each other out. Nelson (2022) suggested that Linstone's schema can be made more inclusive systemically if other viewpoints are added, for example, political, economic, spiritual and ethical.

Ackoff (1999) was clear that contemporary corporations are best viewed as 'social systems' with responsibilities to themselves, their parts, and to the wider systems of which they are part. But he still saw value in the machine and organism metaphors in appropriate circumstances and made use of methods and techniques associated with them in the context of his Interactive Planning methodology. Barabba (2004) found this a powerful combination in helping to turn General Motors round in the 1990s.

Neither Linstone nor Ackoff offered a lens that focuses on 'radical change' or makes use of the 'psychic prisons' or 'instruments of domination' metaphors.

5.3   *Explore* – Process

Explore, the first stage of CSP, aims to provide a rich appreciation of any situation of interest. It does so by examining it through the different lenses provided by five 'systemic perspectives' – **mechanical, interrelationships, organismic, purposeful** and **societal/environmental**. These systemic perspectives – inclusive of the worldviews provided by the key world hypotheses, sociological paradigms and metaphors – enable us to identify the primary and secondary issues we need to address in a situation of interest. Figure 5.1 reminds us of where *Explore* sits in the *EPIC* cycle.

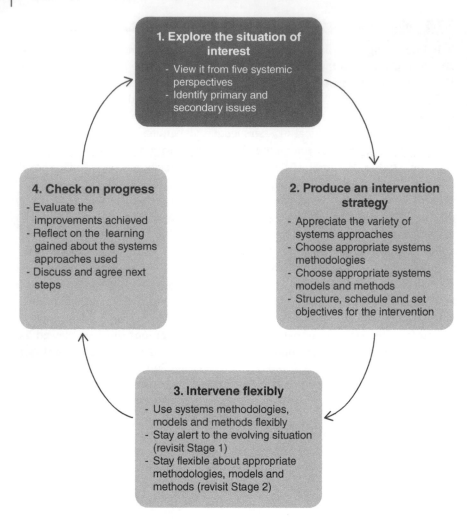

Figure 5.1   The four *EPIC* stages of Critical Systems Practice.

5.3.1   View the Situation of Interest from Five Systemic Perspectives

In suggesting how his four world hypotheses be employed to interpret the world and guide action, Pepper recommended we proceed with 'rational clarity in theory and reasonable eclecticism in practice'. 'Rational clarity' in theory means keeping the world hypotheses discrete. We need to follow his logic in using the five systemic perspectives. This is necessary to retain clarity of thinking and to enable the learning that ensures the continued development of each perspective. They must be treated as self-contained and separate because any attempt to combine them or cherry-pick from them will sow confusion. As they are all equally 'adequate', it also risks 'cognitive loss', the impact of which we have no means of estimating. Having pure theories at our disposal eliminates this risk (Pepper, 1942). In practice, however, 'reasonable eclecticism' is preferred because we need to draw on the benefits all the world hypotheses or systemic perspectives can bring:

> In practice, therefore, we shall want to be not rational but reasonable, and to seek, on the matter in question, the judgment supplied from each of these relatively adequate world theories. If there is some difference of judgement, we shall wish to make our decision with all these modes of evidence in mind, just as we should make any other decisions where evidence is conflicting. (Pepper, 1942, p. 331)

It is clear from this that Pepper does not mean by 'reasonable eclecticism' that we should integrate the different theories. The eclecticism comes from keeping all of them at the forefront of one's mind throughout the course of an intervention;

> Our postrational eclecticism consists simply in holding these four theories in suspended judgement as constituting the sum of our knowledge on the subject. (Pepper, 1942, p. 342)

And, because only world hypotheses can legitimately challenge other world hypotheses, conflict between them is to be encouraged. They act as excellent checks on each other.

It is now time to provide the rational clarity required on the nature of the five systemic perspectives.

5.3.1.1 The Mechanical Systemic Perspective

The mechanical systemic perspective covers Pepper's mechanism, aspects of the functionalist sociological paradigm, the 'machine(s)' metaphor (Ackoff and Morgan) and Linstone's technical perspective. To be clear, it is not the same as the model of the organisation underpinning the classical management theory of Taylor and Fayol. This certainly treats organisations as machines but *not* as systems. The mechanical *systemic* perspective shares an emphasis on goal-seeking but is more sophisticated in adopting an input–output orientation, stressing the importance of the interrelationships between the parts, valuing emergence, incorporating feedback mechanisms and engaging front-line workers in improvement.

The mechanical systemic perspective was most directly influenced by the discipline of engineering. It emphasises goal-seeking above all else. The goal is seen as set from outside the system. Once it is clear, the parts can be organised to achieve the goal as efficiently as possible. Ward summarised:

> A well-designed machine is an instance of total organization, that is, a series of interrelated means contrived to achieve a single end ... A machine consists of a coherent bringing together of all parts toward the highest possible efficiency of the functioning whole, or interrelationships marshalled wholly toward a given result ... The machine is, then, a perfect instance of total rationalization of a field of action and of total organization. (Ward, quoted in Scott, 2003, p. 33)

For Ackoff (1999), the purpose of a mechanical system is achieved as an emergent property of the whole. For example, only a car can transport you from A to B. None of its parts – engine, wheels, frame, etc., – can. Further, the parts must be well integrated. You can't take the best bits from a Mercedes, BMW, and Lexus, and put them together and expect a well-functioning vehicle.

The mechanical perspective pictures the world using an input-transformation-output model. Once the goal is determined, money is found to obtain the inputs of machines, materials and people necessary to carry out the transformation process and organise it as efficiently as possible to produce the desired output. In cases of greater complexity, the world is seen as a 'system of systems' requiring coordination and control. A hierarchical arrangement is envisioned whereby systems are made up of subsystems which, in turn, have their own subsystems. This hierarchy can be decomposed to analyse the behaviour of systems at all levels (Simon, 1962). Things will occasionally go wrong with mechanical systems designs. To counteract this, feedback mechanisms should be in place to drive corrective action. Managers ensure that supplies are obtained, the transformation process is continuously improved and repairs are carried out. Often, involving other staff is seen as essential in bringing about improvement.

Viewing a system of interest through the mechanical perspective places emphasis on efficacy and efficiency. Attention can be directed towards whether the goal is clearly defined and can be achieved. There will be a focus on whether the necessary inputs are obtained at a good price and whether the transformation process is smooth and uses the minimum resources necessary to achieve the goal. Questions will be asked about whether there is sufficient co-ordination and control exercised to ensure that predictable outcomes are obtained from subsystems and from the whole system.

5.3.1.2 The Interrelationships Systemic Perspective
The interrelationships systemic perspective corresponds, in large part, to Morgan's 'flux and transformation' metaphor but, in other respects, stands apart from the world hypotheses, paradigms and metaphors. This is an indication that its articulation and development have largely been an achievement of ST.

An emphasis on interrelationships has been central in ST. It is dominant in the Indigenous tradition mentioned in Chapter 4. The emphasis on 'circular causal relationships' in cybernetics evinces a similar orientation. Donella Meadows captured the essence of this systemic perspective:

> So, what is a system? A system is a set of things – people, cells, molecules, or whatever – interconnected in such a way that they produce their own pattern of behavior over time. The system may be buffeted, constricted, triggered, or driven by outside forces. But the system's response to those forces is characteristic of itself, and that response is seldom simple in the real world. (Meadows, 2008, p. 2)

It was insights derived from control engineering, particularly the investigation of servomechanisms, that gave rise to the formal study of systems based on the interrelationships between their parts. System Dynamics (SD) was the outcome. SD sees the multitudes of variables constituting complex systems as becoming causally related in feedback loops that themselves interact and determine system behaviour. Forrester explained in more detail:

> The structure of a complex system is not a simple feedback loop where one system state dominates the behavior. The complex system has a multiplicity of interacting feedback loops. Its internal rates of flow are controlled by non-linear relationships. The complex system is of high order, meaning that there are many system states (or levels). It usually contains positive-feedback loops describing growth processes as well as negative, goal-seeking loops. (Forrester, 1969, p. 9)

Viewing a system of interest through the interrelationships perspective highlights the need to take account of all the variables that can have an impact on system behaviour. It focuses attention on the important linkages between them and how they become entangled in interacting feedback loops. In complex systems, causes are not easy to identify as resulting from immediately preceding events. They emerge from the structure of the system, and causes and effects are often distant in space and time. It is essential, therefore, to secure a deep understanding of that structure if we are going to make sense of system behaviour. If we can do so, it becomes possible to intervene in a manner that brings favourable outcomes for stakeholders while avoiding unintended consequences.

5.3.1.3   The Organismic Systemic Perspective
The organismic systemic perspective incorporates Pepper's formism and organicism, aspects of the functionalist sociological paradigm, most of Morgan's

'organisms' and 'brains' metaphors, and Ackoff's organism metaphor. It focuses on the ability of systems to survive and thrive by being agile in turbulent environments.

The lineage of the organismic perspective can be traced back to the sociology of Spencer and Durkheim. A more direct influence on contemporary ST stems from von Bertalanffy's concept of organisms as 'open systems' (von Bertalanffy, 1969). Katz and Kahn (1978) provided the classic expression of the organismic perspective in organisation theory, managing to integrate open systems theory and sociological systems theory. They delineated nine characteristics of organisations as open systems and identified five subsystems necessary to meet the functional needs of organisations – 'production', 'supportive', 'maintenance', 'adaptive' and 'managerial'. The perspective is scalable, as Corning (2023) demonstrated when he drew on examples of superorganisms to suggest how to create a more effective global society.

More and more books are being written arguing that organisations should be viewed as 'living systems' rather than machines. The call is always for less hierarchy, more organismic structures to promote adaptation and resilience and employee empowerment. Those of de Geus (1997) and Taleb (2013) are among the best. De Geus argued that seeing a company as a machine implies that it is static; it can change 'only if *somebody* changes it'. The living company, by contrast, like all organisms, 'moves from birth to death, seeking to extend its own potential. *There is no one steering*'.

Four factors, for deGeus, define a living company:

1) Sensitivity to the environment – requiring the ability to learn and adapt
2) Cohesion and identity
3) Tolerance – expressed in decentralisation and building constructive internal and external relationships
4) Conservative financing – allowing a company to govern its own growth and evolution

Taleb wants to create 'anti-fragile' organisations that are not just resilient but improve after unexpected shocks. To do this, leaders must abandon what they have learned from machine thinking and learn from Mother Nature. Biological systems have survived and developed over millions of years without much command and control.

Consultancies have also got the organismic bug. A 2018 McKinsey & Company report argued that organisations need to transform themselves into agile organisations by embracing 'the new [*sic*] paradigm: organizations as living organisms'. Martin Reeves and colleagues, from the BCG Henderson Institute, argued that a shift in business thinking is necessary if organisations are to thrive in an interconnected world (Ramaswamy et al., 2023). This requires learning lessons from biology.

Viewing a situation of interest through the organismic perspective draws attention to the need for agility. An organisation, like an organism, is an open system that depends on its environment. To survive and thrive, it must maintain a dynamic equilibrium with that changing environment. The managerial subsystem is the 'brain' of the organisation which houses memory and should be capable of learning. It is responsible for securing favourable interchanges with the environment. It must also ensure that vital subsystems are working well and that they are controlled and coordinated so that the needs of the whole are met. This is not so easy because these subsystems will need to be partially autonomous, like the heart, lungs, liver, etc., in the body. In a turbulent environment, without some local autonomy, higher management levels would be overwhelmed with matters requiring a decision. They would lack the capacity to address strategic issues. Smuts, writing in 1926, commented on the 'close and intense' synthesis that exists between the whole and parts in an organism compared to in a mechanical system, stating that

> ... in the organic whole, parts and whole reciprocally influence and alter each other instead of merely the parts making up the whole, and in the end it is practically impossible to say where the whole ends and the parts begin, so intimate is their interaction and so profound their mutual influence ... the whole seems to be in each part, just as the parts are in the whole. (Smuts, 1986, pp. 125–126).

5.3.1.4 The Purposeful Systemic Perspective

The purposeful systemic perspective covers Pepper's contextualism, the interpretive sociological paradigm, Morgan's 'cultures' and 'political systems' metaphors, parts of Ackoff's social systems conception, and Linstone's organisational and personal viewpoints. It emphasises that human systems are different because people are self-conscious, attach meaning to the situations they find themselves in, and operate with sophisticated mental models. These models are seen as the main determinant of the way individuals think, act and interact. As Cassirer says, humans operate in a world of symbols and this

> ... transforms the whole of human life. As compared with other animals man lives not merely in a broader reality; he lives, so to speak, in a new dimension of reality. (Cassirer, quoted in Skidelsky, 2008, p. 100)

Social reality emerges from a process in which different symbolic representations, held by different individuals and groups, are continuously negotiated and renegotiated.

Churchman and Ackoff were the primary proponents of the purposeful perspective in the United States. Churchman wanted the systems approach to 'sweep in' as many worldviews as possible when trying to improve social systems. For him, increasing purposefulness in social systems design, by dialectically developing worldviews, is a never-ending process. Ackoff viewed organisations as social systems serving three sets of purposes – their own, those of their parts and those of the wider system of which they are part. Managers should seek to serve purposes at all these levels by developing their organisation's various stakeholders and removing any conflict between them.

Boulding's (1961) reflections on the importance of 'the image' offered another path to the purposeful systemic perspective. He called for a new science of images called *eiconics*. Sir Geoffrey Vickers, in the United Kingdom, was impressed. Vickers (1972) argued that it is impossible to study human systems using the methods of the natural sciences because their components are active individuals using 'appreciative systems' – nets of interrelated fact and value judgements – to attribute meaning to their situation and to decide what to do. The best way to understand human systems is to seek to comprehend the different appreciative systems that people bring to bear on a situation. According to Vickers, human systems can only achieve stability and effectiveness if the appreciative systems of their participants are sufficiently shared to allow mutual understanding to be achieved. Checkland's Soft Systems Methodology (SSM) owes much to Vickers's concept of 'appreciative systems', while his thinking was further enriched by drawing on work from the interpretive sociological paradigm, particularly Husserl's phenomenology and Dilthey's hermeneutics. Here are Checkland and Holwell discussing what an 'organisation' is from this perspective:

> But what causes it, as an entity, to exist? The answer can only be: the readiness of some people, usually large numbers of people, members and non-members alike, to talk and act as if there were a collective entity which could behave like a conscious being, with the ability to do things and then make them happen ... This way of thinking about an organization ... is necessary to make sense of what we all know from observation and experience, namely that members of organizations are not necessarily simply quiescent contributors to the achievement of organizational goals, as the conventional model suggests. (Checkland and Holwell, 1998, pp. 80–81)

Viewing a system of interest through the purposeful systemic perspective suggests that reality is socially constructed and can give rise to stable structures, but just as often produce change and novelty. The world is unpredictable and what happens is subject to multiple interpretations. This perspective alerts leaders and managers to look out for a variety of cultural and political factors that may require attention in a situation of interest. They will look to see if a culture is in place that allows shared purposes to emerge. There needs to be mutual understanding and agreement that the right things are being done, that the system is effective. On the other hand, the culture should not be so strong that it generates groupthink and stifles original thinking and innovation. It may harbour taken-for-granted assumptions which hinder free thought and discussion. They require exposure and challenge. Disagreements can be healthy. However, consideration should be given to whether there are means available for reaching accommodations between individuals and groups with diverse perspectives, thus keeping conflict under control.

5.3.1.5 The Societal/Environmental Systemic Perspective

The societal/environmental systemic perspective covers the radical humanist and radical structuralist sociological paradigms, Morgan's 'psychic prisons' and 'instruments of domination' metaphors, and aspects of his 'organisms' metaphor, and Ackoff's concern with serving the purposes of the environment. It highlights the possibility that some stakeholders and/or the natural environment may be disadvantaged by systems designs.

In its mildest form, the perspective draws attention to the wide variety of stakeholders who might be impacted by systems designs and maintains that organisations should consider not just their own needs but also those, for example, of their suppliers, employees, customers, the communities in which they operate, future generations, non-human species and the environment. The presumption is that all stakeholders should be involved in discussion about any proposed designs and, if they are not (if they are affected but not involved), then action should be taken to ensure their voice is heard. Otherwise, it is asked: How can any systems design be regarded as legitimate? Churchman, Ackoff and Checkland, from their purposeful systemic perspectives, made the case for wide participation in systems design but failed, it must be said, to give much attention to how genuine participation can be brought about in situations where some stakeholders are excluded from or unable to take an equal part in debate. A way forward is to employ Habermas's (1979) critical standard – communication free from domination – to judge whether genuine participation is taking place. In an 'ideal speech situation', 'all concerned parties have as equal a chance of articulating their concerns as possible' (Ulrich 1983) and the better argument should prevail, rather than the wishes of the powerful. Future generations and non-human entities will need to be represented in the debate.

A more radical focussing of the lens questions whether the powerful will bother to take account of the views and interests of the disadvantaged, even if clearly expressed in debate. The sources of advantage and disadvantage in society are seen as deeply embedded in structures and institutions and may be difficult to identify, let alone replace. The argument is made that those disadvantaged by current social arrangements must have more active and committed support from ST if anything is really to change. This systemic perspective was famously developed by Marx in relation to the working class in capitalist society. In *Capital* (Marx, 1961; originally 1867) he sought to provide a systemic explanation of how the capitalist mode of production leads to class struggle between the capitalist class, who own the means of production, and the exploited working class from whose labour profit is extracted. More recently, race, gender, sexual orientation, disability, age, etc., have also been identified as providing foundations for inequality and disadvantage. Different forms of oppression are frequently linked. For example, Stephens (2013) sees patriarchy as responsible for the oppression of both women and the environment. The strong societal/environmental perspective makes the case that improvement can only come about through the empowerment and emancipation of oppressed groups. This demands significant change to the status quo.

Advocates of the societal/environmental perspective, in its strong form, also respond vigorously to the environmental crisis facing the planet. We all depend upon the natural environment and endanger it when we exploit natural resources and create waste. The sustainability of life on Earth relies upon us nurturing the natural world and protecting it for future generations. If we ignore this, pollution and climate change will overcome Gaia's regulatory capacity and our blue planet's ability to sustain human life will be no more.

Viewing a system of interest through the societal/environmental systemic perspective requires asking pointed questions about whether the interests of all stakeholders, including the marginalised, have been considered in undertaking systems interventions. It highlights issues of power, discrimination and inequality. It prompts systems thinkers to seek to give a voice to the disadvantaged, offer them active support and, if necessary, campaign with them. It focuses attention on whether sustainability and environmental matters have been given due weight.

5.3.2 Identify Primary and Secondary Issues

The *Explore* stage ends when a study using the five systemic perspectives is completed and those involved conclude that they can identify the primary and secondary issues in the situation that interests them. This prioritisation usually begins to happen naturally during the process of using the perspectives. In very general terms, the 'primary' issues are those that seem to need most urgent attention – perhaps they appear to get to the heart of the matter and scream out at the participants. The secondary issues are, on the practical grounds that we cannot do everything at once, ruled out for immediate action. Nevertheless, CSP insists, they must be kept in mind because they may assume greater importance if a fresh run through *Explore* brings them to the fore. The use of the five systemic perspectives encourages participants to take a broad look at the situation of interest and to gradually focus on those issues deemed most crucial at that point in its evolution.

5.4 *Explore* – Example: The Early Days of the COVID-19 Pandemic in the United Kingdom

During the initial phase of the COVID-19 pandemic, it is generally agreed that the United Kingdom did not fare well:

> The effect of the pandemic on particular countries has been different at different times ... But in 2020 the UK did significantly worse in terms of covid deaths than many countries – especially compared to those in East Asia even though they were much closer geographically to where the virus first appeared. (House of Commons, 2021, p. 5)

This contrasts with the success of the later vaccine roll-out. Our example takes as the 'situation of interest' the issues encountered by the UK 'health system' (taken to involve Government, the National Health Service [NHS], care homes, health advisors, health professionals, etc.) during the early period of the pandemic and uses the first stage of CSP to explore them. It benefits from describing something we can all easily relate to, even if not in the specific context of the United Kingdom. It suffers because the information remains sketchy, and much is drawn from newspaper reports. The UK COVID-19 Inquiry is in its early days at the time of writing. The example, therefore, should be taken simply as illustrative of how *Explore* would go about unearthing major issues in a complex situation.

Responses to epidemics tend to place significant reliance on epidemiological models. Morin's (2006) work suggests that such models assume 'restricted complexity' and their outputs need treating with extreme caution when a 'general complexity' approach is appropriate. The COVID-19 pandemic, its progress and the responses to it, is a case in point. In the early days of COVID-19, there was a lack of information to feed into the models, for example, on who had the disease, on transmission rates, on processes of infection, on length of immunity after infection, etc. There is no wonder that the modellers struggled. As chaos theory demonstrates, a small change in the weight attached to any variable can have a huge impact on the outcome a model produces. Epidemiological models in the United Kingdom showed total deaths ranging from a few thousand to over a million. Further, there were significant psychological, political, economic and socio-cultural factors at play in determining how the disease might progress. The way individuals, government, politicians, experts, health professionals and communities reacted to the outbreak, to what they were being told, to actions taken to combat it, and indeed to the models themselves, would impact how things went with COVID-19. This is exactly why Morin identifies the fundamental problem of general complexity as 'epistemological, cognitive, and paradigmatic'. Sir John Kay, in his evidence to the Science and Technology Committee, in June 2020 (House of Commons, 2021), expressed his concerns about the limitations of models as predictive devices. Models are inevitably simplifying and, therefore, partial; they encourage the belief that numbers can be put on everything; they don't respond well to change because they tend to assume the world is 'stationary' and linear; and they cannot account for 'reflexivity' – their own impact on how people think and behave. The over-reliance on models during the early phase of the pandemic in the United Kingdom provides a salutary lesson of what can happen if you operate with a restricted complexity viewpoint when general complexity thinking is required (Jackson, 2020).

With this background in place, it is possible to run through the five 'systemic perspectives', employed by *Explore*, to identify the range of interacting issues that hindered the UK health system from responding adequately in the early days of the COVID-19 pandemic.

In terms of the **mechanical systemic perspective**, we would expect a health system to have clear plans in place of how to respond to an emergency, the necessary resources to support the plans, and processes designed to deliver them. In the United Kingdom, there had been a planning exercise related to a possible flu pandemic, but the shortcomings revealed were not addressed. In any case, COVID-19 represented a somewhat different challenge. A robust plan, as England's chief medical officer, Sir Chris Whitty, said to the COVID Inquiry, would have concentrated on the 'building blocks of lots of different capabilities' (Booth, 2023). Clearly, the resources available were inadequate. Hospitals were struggling to cope with existing patient demand. At the beginning of the outbreak, there were shortages of staff, hospital beds, personal protective equipment (PPE) and ventilators. Supply lines for some essential equipment had not been secured. Testing capacity was low. Some microbiology/virology laboratories, necessary to develop and carry out testing, had been closed or outsourced to the private sector. There were no adequate arrangements in place for large-scale 'track and tracing' or a workforce trained to undertake this task. The health system lacked standardised procedures for dealing with emergencies. This was exacerbated because the private sector had become dominant in running care homes.

The **interrelationships systemic perspective** would have drawn to the attention of decision-makers the impact of important relationships that were being neglected. The long-term failure to address the interrelationships between hospitals and the care sector is the most obvious example. It leads to 'bed-blocking' in hospitals because vulnerable patients have nowhere suitable to go following their treatment. As the COVID-19 emergency escalated, it was difficult to provide for the safe discharge of patients. To free up beds, patients were emptied out of hospitals into care homes, many without testing, thus contributing to the spread of the disease among existing residents. The way the NHS was privileged, in what should have been a partnership arrangement, contributed to problems in several ways. For example, the NHS was prioritised for PPE and testing kits. The nature of their employment meant care workers moved between homes. A tragedy began to unfold from the interactions impacting care homes.

From the point of view of the **organismic systemic perspective**, the health system should have been organised with sufficient response capability to deal with crises thrown up by a turbulent environment. The necessary 'variety' (Ashby, 1956) can be built into a system using forms of integration and information management that allow for appropriate autonomy to subsystems. In England, however, the NHS is organised as a hierarchy and decisions about how to respond to the epidemic were taken centrally by the government. This can be compared to the situation in Germany where regions have much more power and responsibility and were able to redirect local resources, for example, to bolster the 'track and trace' system. The situation in the United Kingdom led to the government issuing proclamations which were met with incredulity on the ground because they bore no relation to the reality of what was necessary or could be achieved. Meanwhile, local bodies lacked the information and authority to launch initiatives in response to their own individual circumstances (Harris, 2020). In Leicester, when a second spike in the epidemic occurred, local leaders were unable to access the data needed to implement appropriate action, not that they had the power to do much anyway. The rigidity of the system was reinforced when a centralised 'track and trace' system was introduced, apparently after little or no consultation with local authority public health teams (McCoy, 2020). Successful local systems, developed to monitor the spread of sexually transmitted diseases, could have been repurposed. Of course, the argument for greater decentralisation, explicit in this analysis, needs careful consideration in the light of experiences in the United States, where the lack of a unified response has been blamed for many of the problems encountered. A balance must be achieved. The centre needs to act to coordinate and support local responses and fill gaps in provision when necessary.

You would expect an organisation to possess the capacity of an organism to adapt to a crisis without threatening other core activities essential to its successful functioning, for example, dealing with referrals for cancer screening and providing urgent treatment for serious cases of heart disease and cancer. This was not the case with the UK health system. You would expect an organisation as an organism to learn from past experiences. This occurred in countries such as South Korea, Taiwan and Hong Kong, but nothing seems to have been absorbed into the 'brain' of the UK's health system.

The **purposeful systemic perspective** points to the need for mutual understanding and sufficient alignment of purposes among stakeholders confronting a complex problem situation. In the United Kingdom, this was not always present. The Scientific Advisory Group for Emergencies (SAGE) began by seeking to present a unified view to the government, believing this was better for decision-makers than being exposed to a variety of opinions. This may initially have blinded politicians to the uncertainty of science and to the availability of different options. Eventually, the uncertainty could not be hidden and, once it was clear that 'the science' had little to say on many of the major decisions that needed taking, government could no longer hide behind it. Politics entered the fray with a vengeance. There was chronic indecision at the top. There were unresolved disputes, for example, about the importance of minimising deaths from the disease as against maintaining the health of the economy. The devolved administrations sought to assert their independence. Local politicians began to see the pandemic as a fight for resources. Information presented at the daily press conferences was seen by many as massaged to suit the government's agenda and paint it in a good light. For example, comparisons of the UK's performance against other countries were dropped when it became obvious it was worse. Trust was dissipated. The media weighed in, amplifying the burgeoning set of disputes. Chris Whitty suffered personal abuse in the street.

The purposeful systemic perspective also alerts us to the danger of groupthink. A culture of 'English exceptionalism' was prevalent, manifesting itself in a slowness to learn from other countries already in the throes of the epidemic and to listen to advice from the World Health Organization. Everything the United Kingdom did had to be 'world beating'. Another cultural factor was the 'myth' that surrounds the NHS. Davies (2020) argues that the NHS myth has become 'entangled with a host of other national British icons, many of which hark back to the Second World War'. The myth helped to inform the decision to shift from a policy of track and trace (formally abandoned as early as March 12, 2020) to one of 'flattening the curve' to allow the NHS to cope. The alternative strategy, successful elsewhere, of eliminating the virus through rapidly escalating testing capacity and imposing isolation fell by the wayside. As Chris Whitty stated to the COVID Inquiry, the United Kingdom 'did not give sufficient thought' to stopping COVID in its tracks (Booth, 2023). Groupthink seems to have been present in relation to 'the science' on which the government relied in the early days. It was a very traditional type of science. There are alternatives. For example, complexity theory argues that, if you are confronted by a chaotic situation, you do not spend time finessing mathematics and statistics. You need to act quickly and decisively (Snowden and Boone, 2007). As Taleb and Bar-Yam (2020) put it, specifically in relation to the UK government's response to COVID-19, 'someone watching an avalanche heading in their direction [does not call] for complicated statistical models to see if they need to get out of the way'. But establishment science, the basis for epidemiological models, works that way. And, it seems to have encouraged dithering and delay as mathematical models were argued over and refined. Direct action, such as lockdowns, closure of airports and seaports, and the ramping up of tracking and tracing systems, proved to be effective elsewhere. They were slow to be adopted or were quickly abandoned in the United Kingdom. Other countries looked on in amazement at the endless bickering about the efficacy of facemasks. There was little challenge to the nature of 'the science', even when it was clearly out of its depth. Behavioural scientists were asked to comment on the possible psychological and social impact of actions, but their thinking was constrained by the stimulus-response model that allows them to fit into 'the science paradigm' and makes them attractive to decision-makers. This model detracts from an alternative view that people should be treated as intelligent, as capable of understanding the situation and acting reasonably. The Health and Social Care and Science and Technology Committees of the House of Commons heard that 'red teaming' and structured challenge, as used within the national security community, 'may also be of benefit to the scientific community' (House of Commons, 2021). Chris Whitty supported the idea that 'red teams' outside SAGE had provided more 'challenge' (Booth, 2023).

From the **societal/environmental systemic perspective**, a health system fit to cope with something like COVID-19 ought to have considered in advance and put in place measures to address the effect that inequalities would have on the impact and progress of the disease. In the United Kingdom, insufficient consideration was given to the likelihood that Black, Asian, and minority ethnic groupings, and people with learning disabilities, would be disproportionately affected (House of Commons, 2021). Sir Patrick Vallance, the government's chief scientific officer, told the COVID Inquiry that it was a 'terrible truth' and 'tragedy' that 'pandemics feed off inequality and drive inequality' and said that while 'we did pick up on it, [the knowledge] needs to be embedded right from day one' (Booth, 2023). Questions have also been asked about whether the failure to protect care homes was the result of 'systematic ageism' (see Toynbee, 2020). The ongoing UK COVID-19 Inquiry is revealing that discriminatory attitudes towards women led to their exclusion when important decisions were being taken. Greater diversity might have helped avoid the groupthink previously identified.

I have employed this example to show how *Explore* could have assisted preparedness and initial thinking in response to a complex multi-agency emergency – the COVID-19 pandemic in the United Kingdom. It is perhaps worth concluding this section by reiterating what I see as some strengths of *Explore*. Each of the five systemic perspectives reveals new matters worthy of attention. The different perspectives emphasise alternative accounts of what are the most important issues and their causes. Even if they provide conflicting information and explanations, this can prove helpful in gaining a richer appreciation of the complexity involved and in supporting informed decision-making. In the COVID-19 case, the UK health system faced serious problems from the point of view of all the perspectives and there were no obvious leverage points that could be targeted to generate overall improvement. *Explore* would have identified some primary issues which needed immediate action and some secondary issues deserving of attention when resources allowed. Once the epidemic had started, it could have pointed to where best to direct the response. What were identified as the primary issues would depend on where the greatest impact could be had quickly. For example, a lack of PPE would assume greater immediate significance than a re-organisation of the health service to promote more effective local autonomy.

Science saved us in the end with the development of the vaccine. But CSP could, I think, have played a significant role in improving preparation for the emergency and better informing the early response.

5.5 *Explore* – Issues

In this section, I provide further clarification of the nature of *Explore* by anticipating and responding to some possible criticisms.

While the potential user of CSP will be relieved that there are only five 'systemic perspectives', a critic might wonder why five is the limit. The five perspectives, I would argue, emerge naturally from the review of different theories and perspectives in philosophy, social science, organisation theory and ST. I have cut a swathe through that literature, not always presenting the details, but I believe that the evidence speaks for itself. If other candidate systemic perspectives are presented, they will need to demonstrate the same 'adequacy', the same 'cognitive power' as the five described. That said, there will no doubt be a variety of 'sub-narratives', under each of the systemic perspectives, that may help bring more precision to the analysis in a particular case. For example, Patrick McKenna (2022), during a CSP project to improve the Emergency Relief social service program in Australia, employed 'maze', 'treadmill' and 'income-support top-up' metaphors to support his analysis from the purposeful systemic perspective.

It might be asked whether one of the systemic perspectives could prove so powerful, produce so much evidence in its favour, that the others could reasonably be dispensed with. Pepper, considering this in relation to his world hypotheses, does not rule it out. Perhaps the approach used in the physical sciences, so successful in its own domain, could be extended to other fields. But he is sceptical and offers a warning:

> Certainly, in the past, every attempt to extend the achievement of the physical sciences as a consistent system beyond the subject matter of these sciences has resulted in some form of root-metaphor hypothesis, usually mechanism. (Pepper, 1942, p. 336)

Many more readers, I'm sure, will ask whether the systemic perspectives can be harmonised and amalgamated. For Pepper, the answer is no. They each make compelling cognitive claims, and these are irreconcilable:

> We see that there is much to be said for each of these theories of truth, that they cannot be successfully amalgamated in one view that will do full justice to them all. (Pepper, 1942, p. 347)

Any credible attempt to reconcile world hypotheses, therefore, 'turns out to be the judgement of one of the theories on the nature of the others' (Pepper, 1942). It privileges one theory, leading to 'cognitive loss' in terms of what the other theories have to offer.

Let us, therefore, keep different world hypotheses autonomous and learn about and benefit from what each has to offer. ST can assist in this by making each world hypothesis more 'coherent'. The expression 'systemic perspectives' reminds us that we need well-formulated, interlinked sets of ideas, making up coherent wholes, with which to interrogate situations of interest. Rescher (1979), in his 'coherentist theory of knowledge', notes the tendency of human beings to organise their knowledge in 'cognitive systems'. These cognitive systems are structured frameworks linking various elements of our knowledge into cohesive wholes. They express certain intellectual norms – simplicity, regularity, uniformity, comprehensiveness, unity, harmony and economy. These are norms which people have found useful in developing theories that enable them to think seriously about the world. Cohesive systemic perspectives allow us to maintain 'rational clarity' in theory and provide appropriate depth of analysis. Learning can occur and parallel usage becomes easier when we adhere to such precise theoretical constructions. It is easy to recognise the dangers if we don't. Many popular business books see the 'machine model' of the organisation as inadequate and call for a more organismic model, drawing on lessons from biology and presenting organisations as 'living systems'. Rarely, however, do the authors stick strictly to the organismic perspective. Sensing intuitively that it doesn't quite cut the mustard for their purposes, they 'cheat'. They introduce into their narratives, on an *ad hoc* basis, aspects of the purposeful and societal/environmental approaches. Such eclecticism does nothing for coherence or the promotion of learning.

I have a feeling that the argument so far will be a big disappointment to some systems thinkers. They will be of the view that ST can provide a meta-narrative leading us to the sunny uplands from where the world's problems can be clearly viewed, understood and solved. I think this is nonsense. ST cannot see off philosophical disputes going back millennia and settle sociological arguments that have been around for hundreds of years. We can again turn to Pepper (1942) to develop this point. Pepper uses the term 'hypostatization' for a process in which concepts can lose contact with their root metaphors and become empty abstractions. *Wiktionary* provides an excellent definition of hypostatization: 'to construe a contextually subjective and complex abstraction, idea, or concept as a universal object without regard to nuance or change in character'. This is what some systems thinkers do with 'system' and related concepts. It should be obvious that the concept 'system' has become thin – used to describe everything from double glazing to the universe. But, employing Pepper's language, 'the very emptiness of the concept is used as an argument for its acceptance'. Systems thinkers too often believe it has 'a cosmic glow about it' and demand it is treated with awe. This can soon lead to earthly scepticism and loss of respect. The concept 'system' cannot be provided with a universal definition. The way forward, Pepper would say, is to attach it, and related holistic concepts, to powerful world theories that can give them meaning and significance, and to which they can provide service. The role of ST, as it is understood in CST and CSP, is to enhance useful world theories with its powerful array of holistic concepts. In this way I have, for example, sought to interpret Pepper's 'mechanism' and 'formism', which he sees as essentially analytic approaches, in a more synthetic fashion. The aim is to ensure that ST can, across the spectrum of ways of understanding the world, supply useful systemic perspectives. The role of ST is not to try to replace decision-makers with expert knowledge but to complement their experience and knowledge of context with alternative ways of thinking and new ways of operating in the 'swampy lowlands' (Schön, 1983).

It is reasonable to ask how *Explore* itself can be enhanced. The systemic perspectives, I would argue, are easy to complement with other proven creativity-enhancing devices. They can, for example, be used together with 'Rich Pictures' (Checkland, 1981) to make an *Explore* exercise more stimulating and exciting. Once they have grasped the essentials of the mechanical systemic perspective, participants could be asked to draw a Rich Picture which shows how their organisation is failing as a mechanical system. Then, perhaps, draw another one picturing what it would have to be like to be a successful mechanical system. They could be asked to produce a Rich Picture, based on the societal/environmental systemic perspective, to encourage thinking about who is being discriminated against in tackling an issue in a particular way. There are many fruitful avenues to explore using the combination of systemic perspectives and Rich Pictures.

There is certainly work that needs doing on how to acquire the 'cognitive flexibility' to operate with five systemic perspectives. We will return to this in Part 3 of the book. For now, we rest content with noting two contributions suggesting that, to promote the necessary flexibility, CST and CSP will need to transcend the rational-analytic approach that dominates the Western tradition. Raghav Rajagopalan (2020) argued that CSP ignores 'ways of knowing' – 'experiential' (active), 'presentational' (artistic) and 'practical' (craft) – practised in other cultures for centuries. Holistic systemic knowing requires the embrace of two modes of consciousness – 'intentionality', highlighting the agency of the practitioner, and 'non-intentional' mindful awareness, which sees value in simply 'abiding' and appreciating ecological relationships. The former is dominant in Western thinking, while the Indian philosophical tradition makes room for both. Chowdhury (2019) argued that 'holistic flexibility' requires developing a 'state of mind' that encourages and can underpin flexible and responsible systems practice. This means superseding rational-analytic thinking. He drew upon the five most important 'functions' of the *Nataraja*, an anthropomorphic form of the Hindu god, *Shiva*, to articulate five principles of holistic flexibility – 'system as becoming', 'transformative flexibility', 'responsible practice', 'spiral of learning' and 'pragmatic artistry' (Chowdhury, 2022). In a recent book, Chowdhury (2024) remarked that the greatest contribution that ST can make is as a cognitive process that facilitates more creative and flexible ways of viewing the world. The success of 'holistic flexibility' depends more on nurturing appropriate cognitive skills than on methodologies, frameworks and prescriptions. I largely concur. Developing the ability to see the world through the different 'systemic perspectives' can take us a long way on the ST journey.

I suspect, notwithstanding these warnings about relying too much on rational analysis, that there will be readers hoping for more specific guidance on how to carry out *Explore*. For these people, please remember that the 'systemic perspectives' are only meant to provide a general orientation to an intervention at the first stage of CSP. It is the systems methodologies linked to the systemic perspectives, and set out in the next chapter, that carry the detailed guidance on how to translate the thinking provoked by *Explore* into practice.

5.6 Conclusion

The systemic perspectives, drawn from well-respected classifications of world theories, paradigms, metaphors and viewpoints, capture the essence of those 'experiential gestalts' that have stood the test of time in terms of proving useful to the human species. They all have much to offer. Using them together in *Explore* ensures that this stage has both breadth and depth. As will become apparent in later chapters, they also serve the purposes of later stages of CSP. For example, they are well aligned to the assumptions made by the different systems methodologies which we need to consider during the *Produce* phase and to employ in *Intervene*. The issues the different systemic perspectives bring to attention correspond to those prioritised by the different methodologies.

References

Ackoff, R. L. (1999). *Ackoff's Best*. Wiley.

Ashby, W.R. (1956). *An Introduction to Cybernetics*. Methuen.

Bakewell, S. (2010). *How to Live: A Life of Montaigne*. Chatto & Windus.

Barabba, V.P. (2004). *Surviving Transformation*. Oxford University Press.

von Bertalanffy, L. (1969). The theory of open systems in physics and biology. In: *Systems Thinking* (ed. F.E. Emery), 70–85. Penguin.

Booth, R. (2023). Chris Whitty: UK should have focused more on stopping Covid-type pandemic. *The Guardian*, 22 June.

Boulding, K.E. (1961). *The Image*. Ann Arbor.

Burrell, G. and Morgan, G. (1979). *Sociological Paradigms and Organizational Analysis*. Heinemann.

Checkland, P.B. (1981). *Systems Thinking, Systems Practice*. Wiley.

Checkland, P.B. and Holwell, S. (1998). *Information, Systems and Information Systems*. Wiley.

Chowdhury, R. (2019). *Systems Thinking for Management Consultants: Introducing Holistic Flexibility*. Springer.

Chowdhury, R. (2022). Holistic flexibility for critical systems thinking inspired by the *Nataraja*. *Journal of Management, Spirituality & Religion* 19: 154–185.

Chowdhury, R. (2024). *Holistic Flexibility for Systems Thinking and Practice*. Routledge.

Corning, P. (2023). *Superorganism: Toward a New Social Contract for Our Endangered Species*. Cambridge University Press.

Davies, W. (2020). Flags, face masks and flypasts. *The Guardian*, 16 May.

De Geus, A. (1997). *The Living Company*. Longview Publishing Ltd.

Forrester, J.W. (1969). *Urban Dynamics*. Productivity Press.

Habermas, J. (1979). *Communication and the Evolution of Society*. Heinemann.

Harris, J. (2020). The pandemic has exposed the failings of Britain's centralized state. *The Guardian*, 25 May.

House of Commons – Health and Social Care and Science and Technology Committees. (2021). Coronavirus: lessons learned to date. *House of Commons*, 12 October.

Jackson, M.C. (2020). How we understand 'complexity' makes a difference: lessons from critical systems thinking and the Covid-19 pandemic in the UK. *Systems.* https://doi.org/10.3390/systems8040052.

Katz, D. and Kahn, R.L. (1978). *The Social Psychology of Organizations*, 2e. Wiley.

Kuhn, T.S. (1970). *The Structure of Scientific Revolutions.* University of Chicago Press.

Lakoff, G. and Johnson, M. (1980). *Metaphors We Live By.* University of Chicago Press.

Linstone, H.A. (1984). *Multiple Perspectives for Decision-Making; Bridging the Gap Between Analysis and Action.* North-Holland.

Marx, K. (1961). *Capital.* Foreign Language Publishing House.

McCoy, D. (2020). Countries from Germany to Vietnam got test and trace right, so why didn't England? *The Guardian*, 16 June.

McKenna, P. (2022). Critical systems thinking for the design and improvement of complex social service program outcomes. M.Phil. thesis. Queensland University of Technology.

McKinsey & Company. (2018). *The Five Trademarks of Agile Organizations.* McKinsey.

Meadows, D.H. (2008). *Thinking In Systems.* Chelsea Green Publishing.

Montaigne, M. de. (c 1580). *The Complete Essays* (translated and edited by M.A. Screech, 2003). Penguin Books, Kindle edition.

Morgan, G. (1986). *Images of organization.* Sage.

Morin, E. (2006). Restricted complexity, general complexity. Presented at the Colloquium 'Intelligence de la complexité: épistémologie et pragmatique', Cerisy-La-Salle, France, June 26, 2005. Translated from French by Carlos Gershenson.

Nelson, H.G. (2022). Systemic design as born from the Berkeley Bubble. *Contexts – The Journal of Systemic Design* 1. https://doi.org/10.58279/v1001.

Pepper, S.C. (1942). *World Hypotheses.* University of California Press.

Rae, C. (2020). *William S. Burroughs and the Cult of Rock'n'Roll.* White Rabbit.

Rajagopalan, R. (2020). *Immersive Systemic Knowing: Advancing Systems Thinking Beyond Rational Analysis.* Springer.

Ramaswamy, S., Reeves, M. and Job, A. (2023). Thriving in an interconnected world: the systems of business. *BCG Henderson Institute.* August 24.

Rescher, N. (1979). *Cognitive Systematization: A Systems Theoretic Approach to a Coherentist Theory of Knowledge.* Basil Blackwell.

Sagasti, F. (2019). Renewing strategic planning and management: a paradoxical approach. *Harvard Deusto Business Research* 8: 208–218.

Schön, D. (1983). *The Reflective Practitioner: How Professionals Think in Action.* Temple Smith.

Scott, W.R. (2003). *Organizations: Rational, Natural, and Open Systems*, Fifth edition. Pearson Education.

Simon, H.A. (1962). The architecture of complexity. *Proceedings of the American Philosophical Society* 106: 467–482.

Skidelsky, E. (2008). *Ernst Cassirer: The Last Philosopher of Culture*. Princeton University Press.

Smuts, J.C. (1986). *Holism and Evolution. The Gestalt Journal Press.*

Snowden, D.J. and Boone, M.E. (2007). A leader's framework for decision making. *Harvard Business Review*, November: 69–76.

Stephens, A. (2013). *Ecofeminism and Systems Thinking*. Routledge, Kindle edition.

Taleb, N.N. (2013). *Antifragile: How to Live in a World we Don't Understand*. Allen Lane, Kindle edition.

Taleb, N. N. and Bar-Yam, Y. (2020). The UK's coronavirus strategy may sound scientific. It isn't. *The Guardian*, 25 March.

Toynbee, P. (2020). The ghosts of the care-home dead will come back to haunt this government. *The Guardian*, 1 June.

Tsoukas, H. (2017). Don't simplify, complexify: from disjunctive to conjunctive theorizing in organization and management studies. *Journal of Management Studies* 54: 132–153. https://doi.org/10.1111/joms.12219.

Ulrich, W. (1983). *Critical Heuristics of Social Planning*. Haupt.

Vickers, G. (1972). *Freedom in a Rocking Boat*. Pelican Books.

Woermann, M., Human, O. and Preiser, R. (2018). General complexity – a philosophical and critical perspective. *Emergence: Complexity and Organization*. https://doi:10.emerg/10.17357.c9734094d98458109d25b79d546318af.

6

Critical Systems Practice 2 – *Produce* an Intervention Strategy

> *Generally, the pathos of the interdisciplinary predicament can be seen by the fact that ... we are dealing with an integrated problem with dis-integrated sciences and disciplines. We need a comparable level of integration in our thought and action to achieve effective responses to many of the applied problems we face in the world today.*
>
> (Bhaskar, 2017)

6.1   Introduction

This chapter details what is involved in *Produce*, the second stage of any Critical Systems Practice (CSP) intervention. *Produce* is concerned with the design of an appropriate intervention strategy based on the learning derived from *Explore*. It continues to carry forward the commitments of Critical Systems Thinking (CST) by selecting appropriate systems methodologies, models and methods that will later be used in a pluralist fashion to drive multifaceted improvement in a situation of interest. The success of *Produce* rests on understanding the purposes, strengths and weaknesses of different systems methodologies. Five types of systems methodology are identified and described – engineering, system dynamics (SD), living, soft and emancipatory. These are shown to relate to the five systemic perspectives that were employed to provide an appreciation of the situation of interest in *Explore*. Examples are provided of how different methodologies were chosen as 'dominant' at different times to steer interventions. Finally, some possible objections to what *Produce* suggests are discussed.

Critical Systems Thinking: A Practitioner's Guide, First Edition. Michael C. Jackson.
© 2024 John Wiley & Sons, Inc. Published 2024 by John Wiley & Sons, Inc.

6.2 *Produce* – Preliminaries

The commitments of CST – to systemic pragmatism, systemic critique, systemic pluralism and systemic improvement – must be honoured at each of the *EPIC* stages of CSP.

Produce views the various systems methodologies as offering alternative ways of securing improvement that must prove their worth in the contexts in which they are used. As Rescher had it:

> The proper test for the correctness or appropriateness of anything methodological in nature is plainly and obviously posed by the paradigmatically pragmatic questions: Does it *work*? Does it attain its intended purposes? Does it – to put it crassly – deliver the goods? (Rescher, 1977, p. 3; italics in the original)

The notion that one methodology is better because it has a truer understanding of 'reality' and how to change it is rejected. There is no 'one best way'. Rather, the methodologies, and the systemic perspectives they reflect, provide partial truths and act as critiques of each other. As Pepper (1942) says of his 'world hypotheses', they 'have no difficulty in explaining each other's errors'.

Producing an appropriate intervention strategy necessitates systemic critique – having an appreciation of the strengths and weaknesses of different systems methodologies. However wonderful a favoured methodology may seem to its advocates, it will inevitably focus attention on certain matters and ignore others. This characteristic is closely related to the 'systemic perspective' that a methodology privileges, either knowingly or implicitly. CST has, throughout its history, been committed to exposing the claims to universality of individual systems methodologies and relentless in interrogating them about their theoretical underpinnings and the consequences of these for what they can achieve in practice (Flood and Jackson, 1991; Jackson, 1991, 2000, 2003, 2019). The approach taken here is to relate the systems methodologies directly to the systemic perspectives employed during *Explore*. They are classified according to which systemic perspectives they prioritise.

The *Produce* stage honours CST's commitment to systemic pluralism by considering for use the full range of potentially helpful systems methodologies, models and methods. Informed by the outcomes of *Explore*, and by systemic critique, the aim is to arrive at an intervention strategy that will employ the different systems approaches in combination in a manner that maximises the capacities they possess, as a set, to improve things in a particular context of application. The use together, in a single intervention, of different methodologies and methods is known as 'multimethodological' practice. There are several reasons why it is desirable (Jackson, 1987, 1997; Mingers and Brocklesby, 1997; Mingers, 2014), the main one being that complex situations usually exhibit 'multidimensional' characteristics. Employing a range of methodologies allows a more comprehensive response to heterogeneity. Despite this, there will be circumstances when the 'primary issues' revealed during *Explore* are heavily concentrated in just one area, e.g., are about the ability to be agile and adaptive, as revealed by the 'organismic' perspective. In these circumstances, it is appropriate to employ just one methodology to guide the intervention. Such a decision should be taken self-consciously by decision-makers and permit a change of methodological orientation as the intervention proceeds. This matter is discussed further in Chapter 7 on *Intervene*.

The final commitment of CST is to bring about improvement in situations of interest to stakeholders. The *Produce* stage seeks to ensure the most appropriate choice of systems methodologies, models and methods so that this can be achieved. The various methodologies define improvement in different ways – increased efficiency and efficacy, finding leverage points, agility and anti-fragility, mutual understanding, emancipation, sustainability, etc. Using them in combination ensures that these different aspects of 'improvement' can be pursued in parallel. This matter receives further consideration in Chapter 8 on *Check*.

We can now turn to the details of the *Produce* stage of CSP.

6.3   *Produce* – **Process**

Produce requires participants in the CSP process to appreciate the range of systems approaches, choose appropriate systems methodologies, choose appropriate systems models and methods and structure, schedule and set objectives for the intervention. Figure 6.1 reminds us of where *Produce* sits in *EPIC*.

6.3.1   Appreciate the Variety of Systems Approaches

It can help us appreciate the nature of the various applied systems approaches if we distinguish between *systems methodologies, systems models* and *systems methods*. Although they do different things, they are often confused in the literature.

Systems methodologies translate broad hypotheses about the nature of the world into recommendations for practical action. There are various systems methodologies available, each based upon different assumptions about the world and how best to intervene to change it. It has long been the argument of CST and CSP that if a systems practitioner is familiar with, and uses just one or two methodologies, they are restricting their perspective on what issues are important and how they might be dealt with. This should, therefore, only be done consciously after careful

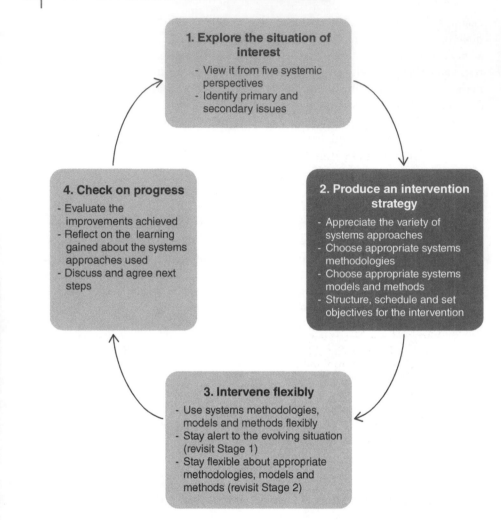

Figure 6.1 The four *EPIC* stages of Critical Systems Practice.

deliberation. Five types of systems methodology can be identified relating to the five systemic perspectives:

1) **Engineering systems methodologies** related to the mechanical systemic perspective (e.g., the Deming Management Method, the Vanguard Method [VM] and Systems Engineering [SE]).

2) **SD** based on the interrelationships perspective.

3) **Living systems methodologies** corresponding to the organismic perspective (e.g., Sociotechnical Systems Thinking [STS] and the Viable System Model [VSM]).

4) **Soft systems methodologies** privileging the purposeful systemic perspective (e.g., Interactive Planning [IP], Soft Systems Methodology [SSM] and Strategic Assumption Surfacing and Testing [SAST]).

5) **Emancipatory systems methodologies** responding to societal/environmental concerns (e.g. Critical Systems Heuristics [CSH] and the Gender equality, Environments and Marginalized voices [GEMs] framework).

Systems Thinking (ST) has done well in formulating a range of methodologies that cover the ground in terms of systemic perspectives and is able, as a result, to respond to whatever issues are surfaced during the *Explore* stage of CSP.

Systems models seek to capture the essence of a situation in ways that make it easier to understand and manipulate. Examples are as follows:

- Fishbone Diagrams
- Value Stream Mapping
- Control Charts
- Computer Simulations
- Causal Loop Diagrams (CLDs)
- Stock and Flow Diagrams
- Rich Pictures
- Conceptual Models

Systems methods are techniques which, if used correctly, should deliver a desired outcome for the practitioner. Examples are as follows:

- Just-In-Time
- Total Quality Management
- Lean
- Six Sigma
- Process Engineering
- System Archetypes
- Agile
- Idealized Design
- CATWOE Analysis
- Dialectical Debate
- Boundary Questions

Other lists are provided by Barbrook-Johnson and Penn (2022) and Williams and Hummelbrunner (2010). The former outlines seven systems mapping/modelling techniques of both a qualitative and quantitative nature. The latter offers 19 systems methods, methodologies and models from which the practitioner is invited to choose. Both these sources conflate methodologies, models and methods in a way that I am not comfortable with. For reasons explained below, I want to insist on the primacy of methodologies. I do, however, accept that the distinction is not always easy to make. Certain models and methods have become so strongly associated with host methodologies that it makes little sense to try to separate them. This is the case, for example, with CLDs and SD, and Rich Pictures and SSM.

6.3.2 Choose Appropriate Systems Methodologies

To *Produce* an intervention strategy, it is essential to start by choosing a systems methodology or methodologies to steer the process. The appropriate choice of systems methodologies will guide the intervention in a way that ensures the issues revealed during *Explore* are addressed in an informed and focussed manner. Systems models and methods should be considered later. They are more flexible and can usually be employed for a variety of purposes in conjunction with different methodologies. Their role is to support the chosen methodologies and attune them to the specific characteristics of the situation of interest.

The proper choice of systems methodologies depends on the primary and secondary issues revealed during *Explore*. It is convenient, as we have done, to classify the systems methodologies according to which systemic perspectives they prioritise. This makes for a smooth transition to the choice of appropriate systems methodologies. For example, if the mechanical systemic perspective proves productive in highlighting significant issues during *Explore*, then it is sensible to privilege a methodology such as SE that pays attention to more technical issues.

The five types of systems methodology are now described. For further information on the philosophy and theory underpinning each methodology, on the methodology itself, on closely associated models and methods, for more examples of use and critique, see Jackson (2019).

6.3.2.1 Engineering Systems Methodologies

Engineering systems methodologies respond well to issues highlighted by the mechanical systemic perspective. They seek the efficient design of input-transformation-output systems in pursuit of externally defined goals. This requires a clear definition of purpose, attention to inputs, the integration of the elements involved in the transformation and close attention to the needs of clients or consumers. Control is maintained by eliminating variations and by feedback mechanisms.

Donaldson set out the essentials of this kind of approach. In his account, all the energy of the whole enterprise must be harnessed towards the achievement of its purpose. This requires those in control to design an appropriate Enterprise Management System:

> Did you design the system, or did it just develop by default? As the owner or leader, you are the architect, the engineer, the artist, the philosopher king who designs the system – or not! (Donaldson, 2017, loc. 185)

In carrying out systems design, leaders must:

> Remember that your enterprise is a system designed to convert inputs into outputs, a term we call *throughput*. The goal is to optimize total system throughput – e.g., to get the highest possible output (in quantity, quality, or some combination) from the chosen inputs. (Donaldson, 2017, loc. 926; italics in the original)

Matters upfront in other systems methodologies – for example, determining the appropriate level of autonomy to give to subsystems ('holons') and aligning stakeholder purposes – receive some attention, but as subordinate concerns to be dealt with as part of designing the perfect mechanical system for efficiently achieving the purpose:

> Here is a key systems-thinking insight you have to become comfortable with: the only way you are really in control is if the *system* is in control, and every holon and employee is doing what they should do. (Donaldson, 2017, loc. 2973; italics in the original)

Donaldson references Deming as 'one of the titans of the management literature' and insists that enterprises are 'systems of systems' ('holarchies'). This points us to two important engineering systems approaches – the Deming Management Method and SE.

In the acknowledgements to *Out of the Crisis* (2018; originally 1982), W. Edwards Deming noted his debt to W. A. Shewhart, H. E. Dodge and G. Edwards, all of the Bell Telephone Laboratories. Their work inspired the Deming Management Method, which has been credited with helping to create the post-WW2 Japanese economic miracle. At the centre of Deming's philosophy is the famous flow diagram where he represents production as a system leading from suppliers, through production, assembly and inspection, to distribution to consumers. Improving this system requires working with suppliers to ensure the quality of incoming materials and equipment; a continuing emphasis on the integration, design, testing and redesign of processes, machines, and methods; and an appreciation of what consumers want. Employing a four-stage process, *Plan, Do, Check, Adjust* (PDCA), to test and implement possible changes, it becomes possible to design a system where all activity is consistent with the purpose, which produces the highest quality for the consumer, and is capable of continuous improvement (Walton, 1994). Testing is essential throughout the process to find any variations in quality that might lead to waste. The aim is to build quality into the product in the first place. The use of statistical control charts is said to reveal that 94% of the variations from what is required are regular and can be traced to the design of the system rather than to 'special causes' (Deming, 2018). This should convince managers that their role is to work to improve the system, not to control workers. Production workers can be brought into an 'undivided bond' with managers and contribute to improving quality if they understand how their work contributes to the overall purpose.

The success of the Toyota Production System (TPS), in which Taiichi Ohno operationalised and extended Deming's thinking, ensured the popularity of this approach in manufacturing. Ideas associated with the TPS include just-in-time manufacturing (producing to customer demand), Lean Production, Value Stream Mapping, the classification and elimination of 'waste', Kanban (a scheduling system), Kaizen (continuous improvement), Total Quality Management, 360-degree Communication, Fishbone Diagrams, Control Charts and many others (Sweeney, 2017). The ideas spread worldwide and inspired the development of other 'lean' concepts such as the 'Theory of Constraints', Six Sigma and Process Engineering.

The VM, developed by John Seddon (2005, 2019), extended the thinking of Deming and Ohno for service organisations. VM honours Deming's principle that the best way to manage an organisation is to treat it as a system. This way of thinking must replace the traditional, 'command and control' approach which emphasises hierarchy, the separation of decision-making from work and measures based on budgets, standards and targets. Concentrating on the horizontal flow of work delivers good service to customers and ensures efficiency. They are satisfied the first time, and 'failure demand', which paralyses traditional organisations as customers return again and again desperate to get what they want, is hugely reduced. The VM has three stages: *Check, Plan* and *Do*. The first stage, *Check*, is an analysis of how the current system performs from the perspective of customers – does it cope well with the demand placed upon it? The flow of the work through the system is mapped with a view to distinguishing activities which contribute to achieving customer purpose from 'waste'. *Plan* starts with rethinking the purpose of the system from the customer's point of view and considering how to redesign it to best achieve customer purpose. The system's principles followed in the redesign include 'design against demand', 'only do value work', 'pull on expertise as needed' and 'IT should support the work'. *Do* sees changes introduced incrementally taking account of customer feedback. According to the VM intervention methodology, the three stages should be done by the leaders together with the people who do the work. The leaders will then see for themselves the dysfunctions of 'command and control' thinking and, hopefully, adopt the ST mindset of working on the system to ensure it supports the staff carrying out the work. If this is achieved, Seddon (2019) argued, it is possible to create innovative, adaptive and energised organisations that behave and learn according to what their customers want. The VM is used extensively in the public and increasingly in the private sector. It has achieved some remarkable results (Zokaei et al.,2011; Jackson, 2019). It can struggle when it is difficult to define customer purpose, when the purpose of a subsystem undergoing redesign is difficult to harmonise with others and because of internal politics (Jackson et al., 2008).

SE offers a solution to the harmonisation issue. Hall (1962) provided a classic exposition based on his experiences at the Bell Telephone Laboratories. He charged the systems engineer with co-ordinating a multidisciplinary team to clarify overall objectives and ensure the optimum integration of subsystems into a system to realise those objectives. Models are used to test potential solutions and control measures put in place to appraise the performance of the system once it is implemented. SE was rapidly taken up as a methodology in defence, space, aerospace, energy and manufacturing and had demonstrable success in helping to realise large-scale projects such as the Apollo moon landings.

The high-profile economist, Mariana Mazzucato (2021), saw the Apollo programme as a model of effective practice from which many lessons can be learned. It had the government in the driving seat, but it catalysed dynamic partnerships between different sectors and stimulated private-sector investment. It was outcome-driven rather than cost-oriented, imagining a different world and encapsulating a determination to get there. Overall guidance was needed to prevent mission drift, but significant freedom was allowed to collaborating entities to think freely, be flexible and innovate. The result was a 'dynamic, creative, experimental organization'. Mazzucato believes we should take inspiration from the Apollo programme and create a 'mission economy' that will enable us to better manage the challenges we face today – climate change, pollution, inequality, social mobility, ageing, etc. Governments need to be bold, seeking widespread public support for missions of societal relevance. 'Mission maps' should be constructed which translate broad aspirations into clear, targeted missions. These should then be broken down into a portfolio of relevant projects to inspire participation from many different sectors and gain business investment. Systems management and SE approaches should be employed to ensure a focus on the goal, integration of the parts, a multidisciplinary approach and a problem-solving orientation. This should guarantee that 'the whole system is more than the sum of its parts'. The influence of the idea of a 'mission economy' can be seen in the UK Government's document on Levelling Up the United Kingdom (Department for Levelling Up, Housing and Communities, 2022) and in its commitment to four 'health missions' to address cancer, mental health, obesity and addiction. These are supposed to be conducted using the 'vaccine taskforce model' (UK Government, 2022). Reeves et al. (2023) noted that the successful Pfizer 'Lightspeed' project, to rapidly develop a COVID-19 vaccine, shared many characteristics with the Apollo project, especially in its ability to manage the tensions between 'control and ingenuity'.

The opportunities for SE seem vast. The International Council on Systems Engineering (INCOSE) is committed, in its Vision 2035, to extending SE beyond its traditional domains of competence to tackle major societal challenges (INCOSE, 2021). However, little has been done in SE to address the methodological shortcomings identified by Hoos in 1974 (inappropriate when problems are 'essentially human and social'), Kiss and Tomlinson in 1984 ('incomplete, and often incorrect, methodology') and many more. As Mazzucato points out, we cannot simply cut and paste the lessons from Apollo to 'wicked' social and environmental problems. SE is very successful when the complexity confronted is predominantly technical, and in those rare cases where social, economic, political, environmental and technical requirements happen to align and are skilfully managed. The successful project to transform the Segura River (in Southern Spain) from the 'most polluted to the best quality in its homeland' was one such case (Rodenas and Jackson, 2021). However, SE has long been known to struggle when confronted by complex socio-technical systems when there are unclear boundaries, multiple stakeholders with different interests, environmental turbulence and power relationships. While it can pay attention to these factors, it has no way of addressing them appropriately within the confines of its existing methodology.

There are a few within SE willing to challenge the existing methodology (Carayannis and Forbes, 2001; Sillitto, 2012; Potts et al., 2020; Haskins, 2021). There is certainly more recognition that SE must be applied more participatively, flexibly and pragmatically if it is to succeed in a wider range of domains. A reformulation of SE for healthcare (Royal Academy of Engineering, Royal College of Physicians and Academy of Medical Sciences, 2017) sees SE as a holistic approach centred on people, systems, design and risk, and advocates using a series of prompting questions to encourage the application of SE principles. Nevertheless, there is still more to be done, which will require recognising what other systems methodologies are better at.

6.3.2.2 System Dynamics

SD responds to the issues raised by the interrelationships systemic perspective. According to Meadows et al.:

> The basis of the method is the recognition that the *structure* of any system – the many circular, interlocking, sometimes time-delayed relationships among its components – is often just as important in determining its behavior as the individual components themselves. (Meadows et al., 1972, p. 31; italics in the original)

Jay Forrester (1971a), the originator of SD, argues that understanding the underlying structure of a system requires combining the power of the human mind with the capabilities of modern computers. The human mind is best in the early stages of the SD methodology, structuring the problem, recognising the variables involved and considering the linkages between them. Here, CLDs are often employed to help visualise the causal relationships between variables and explore possible positive and negative feedback loops. Figure 6.2, for example, shows a CLD constructed as part of a SD study of the Malaysian health system to illustrate the impact of regulating traditional medicines.

The middle stages of the SD methodology require the development of computer simulations because the human mind is deemed inadequate for grasping the dynamic, often counterintuitive behaviour to which the interacting loops and the lags give rise. The computer simulations are derived from quantified Stock and Flow diagrams. Figure 6.3 shows a basic Stock and Flow model developed as part of the Malaysian study to calculate the impact of a lack of capacity planning.

Various software packages – Vensim, STELLA/iThink and AnyLogic – have been developed to assist in the transition to computer simulations. The human

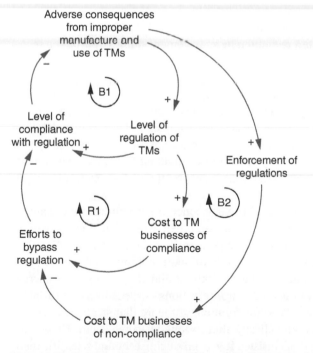

Figure 6.2 Example of a CLD. Regulation of traditional medicines creates costs to traditional medicine businesses, which some actors attempt to bypass (R1), creating a race to close regulation loopholes (B1) and enforce existing regulations (B2).
Source: Adapted from Martins et al., 2021, p. 398.

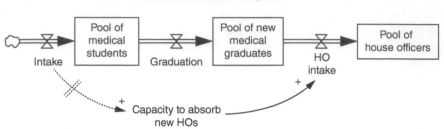

Time for medical education: five years

Time for information flow: near-instantaneous

Figure 6.3 Example of a Stock and Flow diagram. Employment planning did not reflect student intake rates. The dotted arrow indicates this lack of information flow and the missed opportunity to adjust the capacity of the health system to receive new medical graduates. The delay mark on the dotted arrow reflects the time required for the system to adapt to increased capacity. *Source:* Adapted from Martins et al., 2021, p. 297.

mind returns in the final stages of the methodology to decide what action to take to improve the system from the point of view of the stakeholders.

Forrester aimed to create a revolution in management studies by bringing scientific rigour to the field:

> People would never send a space ship to the moon without first testing prototype models and making computer simulations of anticipated trajectories ... Social systems are far more complex and harder to understand than technological systems. Why then do we not use the same approach of making models of social systems and conducting laboratory experiments before adopting new laws and government programs? (Forrester, 1971b, p. 53)

With such a revolution in mind, his early concern with 'industrial dynamics' expanded to embrace first 'urban dynamics' and then 'world dynamics'. The problem, of course, is the very complexity of the social systems to which Forrester alludes. With these systems, it is incredibly difficult to know if all the elements generating system behaviour have been captured and to quantify their current settings and the force they impart in their interactions – especially as the variables will include human beings. We know from chaos theory that small changes in a system's initial conditions can radically alter its long-term behaviour. These criticisms would be damning if SD insisted it was producing accurate scientific models of the way social systems behave. If, however, SD is interpreted from a pragmatic rather than representational standpoint, its prospects of providing a useful service to decision-makers are greatly enhanced.

In an interesting paper, Malczynski and Lane (2023) described an encounter between Forrester and Isaac Asimov, the renowned science fiction writer, at a workshop in 1975. At the event, Asimov explained that, in his *Foundation* trilogy, he had anticipated Forrester's ideas by more than 30 years. In the first volume of the trilogy, Hari Seldon creates the fictional science of psychohistory, capable of predicting the future and enabling an elite group to manipulate events. Forrester was having none of it and pointed out that the success of SD required an informed public capable of understanding the modelling. David Lane (2022), reflecting on the 60th anniversary of the publication of *Industrial Dynamics*, emphasised the practical purpose, requiring close engagement with stakeholders, that always dominated Forrester's thinking. He found, even in that early work, albeit in embryonic form, the idea that models are artefacts constructed to be useful in specific contexts, helpful for organising thinking and structuring inquiry.

It was the unfounded belief that SD built models for the purpose of prediction and control that plagued the reception of the best-known product of SD – the report to the Club of Rome based on Forrester's *World Dynamics* and published as *The Limits to Growth* (Meadows et al., 1972). Its foremost conclusion stated starkly that:

> If the present growth trends in world population, industrialization, pollution, food production, and resource depletion continue unchanged, the limits to growth on this planet will be reached sometime within the next one hundred years. The most probable result will be a rather sudden and uncontrollable decline in both population and industrial capacity. (Meadows et al., 1972, p. 24)

To many readers and commentators, this seemed to be a deterministic vision of doomsday just around the corner. It provoked uproar and was heavily criticised for giving too little weight to the likely scientific and technological advances that would avert catastrophe. It was, of course, nothing of the sort. Rather, it was an invitation to explore what changes were necessary to make a sustainable future possible. A timely call to action – and one that has scarcely been heeded 50 years later.

Today, it is generally accepted that SD models are best used in a practical, actionable and participatory manner as thinking tools to enable decision-makers 'to steer and nurture the change we want' (Barbrook-Johnson and Penn, 2022). In 1990, Peter Senge, in his hugely successful book *The Fifth Discipline*, dropped any pretence to rigorous modelling and promoted a qualitative form of SD (the 'fifth discipline' of the title) as the key to creating 'learning organisations'. Certain 'system archetypes' were identified deriving from relationships that occur frequently between reinforcing feedback loops, balancing loops and 'delays'. In the 'tragedy of the commons' archetype, agents seeking to maximise personal gain are likely, over time, to deplete the resources on which they all depend. Overfishing provides a ready example. Once mastered, the archetypes are supposed to open the door to ST, allowing those concerned to change their mental models, engage in team learning and develop a shared vision. The various system archetypes were illustrated in the book by CLDs, and it has since become common to extract CLDs from the full SD methodology. They lend themselves easily for use with stakeholders to gain a shared appreciation of the interrelationships involved in a situation of interest and to facilitate discussion of any unintended consequences and potential leverage points for change. For example, the Munro Review of Child Protection (Munro, 2010) identified causal linkages from the increasingly prescriptive regime being imposed to various poor outcomes, such as a reduction in professional discretion and lower public regard for child protection workers. The clear representation of these linkages in a CLD had sufficient resonance in the social work profession, and with politicians, to provoke legislation designed to create a more 'child-centred system'.

There remain many in SD who regard it as essential to go to the next stage of the methodology and engage in computer simulation and testing. Only then, they believe, can the deeper level of learning be obtained that makes it possible to properly inform policy decisions. Lane (2008) regarded computer simulation as necessary in all but the simplest of cases. John Sterman argued that 'simulation is essential':

> Qualitative maps are simply too ambiguous and too difficult to simulate mentally to provide much useful information on the adequacy of the model structure or guidance about the future development of the system or the effects of policies. (Sterman, 2003, p. 357)

Sterman (2000) is the leading authority on the use of SD for gaining insight into the behaviour of 'business systems', and we should pay careful attention. There will be occasions when the real world remains sufficiently stable for quantitative SD to capture some of its key characteristics in a manner that can inform decision-makers and provide them with traction in bringing about desirable change. Even those who insist on computer models, however, are clear that the aim of SD is to help solve problems. Clients must be involved in the modelling process and be able to engage with the models to enhance their understanding of counterintuitive behaviour and test the impact of potential interventions (Sterman, 2002). Thompson and Tebbens (2008), discussing how SD modelling influenced global health policy related to the eradication of polio, emphasised that gaining influence with policymakers required them to downplay the modelling and engage with a wide range of stakeholder interests. You don't want a client reacting like Stan McChrystal, leader of American and North Atlantic Treaty Organization (NATO) forces at the time, when confronted with an SD model of the conflict in Afghanistan: 'When we understand that slide, we'll have won the war'.

With so few women prominent in the early development of ST, it is worth emphasising the role played by Donella Meadows in the history of SD. She was lead author of *The Limits to Growth* and reflected on why its message was not acted upon:

> We were at MIT. We had been trained in science. The way we thought about the future was utterly logical: if you tell people there's a disaster ahead, they will change course. If you give them a choice between a good future and a bad one, they will pick the good. They might even be grateful. Naïve, weren't we? (Meadows, quoted by Raworth, 2023)

Following that experience, she became convinced that SD had to be taken out of the realm of 'computers and equations' and focussed on enhancing the ST skills of policymakers (Meadows, 2008). She lived by the principles of sustainability (a word coined by the *Limits to Growth* team) herself and believed that if people understood ST, they could live more harmoniously with the planet. Her book *Thinking in Systems* (2008), published after her too-early death, offers the most elegant introduction to SD, sets out her vision of 'dancing with systems' rather than seeking to control them, explores system archetypes and describes, in order of importance, 12 'leverage points' that can be used to cultivate desirable system change. The most important is

> ... to keep oneself unattached in the arena of paradigms, to stay flexible, to realise that *no* paradigm is 'true', that every one, including the one that sweetly shapes your own worldview, is a tremendously limited understanding of an immense and amazing universe that is far beyond human comprehension. It is to 'get' at gut level the paradigm that there are paradigms, and to see that that itself is a paradigm, and to regard that whole realization as devastatingly funny. It is to let go into not-knowing, into what the Buddhists call enlightenment. (Meadows, 2008, p. 164; italics in the original)

Donella Meadows has been deservedly called by Kate Raworth, author of *Doughnut Economics*, the 'mother of systems thinking'.

6.3.2.3 Living Systems Methodologies

Living systems methodologies respond to issues highlighted by the organismic systemic perspective. They treat organisations as biological entities seeking to survive and expand their potential. This requires their vital subsystems to function well in support of the whole system and for that system to be capable of evolving in response to environmental change. The viability of the system and its ability to reconfigure itself to take advantage of new opportunities become the central concerns.

The growth of interest in the organismic perspective led, at the Tavistock Institute of Human Relations in the UK, to the development of Sociotechnical Systems Thinking (STS). STS sees organisations as pursuing primary tasks that can best be realised if their social, technological and economic dimensions are jointly optimised and if they are treated as open systems interacting with their environments. The Tavistock researchers (Emery, Trist and Rice were key figures) also emphasised that complex organisations, like organisms, need to operate with semi-autonomous parts if the whole is to cope with the massive variety of the environment. Considerable effort went into determining how semi-autonomous work groups could best be designed to free up senior management to attend to 'boundary management' rather than supervisory responsibilities. STS methodologies were developed and used to transfer the ideas into practice through large action-research projects. Among the best known are the Norwegian Industrial Democracy Project (Emery and Thorsrud, 1969), the design of Volvo's car plant at Kalmar (Gyllenhammer, 1977) and Shell's 'new philosophy of management' (Hill, 1971). STS was ahead of its time and has much contemporary relevance.

I shall, however, concentrate on Beer's Viable System Model (VSM) because I believe it offers the most useful vehicle for pursuing a living systems approach. The VSM manages to express and integrate the findings of many decades of research in the organismic tradition of social and management theory. Looking to build organisations capable of 'regeneration, growth and adaptation', Beer ruled out mechanical analogies and looked to 'naturally occurring systems' for inspiration (Beer, 1967). He concluded that the human body, controlled by the nervous system, represented the richest and most flexible viable system of all. Following this logic, Beer, in his book *Brain of the Firm* (1972), delved into neurophysiology to uncover the essential subsystems that must be present in any viable system and how they must be organised to ensure the agility of the system in the face of a changing environment. Martin Pfiffner presented the advance made by the VSM over previous management theories in the following terms:

> If we use the organism as a metaphor, then organization charts (Organization 1.0) were used to design the anatomy, business processes (Organization 2.0) the physiology of organizations. We have come a long way with this approach, but it no longer suffices. In today's new world, the information age, we need to shape the neurology – the organization of control and communication, and thus the management of organizations as a whole. (Pfiffner, 2022, p. 26)

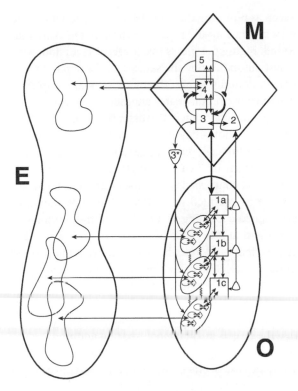

Figure 6.4 Beer's VSM highlighting the managerial and operational elements of an enterprise, its environment and the linkages among them, at two levels of recursion. *Source:* this representation courtesy of 'Metaphorum'.

Figure 6.4 is a diagram of the VSM, with 'M', the square, containing the managerial elements of the enterprise; 'O', the oval, containing its operational elements; and 'E', the amoeba shape, representing its overall environment. Beer sees the viability of systems as depending on their establishing appropriate relationships of control and communication among these three elements.

An enterprise must learn to co-evolve with its environment, exploring the possibilities offered and adapting itself as necessary. To do this, it needs to match the 'variety' of the environment, a difficult task given its massive complexity. It will have to engage in 'variety engineering'. The most effective way of increasing the enterprise's own variety is to allow autonomy to subsystems, ensuring problems are addressed as closely as possible to the point where they manifest themselves and allowing senior management to concentrate on more strategic matters. The VSM facilitates this by representing complex systems in terms of 'recursive' levels – system, subsystems, sub-subsystems, etc. As with a series of Russian dolls, systems at different levels are seen as retaining the same basic characteristics. The VSM can then be used to model systems at all levels of recursion, ensuring that they are all viable and empowered. Figure 6.4 shows two levels of recursion, with the overall system and the subsystems exhibiting the same organisational form.

Providing subsystems with the autonomy to absorb environmental complexity solves one problem for senior management but creates another. There is a danger that the enterprise will fall apart. Overall cohesion is also essential. The VSM offers a solution that grants the maximum autonomy possible to the parts consistent with overall systemic cohesion. It does this through the arrangement of five functional elements, Systems 1–5. These are shown in Figure 6.4. System 1 consists of the various subsystems of the organisation concerned with *implementation*. These are the primary activities that produce its products or services. Three are shown in Figure 6.4. Each subsystem is designed according to the VSM, with its own local-ised management (1a–1c), to ensure that it is viable in its own right. Systems 2–5 are support services to System 1. System 2, *co-ordination*, ensures that the parts of System 1 do not tread on each other's toes. System 3, *cohesion*, promotes synergy by agreeing on targets with the parts of System 1 which are compatible with the over-all purpose of the organisation and negotiating with them about the resources they need to achieve those targets. Once this 'resource bargain' is struck, System 3 steps back, occasionally checking that the targets are being realised and auditing System 1 to ensure agreed-upon procedures are being followed (System 3* is an audit func-tion). It only intervenes directly in the case of emergencies, taking corrective action itself or letting senior management know of urgent problems through an acceler-ated information link called, by Beer, an 'algedonic' (pain/pleasure) channel (not shown in Figure 6.4). While Systems 1–3 concentrate on the 'inside and now', max-imising the performance of the organisation as currently constituted, System 4, *development*, focusses on the 'outside and future', making the case for innovation and change in response to what is happening externally. For this purpose, it must have adequate models of the relevant external environment and of the operational elements. It serves System I by ensuring the continued relevance of System 1 activi-ties. System 5, *policy*, is responsible for reconciling the potentially antagonistic demands made by Systems 3 and 4 – for stability and change – and articulating the identity of the whole system to the wider system of which it is a part. The VSM identifies the information flows required to establish proper communication and control between its different elements and with the environment.

It is easy to see the potency of this formulation. Schumacher contemplated the question of how 'big' organisations should be and, concluding that there is no single answer, asked himself what is really needed:

> In the affairs of men, there always appears to be a need for at least two things simultaneously, which, on the face of it, seem to be incompatible

and to exclude one another. We always need both freedom and order. We need the freedom of lots and lots of small, autonomous units, and, at the same time, the orderliness of large-scale, possibly global, unity and co-ordination. (Schumacher, 1973, p. 49)

The VSM offers a convincing account of how the tensions between freedom and order can be managed in an enterprise. A remarkable achievement and the notion of recursion enables the same logic to be extended from the local to the global level. Espinosa and Walker (2017) argued that to achieve a global economic system capable of learning to co-evolve sustainably with its environment, eight levels of recursion should be recognised and integrated using the logic of the VSM. These are individual, family/household, neighbourhood/community (urban and rural), town/municipality, eco-regional, national, continental and global. They went on to articulate each level of recursion in terms of the issues that need to be resolved, asking what is involved in an individual, family unit, etc., attempting to live sustainably. This represents exactly the kind of world-order, based on 'democratic federalism with organized decentralization of power', that Gare (2023) sees as appropriate if the Radical Enlightenment is to progress. He quotes Ho and Ulanowicz to make the point:

> We can deal with sustainable economic systems by embedding the global economic system in the global ecosystem ... Ideally, the intricate structure of the global economy should look like the many nested sub-cycles that make up the organisms' life cycle ... And each national economy, in turn, would have its own intricate structure that is self-similar to the global. If the entire global system is to be sustainable, there has to be a proper balance between the local and the global, the same kind of reciprocal, symmetrical coupled relationship that one finds in organisms ... Furthermore, the global economy is coupled to the global ecosystem, which too, has to have its own balance ... so that both can survive. (Ho and Ulanowicz, quoted in Gare, 2023, p. 67)

The VSM can be employed to design new viable systems or to diagnose the faults of existing ones. In both cases, it is necessary to pay particular attention to the 'pathologies' that can impact system viability (Beer, 1989). Here are some examples. The levels of recursion must be specified appropriately – an important activity relegated to a low level of recursion will not receive the managerial attention or resources it needs. A system will perish if any of the five necessary functions are missing and/or the appropriate information flows are not well-designed. An organisation is in trouble if System 5 does not embody the purposes of the whole system. An organisation that is System 4 dominated will be subject to 'flights of imagination'. An organisation that is System 3 dominated will suffer from 'narrow tunnel' syndrome and be incapable of recognising and adapting to changes in the environment. An organisation that does not allow sufficient autonomy to System 1 elements will lack the capacity to manage environmental variety. One that grants too much will lack overall coherence and drift and splinter. An organisation that allows any of the Systems 2–4 to develop a life of its own, at the expense of serving the needs of System 1, will be threatened by the dead hand of bureaucracy.

The VSM is a model, but it is not representative of anything in the real world. It does not specify business units or departments. Successful adaptation is the goal it prizes. According to Pickering's (2010) pragmatist reading, the VSM shows how a 'dance of becoming' can be established between an organisation and its environment during which they explore each other's possibilities, establishing mutually satisfactory relationships along the way. It is impossible to predict what will happen. We simply observe where the performance staged by the VSM takes us. It was this thinking that inspired the composer, musician and ex-Roxy Music star Brian Eno when experimenting with 'self-generating music'. Referring to *Brain of the Firm*, he wrote:

> Stafford's book hooked me with one sentence: *Instead of specifying it in full detail, you simply ride on the dynamics of the system to where you want to go* ... And the lovely thrill of it was that the system could produce beautiful things which you had never even conceived of in advance – which hadn't ever existed in any mind. (Eno, 2009, p. 8; italics in the original)

As a model, the VSM needs embedding in a suitable methodology if it is to be successfully implemented. Beer (1972, 1979, 1985) articulated three main phases – establishing the identity of the organisation, 'unfolding' its complexity through different levels of recursion and applying the principles to ensure viability. Pfiffner highlighted the main issue any such methodology will face:

> A reorganization can therefore be compared to a surgical intervention in the anatomy of an organism, yet unlike surgery, the patient is wide awake (fully conscious and unanaesthetised) during reorganization: He or she sees what is coming and reacts accordingly. (Pfiffner, 2022, p. 409)

How are the stakeholders of the organisation to be convinced to accept conclusions drawn from what can appear to be a utopian, rationalistic and overly prescriptive model? The way this issue is addressed, by VSM practitioners, tends to depend on how 'scientific' they believe the principles underpinning the model are. Beer (1989) certainly thought he was doing science and argued that other scientists had verified his findings. On this reading, little methodological sophistication is required in translating VSM theory into practice. We simply need to decide on a goal, apply the principles in a logical order and make recommendations. Hoverstadt (2008) agreed, stating that 'the basic methodology for the VSM is so simple that it hardly warrants the term'. Pfiffner (2022) believed that the VSM can be used, in all cases, to design the 'ideal organisation' to serve the customer, although some work may then have to go into persuasion. Others, however, believe that it is necessary to ease the implementation of VSM recommendations by being less prescriptive and involving stakeholders throughout an intervention. Raul Espejo's Viability Planning (VIPLAN) methodology has a 'learning loop' as well as a 'cybernetic loop' (Espejo and Reyes, 2011). Angela Espinosa has developed a 'Self-transformation Methodology' which aims to use the VSM as a metalanguage to support individual and organisational learning. She has done more than anyone to present the VSM as

> ... a humane and emancipatory approach that challenges autocratic management structures, and empowers workers and citizens ... [which] fully respects and promotes cultural and ethical values .... (Espinosa, 2023, p. 63)

Both these methodologies encourage reflection and the emergence of collective agreements on roles, activities and structures. However, it is still necessary to validate the 'healthiness of such configurations' using the VSM criteria (Espinosa, 2023). The methodologies hide the science and prescription, but they remain in the background. Stakeholders are encouraged to come by themselves to the 'right' VSM conclusions. To paraphrase the infamous football manager Brian Clough on listening to players' opinions: 'We talk about it for 20 minutes and then decide I [or Beer] was right'.

The most ambitious project carried out using the VSM was for President Allende of Chile. *Project Cybersyn* ('cybernetic synergy') employed the model to help manage the industrial economy of the country in a way that supported the aims of the democratically elected socialist government (Beer, 1981; Medina, 2014). The year 2023 marked the 50th anniversary of the brutal military coup that overthrew Allende and his government. That anniversary, and the release of a nine-episode podcast on the project (Morozov, 2023), has inevitably sparked new interest in Beer and his work. Fortunately, there are many excellent secondary sources available alongside Beer's own writings. They have different strengths. Espejo's work prioritises detailed exegesis (Espejo and Schwaninger, 1993; Espejo et al., 1996; Espejo and Reyes, 2011); Espinosa's use of the VSM to support sustainability (Espinosa and Walker, 2017; Espinosa, 2023); Pfiffner's (2022) applications to business; Hoverstadt's (2008) accessibility to managers; and Pérez Rios (2012) classifying and explaining the possible 'pathologies of organisation'. Between them, these books contain numerous examples of the VSM in action (see also, Espejo and Harnden, 1989).

For such VSM advocates as Pfiffner (2022), if something is wrong in an organisation, the issue is likely to be the result of its 'nervous system being wrongly wired'. For example, 'communication and other supposedly cultural problems' usually stem from a poor control system:

> I have often seen executives locate the problem in the people they are dealing with, for example. After illuminating matters with the Viable System Model, they recognized the underlying, structural problem was forcing these people into their behaviors. (Pfiffner, 2022, p. 66)

Soft systems thinkers believe otherwise.

6.3.2.4 Soft Systems Methodologies

Soft systems methodologies respond to issues highlighted by the purposeful systemic perspective. They engage with the emergent properties arising at the people and sociocultural levels of Boulding's hierarchy of complexity (levels 7 and 8). Humans operate in a world of symbols. People use symbols to create sophisticated mental models which shape what they think and how they act. Social reality is full of symbolic constructions offering alternative visions of how the world is and what it could be like. The shift in systems approach necessary to embrace and respond to these emergent properties is massive. This is indicated by the four 'principles' with which Churchman (1979) concluded *The Systems Approach*:

- The systems approach begins when first you see the world through the eyes of another.
- The systems approach goes on to discovering that every world view is terribly restricted.
- There are no experts in the systems approach.
- The systems approach is not a bad idea.

The burning question was how to take these ideas forward in a way that makes a real difference, because:

> A philosophy committed to wanderings through metaphysical mazes of its own construction is condemned to a role within society of complete ineffectiveness. (Churchman and Ackoff, 1946)

The three soft systems methodologies I outline here answer that question in different but complementary ways. These can be correlated with the purposeful systemic imperatives of seeking widespread agreement on purpose, learning what changes are feasible and desirable and challenging 'groupthink'.

Russ Ackoff (1999a) argued that, given the greater complexity of the 'systems age', we need to alter the way we think about organisations. In the past, it had been tempting to regard them either as machines serving the purposes of their creators or owners or as organisms serving their own purposes. However:

> Our society and the principal private and public organizations that it contains have reached a level of maturity that eliminates whatever effectiveness applying deterministic and animalistic models to social systems may once have had. (Ackoff and Gharajedaghi, 1996, p. 22)

Today, organisations must be viewed as 'purposeful systems' serving their own purposes, those of their parts and those of the wider system of which they are part. Managers can serve stakeholder purposes at all three levels by adopting a new approach to planning that Ackoff (1981) called IP. IP is a participative, continuous, holistic process in which stakeholders design a desirable future for their organisation and invent ways of bringing it about. It has five phases. The first, 'formulating the mess', alerts stakeholders to the future awaiting them if existing plans, policies and practices continue in the current environment. It is meant to act as a wake-up call. The second phase, Idealized Design, is the unique and most essential feature of Ackoff's approach and is the design of the enterprise that the stakeholders would replace the existing system with today if they were free to do so. Fundamentally, Ackoff (1999b) was not interested in forecasting the future but in creating a desirable future through action, and IP responds directly to the admonition of the romantic poet William Blake:

> I must Create a System, or be
> enslav'd by another Man's;
> I will not Reason and Compare:
> my business is to Create.
> (Blake, 1815)

Idealized Design provides a means of removing the 'mind-forg'd manacles' against which Blake railed. The aim is to release maximum creativity among stakeholders in pursuit of the purposes they seek through their engagement with the organisation. A compelling Idealized Design leads existing problems to 'dissolve' because the system and/or environment which give rise to them are radically reconceptualised. Petty differences between stakeholders will be overcome. The remaining three phases of IP are directed at realising the Idealized Design as closely as possible. The outcome of IP is not a fixed 'utopia' but an 'ideal-seeking system' that will be in constant flux as it responds to changing values, new knowledge and information and buffeting from external forces.

Ackoff demonstrated the effectiveness of IP as a practical systems methodology in hundreds of projects with government agencies and organisations of all types – for example, Bell Telephone Laboratories, Alcoa, General Electric, Anheuser-Busch, and with leaders of the black ghetto in Mantua, Philadelphia, from whom he borrowed the subtitle for a book (Ackoff, 1981): 'Plan or be Planned for'.

Peter Checkland's SSM was crafted at Lancaster University, in the UK, based on experience derived from an extensive action research programme (Checkland, 1981; Checkland and Scholes, 1990; Checkland and Holwell, 1998; Checkland and Poulter, 2006). SSM is an approach to tackling wicked problems which takes users on a learning journey from finding out about a problematic situation to making changes they deem to be both feasible and desirable.

In its definitive form, the methodology consists of an iterative learning cycle comprising four essential activities, as shown in Figure 6.5.

The first activity involves *Finding Out* about the initial problematical situation. The usual method employed is for participants to draw pictorial representations of the 'real-world' situation as they perceive it. These drawings are called Rich Pictures. There are no fixed rules for drawing Rich Pictures. They can end up being formal, cartoon-like or artistic. Figure 6.6 represents an artistic variant employed to support strategic planning by the Winner group of charities based at Preston Road Women's Centre, Hull.

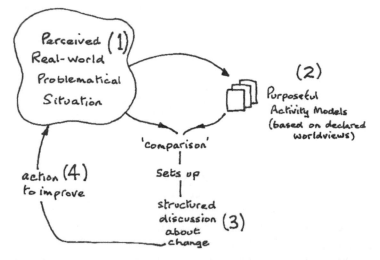

Figure 6.5 The iconic representation of Soft Systems Methodology's learning cycle. *Source:* Reproduced from Checkland and Poulter (2006)/with permission of John Wiley & Sons.

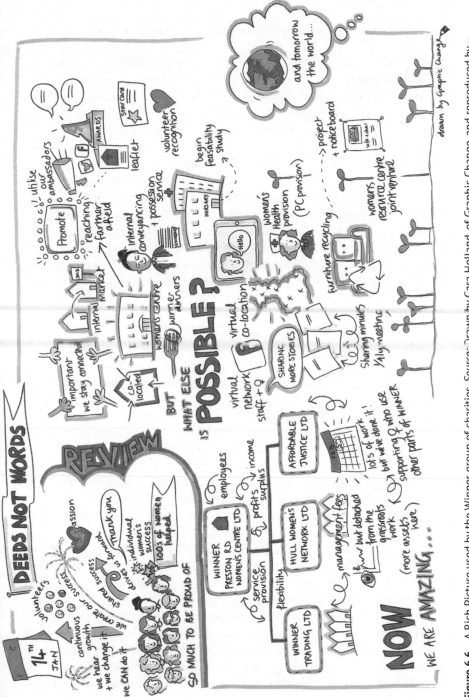

Figure 6.6 A Rich Picture used by the Winner group of charities. *Source:* Drawn by Cara Holland, of Graphic Change, and reproduced by permission of Winner Trading Ltd.

Lisa Hilder, trustee of the group, comments on their use of Rich Pictures:

> The Winner group of charities has been using Rich Pictures to support its strategic planning and development for the last ten years – a period which has seen the group grow and mature, increasing services and activities supporting women and children fleeing and recovering from domestic abuse. During that time the group has grown from a core charity with a trading subsidiary to a conglomerate of seven charities all focussed on a common goal – holistic support and recovery for the client group and with a cumulative turnover of around £2.8 million per annum. The group directors meet annually and conduct a facilitated session, supported by a graphic artist, which is a creative space to reflect on achievements and vision for short-, medium-, and long-term goals which are then captured graphically and most importantly **accessibly**, enabling a clear, shared understanding of what comes next. The resultant rich pictures are displayed in the women's centre (home for the group) for all staff, volunteers, and visitors to see, enabling quick and easy digestion of the strategy and over time, telling a colourful and powerful story of how strategy has been turned into action and delivered demonstrable impact. (Hilder, 2023, personal communication; emphasis in the original)

The second activity consists of delineating some Root Definitions relevant to the situation of interest and turning them into *Purposeful Activity Models*. Each Root Definition must clearly reflect a particular worldview and specify the transformation that the activity model is to carry out. It will take the form of 'a system to do P (the *what*), by Q (the *how*), in order to help achieve R (the *why*)' (Checkland and Poulter, 2006). Root Definitions can be checked for completeness against the elements of CATWOE. Do they specify the **C**ustomers, **A**ctors, **T**ransformation, **W**orldview, **O**wners and **E**nvironmental Constraints of the system? If the Root Definitions are well-formulated, it is relatively easy to turn them into Purposeful Activity Models. These intellectual devices are one-sided representations (each based on a single worldview) which set out the activities required to carry out the transformations named in the Root Definitions. Figure 6.7 shows a Purposeful Activity Model and its Root Definition, employed in an SSM intervention conducted by Checkland and Holwell in the central research and development laboratories of a multinational science-based company.

The third activity uses the models to question the problematical situation and to structure a *Discussion/Debate* about possible changes. This is often orchestrated around comparing the Rich Picture(s) and the various activity models. If an accommodation can be reached on changes that are systemically desirable (according to the models) and culturally feasible (according to the participants), then *Action to Improve* the situation, the fourth activity, can be defined and implemented.

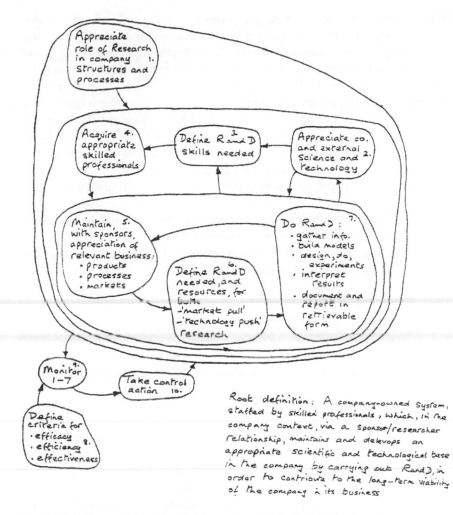

Figure 6.7 A Purposeful Activity Model, together with its Root Definition, relevant to carrying out R&D in a company. *Source:* Reproduced from Checkland and Holwell, 1998/with permission of John Wiley & Sons.

SSM is very flexible and can be used to address 'problematical situations' wherever they are found. It requires no clear definition of purpose. Often it produces Robinson's (2015) definition of 'good action' – 'in retrospect it appears inevitable'. The learning process that SSM facilitates alters perceptions and cultural settings to such a degree that changes, seemingly inconceivable at the beginning of the process, come to appear obvious and necessary to participants. Furthermore, it maps naturally onto the normal managerial process of considering a 'mess', suggesting ways forward and seeking agreements for action. It can act as a template for comparing other similar frameworks that seek to encourage creativity and learning in organisations. One example is Nonaka's SECI model of knowledge conversion – Socialisation, Externalisation, Combination and Internalisation (Nonaka and Takeuchi, 1995). Another is Reeves and Fuller's (2021) process for fostering imaginative potential in companies – challenge existing ways of thinking, develop explicit mental models of alternative futures, compare these with reality and test their attractiveness to people. A third is provided by Kay and King's (2020) exposition of the 'narrative paradigm' as a better way of taking decisions in the context of radical uncertainty – asking what is going on, constructing stories that provide explanations, persuading others and developing mutual understanding that can lead to action.

Mason and Mitroff (both members of the 'Berkeley Bubble') launched a research program in 'dialectical pragmatism', drawing on Churchman's philosophy, from which their SAST methodology emerged. Most organisations fail to deal with wicked problems, they argued, because they find it difficult to challenge accepted ways of doing things (Mason and Mitroff, 1981). They are subject to 'groupthink'. The SAST methodology seeks to exploit any divergent worldviews that exist in organisations to surface alternatives to the existing strategic direction. Groups with different perspectives on a particular policy or problem are formed. Each then engages in 'assumption surfacing', uncovering, mapping and analysing the key assumptions upon which their preferred strategy or solution rests. This is facilitated by 'stakeholder analysis' – each group asking what assumptions about stakeholders underpin their perspective. The groups are brought together and encouraged to conduct a 'dialectical debate' in which the assumptions underpinning the differing positions are ranged against one another. The aim of the final, synthesis stage is to achieve a compromise on assumptions from which a 'higher' level of strategy can be derived. The new strategy should bridge the gap between the different strategies of the groups and go beyond them as well.

SAST has proved its worth in many settings, including in major projects for the US Census Bureau (Barabba and Mitroff, 2014). If it is less heard of today, that is probably because it has been reinvented in the form of Red Teaming (Hoffman, 2017), which originated in the Israeli and US militaries. The idea arose that, had they been able to 'think like the enemy', they could have anticipated and taken action to prevent crises such as the Yom Kippur War and the attack on the World Trade Center. Red Teaming involves establishing a 'red team' in an organisation to champion contrarian thinking and expose favoured worldviews and strategies to alternative perspectives. It spread rapidly to the Canadian, Australian and UK armed forces and into fields such as cybersecurity, airport security, intelligence, government and business. In the Report of the Health and Social Care and Science and Technology Committees to the UK House of Commons, 'Coronavirus; lessons learned to date' (House of Commons Report, 2021), the question was asked: 'Was there sufficient challenge to scientific advice during the first weeks?' The answer: 'We heard that "red teaming" and structured challenge ... used within the national security community ... may also be of benefit to the scientific community'. Championing its use in business, Bryce Hoffman wrote:

> Red teaming challenges your plans and the assumption upon which they are based. Red teaming forces you to think differently about your business and consider alternative points of view. Red teaming makes critical and contrarian thinking part of your company's planning process and gives you a set of tools and techniques that can be used to stress-test your strategy. (Hoffman, 2017, p. 50)

This is undoubtedly true. But it could be further enhanced if it took account of the underpinning philosophy, the supportive methodology and methods and the history of use of SAST.

6.3.2.5 Emancipatory Systems Methodologies

Emancipatory systems methodologies respond to issues highlighted by the societal/environmental systemic perspective. They seek to ensure that no stakeholders or affected parties are disadvantaged by systems designs and that environmental concerns are given due consideration. In *Systems Approaches to Management* (Jackson, 2000), I identified two forms of emancipatory practice, labelled 'emancipation through discursive rationality' and 'emancipation as liberation'.

The former finds expression in Habermas's (1979) writings, setting out a new basis for critique – communication free from domination. As previously explained, this requires an 'ideal speech situation' in which all concerned have an equal chance to participate and represent their interests. Werner Ulrich's CSH (1983) is a systems methodology which draws upon Habermas's thinking but gives it a practical twist. CSH can be used by systems designers and concerned citizens to interrogate an actual or proposed system design without having to wait for an ideal speech situation to be established. Any system design will be based on assumptions reflecting the values and information available to those involved in the design. 'Boundary judgments' are made which limit the options considered and potentially disadvantage some stakeholders. In Ulrich's view, for a design to be 'rational', the assumptions on which it rests need to be exposed and questioned. This is the purpose of CSH. Ulrich drew heavily upon the thinking of his PhD supervisor, Churchman, in developing a methodology which employs Boundary Critique to expose the selective 'boundary judgments' influencing systems designs. A set of 12 questions was proposed which can lay bare their partiality. These questions were arranged according to four sources of influence on any design – Who benefits? Who are the decision-makers? Who provides expertise? and Who represents those affected but not involved? They can be used by those involved to reflect on their own designs, using the questions to ensure proper consideration is given to the concerns of all stakeholders. If the UK Post Office had thought about what sub-postmasters had to say about its Horizon computer system, it could have avoided committing what has been described as 'the most widespread miscarriage of justice in UK history' (see Wallis, 2022). Neil Hudgell, of Hudgell's Solicitors, who now represent the majority of the criminally convicted claimants, has said:

> Commonsense should have led the Post Office to distrust the Horizon system. With systems thinking, it would have avoided causing suffering to thousands of Sub-postmasters and saved the country hundreds of millions (Hudgell, 2013, personal communication).

What is most radical about CSH is Ulrich's insistence that the views of those affected by systems designs, but not involved in the decision-making, must be considered before any design can be regarded as legitimate. If this is not done by the designers, marginalised stakeholders can use CSH themselves to engage in 'emancipatory boundary critique', forcing the involved to reveal the undisclosed assumptions underpinning their proposals.

CSH has been extended from its original focus on giving a voice to marginalised groups to ensuring representation for those simply unable to 'speak', for example, future generations, other species and the natural environment. Stephens et al. (2019) have specifically addressed the need to provide 'ecological justice for nature'. They argued that CST has had an anthropological bias that has led it to marginalise nonhuman entities. How can CSH secure a hearing for the interests of these stakeholders? A potential way forward was explored by Cunico et al. (2023) who report research on a possible new role in facilitation – the New Devil's Advocate – in which some facilitators act on behalf of missing stakeholders rather than maintaining a neutral stance. The potential importance of CSH in supporting this role is apparent when we consider, for example, the Welsh Government's passing of the 'Well-being of Future Generations (Wales) Act 2015'; the Te Urewera National Park and the Whanganui River, in New Zealand, being granted the same legal rights as people (thanks to the lobbying of Māori groups); and the Mexican government being the latest to consider new laws to criminalise

> ... any unlawful or wanton act committed with the knowledge that there is a substantial likelihood of severe and either widespread or long-term damage to the environment. (Kaminski, 2023)

The second type of emancipatory practice, which I called 'emancipation as lib-eration', contains an implicit critique of CSH. It questions whether the powerful will bother to take account of the views and interests of the disadvantaged how-ever well those are expressed. 'Emancipation as liberation' thinkers fail to see how the force of the better argument can prevail in a world of gross inequalities where the exercise of coercive power is ubiquitous. As Ray, referencing Bronner, had it:

> This is because choosing among generalizable concerns is always a politi-cal question that is resolved in the realities of compromise, violence and structural imbalance of power. Thus, distortions will enter from outside the field of argumentation – although discursive rules are followed by the American legal system, one in four African-Americans is in jail, awaiting trial or on probation. (Ray, 2004, p. 318)

'Emancipation as liberation' thinkers believe they can recognise oppression and disadvantage when they see it and want to campaign alongside those who suffer to get things done. Their commitment to action is often bolstered by a theory that seeks to explain the sources of inequality and discrimination in systemic terms and indicates how best to confront the forces that prevent participative decision-making and rational argumentation from taking place.

The origin of this kind of thinking lies in Marx's later work which provided a theoretical explanation of how the working class is exploited in capitalist society and what can be done about it. Multiple theories now exist offering explanations of the oppression and marginalisation of other sections of society on the grounds of gender, race, sexual orientation, disability, etc. For example, 'critical race the-ory', currently the subject of much debate in the United States, seeks to unveil the way institutions, such as the legal system, function to propagate inequalities between White and non-White people. Getting rid of racism is not simply a matter of changing personal beliefs. It requires a radical shift in the way institutions function.

The 'emancipation as liberation' form of critique can also be developed from the perspective of the natural world. Capra (1996) provided a new theory of 'social ecology' that would, he hoped, allow us to reconnect with the web of life and build sustainable communities, meeting our current needs without dimin-ishing the opportunities available to future generations. He proposed new soci-etal arrangements that promote 'maximum sustainability' based on learning from the principles underpinning the pattern and structure of the ecological sys-tem. David Attenborough, always an intuitive systems thinker, has become more radical in his old age. He suggested (Attenborough, 2022) that we are nearing a 'global ecological breakdown' because we are reaching 'tipping points' in many of the systems upon which life on earth depends. Drawing on Kate Raworth's concept of 'doughnut economics', he argued that we need to restore the stability of the planet by acknowledging nine 'planetary boundaries' (climate change, ocean acidification, biodiversity, etc.). While respecting these boundaries, we also need to set out various minimum requirements for human well-being (good housing, healthcare, education, etc.) and seek to raise everybody to these levels. These two things will require us to move beyond the worship of growth; develop and use only clean energy sources; re-wild the oceans and land; give more space back to the living world; plan for a peak human population; and live more balanced lives in a circular rather than linear economy, copying systems in the natural world.

The concept of 'intersectionality' refers to the way in which different forms of discrimination and disadvantage are interlinked. The Independent Commission for Equity in Cricket found systemic discrimination in English cricket 'against women, people of colour and people from poorer backgrounds' (Liew, 2023). You have very little chance of progressing in the game if you are a working-class, Asian woman. In response to one type of intersectionality, Anne Stephens (2013) sought to bring together eco-feminism and CST in a holistic approach that addresses the linked oppressions of women and the environment. These linked oppressions, she argued, flow from a patriarchal perspective based on positivism and dualism. Perhaps it is no coincidence that, as Shafak (2023) noted, women are leading the battle to save the world's forests. Stephens suggested employing five 'feminist-systems thinking principles' during participatory action research, which are as follows:

- Be gender sensitive
- Value the voices from the margins
- Centre nature
- Select appropriate methods/methodologies
- Bring about social change

This work has been developed by Stephens and Ellen Lewis (Stephens et al., 2018) into a systems methodology known as the Gender equality, Environments, and Marginalized voices' framework (GEMs). GEMs is said to be a bottom-up and generative approach to complex systemic intersectional analysis and advocacy. Lewis and Stephens (2022) describe how they are wary of preconceived categories and seek to work with people on the ground to explore three broad 'fields' – gender equality, environments, and marginalized voices. Gender covers all forms of discrimination and barriers arising due to all types of gender identity as the individual defines it. Environments covers human-made and natural landscapes, ecological systems and non-human species, seeking to give them a voice through the people most able to speak on their behalf. Marginalized voices is a field used to identify acute and persistent discrimination and disadvantage called out by those whose lives are impacted. The emphasis is placed on the view-points of those affected and on mutual capacity building:

> The GEMs framework blossoms when actively deconstructed by stakehold-ers [helping to] structure problems, evaluate complex situations and advo-cate for the rights of people as well as environmental systems and species. (Lewis and Stephens, 2022, p. 4)

GEMs has been used in the evaluation of global development programs and also in projects concerned, for example, with the prevention of violence against women and children, agricultural resilience in the face of climate change, water sanita-tion and hygiene and training for health workers in addiction management.

6.3.3 Choose Appropriate Systems Models and Methods

Once agreement has been reached about which systems methodology or method-ologies to employ at the start of the intervention, it is time to decide on the systems models and methods to use. The criteria for choice are that they can be used in support of the principles of the guiding methodologies and are suitable and helpful in the context. CSP encourages the maximum flexibility possible. For example, it is happy to see particular methodologies 'partitioned' or 'decomposed' (Midgley, 1990) to give the practitioner access to the range of methods they contain to use in sup-port of other systems methodologies. Methods that originate from outside ST, per-haps from 'soft operational research' (Rosenhead and Mingers, 2001), can also be considered. Of course, the practitioner should be guided by what they have learned in previous interventions about which models and methods are best for supporting the chosen methodologies. Some may carry theoretical baggage, which makes them less useful for providing service to certain methodologies. For example, Stock and Flow diagrams are unlikely to be helpful in a soft systems intervention.

6.3.4 Structure, Schedule and Set Objectives for the Intervention

The intervention strategy can now be designed and scheduled. Even though CSP is premised on the belief that complex problems are never solved absolutely, con-sideration usually needs to be given to the precise objectives and specific meas-ures of success of the scheduled intervention. The first iteration through *Produce* ends when this is done.

The *Explore* stage of CSP, used in any complex situation of interest, will reveal a host of issues worthy of attention. Looking at the early stages of the COVID-19 pandemic in the United Kingdom, in Chapter 5, threw up materials, staffing, pro-cess, organisational, cultural and inequality issues, all of which confronted decision-makers at the same time. This suggests that it will always be necessary to use several methodologies in parallel. However, doing this can cause confusion, lead to much upheaval and extend beyond whatever resources are available. In normal circumstances, it is better to start with one or two methodologies that address the greatest number of primary issues. As the intervention proceeds, priorities change, the problem situation develops and other issues come to the fore, we need to be sufficiently alert to bring other methodologies into play. These matters will be considered in greater depth when looking at the next stage of CSP, *Intervene*, in the following chapter.

6.4   *Produce* – Examples

This section provides three examples of how *Produce* works, spanning more than 30 years of the history of CSP. Two use the earlier language of 'metaphors' rather than that of 'systemic perspectives'. I retain the original language in these cases. The job of translation to the new terminology should pose no problems.

The first project took place in North Yorkshire Police (NYP) and was concerned with information systems development. It was carried out by a Chief Inspector, Steve Green, under my supervision. I have reported on this project before (Jackson, 2019), but some of the highlights are worth repeating as they were formative in the development of the *Produce* stage. CSP, at that time, called for a situation of interest to be viewed through a variety of systems metaphors. Metaphor analysis revealed the need to shift NYP from a machine type to a more organic type of structure. In changing times, it had to pay more attention to its diverse environments and to communication with the various publics it served. The existing information systems were designed to reinforce 'command and control' rather than promote responsiveness at the local level. Making NYP more of a 'living system' seemed the obvious way forward. We therefore pressed ahead with the VSM as the 'dominant methodology' and made recommendations for a more devolved structure supported with appropriate information systems. Each of seven new territorial divisions was to be given considerable autonomy, developing its own statement of purpose and environmental scanning and planning capabilities. These recommendations were written up in a discussion document, *Divisional Autonomy – The Viable System Perspective*. This was not well received. We had been alerted, by other metaphors, to the difficulty involved in changing NYP's culture and to unhappiness with previous efforts at consultation but had ignored these warnings. The recommendations proved culturally and politically unacceptable. With this learning, we rapidly backtracked and produced a new intervention strategy based on SSM. Rich Pictures were drawn, and four Purposeful Activity Models were taken forward for discussion. Three of these addressed issues that had troubled participants about the recommendations derived from the VSM and the fourth was directed at the consultation issue. Following the philosophy of SSM – the new 'dominant methodology' – the intervention proceeded in as participative a way as possible. A new report was prepared containing many of the conclusions derived from the original VSM analysis but expressed in the shared language that emerged during the SSM process. The intervention proved successful, with the coherent set of changes validated by the VSM enacted in a situation in which SSM had helped ensure they would be perceived as feasible and desirable. The initial choice of the VSM as the dominant methodology was unfortunate. However, the flexibility of CSP allowed us to change tack and elevate SSM to a position of dominance at a later stage. We learned lessons about being more sensitive to the issues raised by all the 'systemic perspectives' and using methodologies in combination where necessary.

The second example, based on a paper by Arina Elyasi and Ebrahim Teimoury (2023), details the use of CSP to help improve the sustainability of the rice supply chain in Iran. This is vital given the importance of rice to the food safety of the country. It is plagued by complexity because of the volatility of the situation and the interacting economic, social and environmental dimensions of sustainability. The authors considered the use of multi-objective linear programming or SD to address the issues involved but argued that one systems methodology alone would 'be unable to tackle the system's complexity'. What was needed was CSP, which allows multiple systems methodologies to be employed in combination. Interviews were conducted, and a metaphor analysis of the results revealed that most insight was provided by the interrelationships (a set of linked economic factors), purposeful (various stakeholder issues) and societal/environmental perspectives. The intervention strategy that followed required the use of SD, SSM, IP and CSH. The interactions of the economic factors impacting the rice supply chain were captured first in a CLD and then, via a Stock and Flow diagram, converted into a computer simulation, which allowed the testing of possible policy options. The best way to ensure sustainability was to increase the guaranteed price for rice produced locally. The use of soft and emancipatory systems methodologies gave proper attention to the social and environmental aspects of sustainability. SSM (Rich Pictures, CATWOE, etc.) guaranteed that the interests of the various stakeholders were considered, and CSH ensured that environmental concerns were foregrounded. It then became possible to follow IP in developing an Idealized Design for the supply chain, set objectives and suggest the means necessary to achieve the 'ideal' state. The authors concluded that:

> Further ... research can be conducted by utilizing the CSP meta-methodology to study other strategic supply chains, such as poultry and wheat, to improve their sustainability. (Elyasi and Teimoury, 2023, p. 467)

Our final example rests on Patrick McKenna's (2022, 2024) work seeking to use CSP to improve the outcomes of Australia's Emergency Relief Program (ERP). The ERP was intended to help people through immediate financial crises with one-off payments, assisting them to become self-reliant. In 2019–2020, it was administered through 197 community organisations and supported 443,475 beneficiaries. The results were varied. For many individuals, the ERP worked. Others, however, became dependent on the payouts or found their situation deteriorating. Exploring this 'wicked problem' using the 'systemic perspectives', it became clear that the mechanical and societal/environmental lenses provided the most insight. The first of these identified a lack of clarity about the best service delivery model for getting the intended results. The second, that the service only benefited a proportion of its intended clients. Others did not have their needs met. The intervention strategy, therefore, employed an 'engineering' methodology, known as Program Logic (PL), and an 'emancipatory systems methodology', CSH. PL is the best practice approach to social services design and evaluation in Australia. It is meant to 'identify and link the purpose, inputs, outputs and outcomes of a program' (McKenna, 2024). In other words, to improve efficiency and efficacy. Using PL, it was possible to demonstrate that the best results, in terms of the measures used, were obtained when all aspects of ERP provision were integrated and co-located with the complementary services to which clients were often referred. McKenna was able to construct a 'Service Integration Grid' – an ideal arrangement of services that providers could aspire to move towards. CSH proved its worth by revealing the 'blind spots' in this approach and offering an alternative vision of what improvement could be about. It asked the vital question: Who does ERP serve? It certainly sought to serve the needs of those experiencing short-term financial issues. Other potential beneficiaries, however, who didn't share the goal of self-reliance, were excluded from benefit by the way in which the system was designed. For example, single mothers who put childcare before working, indigenous people with cultural priorities such as kinship care and the terminally ill. They had different perspectives, and their voices were not heard. One-off payments were of little use to them. Either they became dependent on the service or avoided it altogether because they were unwilling to follow up on referrals that seemed irrelevant to them. The situation was exacerbated by the government directive that ERP programs be evaluated based on the numbers seeking further payments – a low-level counting as success. Inevitably, this led to providers engaging in 'creaming', only working with those likely to achieve the required outcome, and 'parking', avoiding those unlikely to do so. Improvement for stakeholders whose interests were not currently met would require a reorientation of the system to serve the wider goals of preventing people from suffering long-term disadvantage and potentially becoming homeless. Different performance indicators would be necessary. McKenna suggested this would require the engagement of beneficiary groups in a more collaborative governance model. He concluded:

> For complex social services, Program Logic should be used in combination with other systems methodologies from the pluralist and/or coercive paradigms, such as Critical Systems Heuristics. This highlights the weakness in a single method approach to systemic evaluation and the strength of a multimethodology such as Critical Systems Practice. (McKenna, 2024, forthcoming)

6.5 *Produce* – Issues

The five types of systems methodology described offer ways of intervening consistent with the worldviews expressed in the five systemic perspectives, which themselves represent 'adequate' world hypotheses in Pepper's (1942) terms. For those inclined to scepticism or cynicism, this may seem forced. To Rescher, however, nothing could be more natural:

> This is something only natural and to be expected because *if we did not succeed in this cognitive venture we wouldn't be here.* The rationale for this is fundamentally Darwinian: rational guidance is necessary for successful action; successful action is crucial for the survival of creatures constituted as we are; accordingly, our survival is indicative of cognitive competence. (Rescher, 1977, p. 126; italics in the original)

The survival of the human species, adequate systemic perspectives and the existence of appropriate systems methodologies are intimately linked. The five perspectives and associated methodologies represent different ways of seeing and intervening that make a difference. They should be continually refined, but there is little point in inventing new ones unless they can also demonstrate 'adequacy' and make a difference.

I have concentrated on certain systems methodologies within the 5 broad types – around 10, in fact. I view these as being philosophically sound, thoroughly researched and with a good track record of application (see Jackson, 2019). There is inevitably an element of personal bias involved. A case could be made that I should have included, for example, Miller's (1978) work on Living Systems Theory; the Structured Democratic Dialogue approach developed by Warfield and Christakis (Laouris and Dye, 2023); and Beer's (1994) Team Syntegrity.

There will be controversy, no doubt, about whether all the methodologies discussed are truly systemic. Are not 'engineering systems methodologies', for example, better described as 'systematic'? In my view, all those included relate to valuable systemic perspectives and, in terms of their favoured perspective, make proper use of systems ideas. They are all, I maintain, systems methodologies. They correspond to what I believe ST can deliver. ST provides existing 'adequate' world hypotheses with a holistic orientation and enriches them with an armoury of systems concepts that they can use according to their own rationale. Methodologies then allow the translation of the systemic perspectives that result into guidelines for practical action.

Another possible line of criticism is that I have misrepresented certain methodologies in the process of pigeonholing them. It could be argued that I have attached SD to the interrelationships perspective when it can equally well serve the purposeful systemic perspective. Fred Emery (1969) believed that STS, as it developed, left behind the world hypothesis of 'organicism' in favour of 'contextualism' – an argument forcefully supported by Merrelyn Emery (2010). The VSM, as its name says, is a model rather than a methodology and can be aligned with methodologies reflecting different theoretical underpinnings. Some (e.g., Harnden, 1989) prefer to see it as a 'hermeneutic enabler', aligning it with the purposeful rather than the organismic systemic perspective. Ulrich's CSH is not just an emancipatory systems methodology. It can also play a role as a soft systems methodology, illuminating different perspectives and creating greater mutual understanding. I have made a reasoned choice for where the various methodologies and closely associated models best fit and justified it elsewhere (Jackson, 2019). In general, the basis of the choice has been what the methodology does best and, therefore, how it is most usefully employed. As Lane noted, referring to SD, methodologies can lose their focus and power if moved too far from their original roots:

> [While] acknowledging and responding to the contribution of subjectivism, system dynamics cannot move too far in this direction without losing most of what is distinctive and – more to the point – effective about the approach. Indeed, if placation of subjectivists involves the denial of the relevance of causal laws, causal explanations and the grand structural claim of system dynamics then the field should stop placating and start declaiming. (Lane, 2000, p. 15)

Following this logic, it is easy to argue that STS and the VSM have made their major contributions under the sway of organicism. And that the 'scientific' knowledge claimed to be embedded in them limits the range of possible debate when they are employed as soft systems approaches. In the case of CSH, Ulrich may not have intended that it be used exclusively to address issues of coercion, but that is where it has found its niche. This is not chance. It lacks the sophistication of, for example, SSM if used to serve the purposeful systemic perspective but

> ... is unique in that it defines a mechanism for better understanding and addressing power dynamics, and for considering individuals and groups adversely impacted. (Hutcheson et al., 2023, p. 6)

I have interpreted the various methodologies according to the pragmatist philosophy embraced by CSP. The models supporting these methodologies should, therefore, be judged in terms of usefulness rather than as representations of the 'real world'. That said, a model – whether mechanical, Stock and Flow, organismic – will sometimes seem to capture aspects of reality to the satisfaction of participants and the real world allow itself to be manipulated according to the logic of the model. For a time, the model can act in a representational manner. This will only be temporary. The world changes, in part due to the influence on it of models made of it.

The emphasis, in CSP, on pursuing improvement through a range of strictly defined systems methodologies will be irritating to some. They will think one methodology can do the job. For example, SD is often represented, by its advocates, as the essence of ST. For them, it is the only methodology needed. However, this implies, as we saw Morin (2006) arguing, that a 'restricted complexity' approach is appropriate in a world of multidimensional complexity which only allows for partial truths. Addressing the world as though it consists of interrelationships between feedback and feedforward loops and lags can sometimes prove helpful. It is limiting, nevertheless. Far from being able to stand above and model complexity, SD is adrift in the sea of complexity. As Etiënne Rouwette insisted:

> System dynamics projects in organizational contexts are impacted by power and politics. Case studies show how decision makers' interests influence both the modelling process as well as the implementation of recommendations. (Rouwette, 2022, p. 1)

Similar arguments hold against all types of systems methodology. As we have argued, the five systemic perspectives to which they pay respect provide a variety of 'adequate' partial truths. It is necessary to have the same variety available in terms of systems methodologies. This variety offers the possibility of a 'general complexity' approach to the multidimensional complexity decision-makers increasingly confront. Those who employ just one, favoured methodology should reflect on how this limits the way they are able to look at the world and how it restricts their attempts to improve it.

Some believe that integrating the best parts of different systems methodologies will produce a superior methodology capable of gaining purchase on a wider range of issues. The strategy fails because the methodologies represent alternative systemic perspectives offering different insights into the nature of the world and how to change it. To avoid contradictions, any attempt at integration will see one methodology dominating at the expense of the others. There will be a loss of practical benefit in terms of what the less privileged methodologies have to offer. I have never come across an attempt to integrate systems methodologies when it has not been obvious which methodology, and associated worldview, is dominant. It is far better to get the maximum benefit from each and employ them as critics of each other.

Finally, CSP reasons that the methodology(s) that appears most relevant to managing the primary issues, revealed during *Explore,* should be chosen to lead the intervention. An alternative view (Midgley, 2000) is that systemic intervention should, in all cases, begin with an emancipatory methodology such as CSH. If this is not done, it is argued, the use of other methodologies might serve a restricted set of interests and the intervention will be compromised. The response is that CSP always considers the position of the disadvantaged and marginalised at the *Explore* stage using the societal/environmental lens. Having done this, it weighs the immediate importance of the issues raised by that lens against those surfaced by the other systemic perspectives. After all, an organisation may be performing well in this respect and other priorities be temporarily more pressing, for example, saving the organisation from going out of business. CSP ensures a constant review of the priorities embedded in the methodologies it employs, challenging them using alternative systemic perspectives. Employing CSP means that we never forget Sartre's injunction that the 'truth' can only be established by looking at the world through 'the eyes of the least favoured', from the point of view of 'those treated the most unjustly' (see Bakewell, 2017).

6.6 Conclusion

Keats's concept of 'Negative Capability' is very relevant to the CSP practitioner:

> I mean Negative Capability, that is, when a man is capable of being in uncertainties, mysteries, doubts, without any irritable reaching after fact and reason. (Keats, 1899, p. 277; originally 1817)

According to the Keats' Kingdom website:

> The concept of Negative Capability is the ability to contemplate the world without the desire to try to reconcile contradictory aspects or fit it into closed and rational systems. (Keats' Kingdom, 2021)

It is a mindset that rejects philosophical certainties and encourages flexibility and openness. It allows us to creatively explore the world and to be receptive to its potentialities. The third and fourth stages of CSP continue cultivating this mood. However, the issues we face also demand action. We should be informed and confident enough, after going through *Explore* and *Produce*, to take the plunge.

References

Ackoff, R.L. (1981). *Creating the Corporate Future*. Wiley.

Ackoff, R. L. (1999a). *Ackoff's Best*. Wiley.

Ackoff, R.L. (1999b). A lifetime of systems thinking. *The Systems Thinker* 10: 1–4.

Ackoff, R.L. and Gharajedaghi, J. (1996). Reflections on systems and their models. *Systems Research and Behavioral Science* 13: 13–22.

Attenborough, D. (2022). *A Life on Our Planet*. Ebury Press.

Bakewell, S. (2017). *At the Existentialist Café*. Vintage.

Barabba, V.P. and Mitroff, I.I. (2014). *Business Strategies for a Messy World: Tools for Systemic Problem-Solving*. Palgrave Macmillan.

Barbrook-Johnson, P. and Penn, A.S. (2022). *Systems Mapping: How to Build and Use Causal Models of Systems*. Palgrave-pivot.

Beer, S. (1967). *Cybernetics and Management*, 2e. English Universities Press.

Beer, S. (1972). *Brain of the Firm*. Allen Lane.

Beer, S. (1979). *The Heart of Enterprise*. Wiley.

Beer, S. (1981). *Brain of the Firm*, 2e. Wiley.

Beer, S. (1985). *Diagnosing the System for Organizations*. Wiley.

Beer, S. (1989). The viable system model: its provenance, development, methodology and pathology. In: *The Viable System Model: Interpretations and Applications of Stafford Beer's VSM* (eds R. Espejo and R.J. Harnden), pp. 11–37. Wiley.

Beer, S. (1994). *Beyond Dispute: The Invention of Team Syntegrity*. Wiley.

Bhaskar, R. (2017). *The Order of Natural Necessity*. CreateSpace Independent Publishing Platform.

Blake, W. (c.1815). *Jerusalem*.

Capra, F. (1996). *The Web of Life: A New Synthesis of Mind and Matter*. Harper Collins.

Carayannis, E. and Forbes, J. (2001). A pragmatic representation of systems engineering based on technological learning. *Technovation* 21: 197–207.

Checkland, P.B. (1981). *Systems Thinking, Systems Practice*. Wiley.

Checkland, P.B. and Holwell, S. (1998). *Information, Systems and Information Systems*. Wiley.

Checkland, P.B. and Poulter, J. (2006). *Learning for Action: A Short Definitive Account of Soft Systems Methodology and Its Use for Practitioners, Teachers and Students*. Wiley.

Checkland, P.B. and Scholes, J. (1990). *Soft Systems Methodology in Action*. Wiley.

Churchman, C.W. (1979). *The Systems Approach*. Dell Publishing.

Churchman, C.W. and Ackoff, R.L. (1946). Varieties of unification. *Philosophy of Science* 13: 287–300.

Cunico, G., Zimmermann, N. and Videira, N. (2023). Playing the new devil's advocate role in facilitated modelling processes to address group homogeneity. *Journal of the Operational Research Society*. https://doi.org/10.1080/01605682.2023.2263101.

Deming, W.E. (2018). *Out of Crisis*. MIT Press.

Department for Levelling Up, Housing and Communities. (2022). *Levelling up the United Kingdom*. UK Government.

Donaldson, W. (2017). *Simple Complexity: A Guide to Systems Thinking*. Morgan James Publishing, Kindle edition.

Elyasi, A. and Teimoury, E. (2023). Applying critical systems practice meta-methodology to improve sustainability in the rice supply chain of Iran. *Sustainable Production and Consumption* 35: 453–468.

Emery, F.E. (Ed) (1969). *Systems Thinking*. Penguin.

Emery, M. (2010). Refutation of Kira & van Eijnatten's critique of the Emerys' open systems theory. *Systems Research and Behavioral Science* 27: 697–712.

Emery, F.E. and Thorsrud, E. (1969). *Form and Content in Industrial Democracy*. Tavistock.

Eno, B. (2009). Foreword. In: *Stafford Beer – Think Before you Think, Social Complexity and Knowledge of Knowing* (eds D. Whittaker), pp. 7–12. Wavestone Press.

Espejo, R. and Harnden, R. (Eds) (1989). *The Viable System Model: Interpretations and Applications of Stafford Beer's VSM*. Wiley.

Espejo, R. and Reyes, A. (2011). *Organizational Systems: Managing Complexity with the Viable System Model*. Springer-Verlag.

Espejo, R. and Schwaninger, M. (1993). *Organisational Fitness: Corporate Effectiveness Through Management Cybernetics*. Campus.

Espejo, R., Schuhmann, W., Schwaninger, M. and Bilello, U. (1996). *Organizational Transformation and Learning: A Cybernetic Approach to Management*. Wiley.

Espinosa, A. (2023). *Sustainable Self-Governance in Businesses and Society: The Viable System Model in Action*. Routledge.

Espinosa, A. and Walker, J. (2017). *A Complexity Approach to Sustainability: Theory and Application*, 2e. World Scientific.

Flood, R.L. and Jackson, M.C. (1991). *Creative Problem Solving: Total Systems Intervention*. Wiley.

Forrester, J.W. (1971a). *World Dynamics*. Productivity Press.

Forrester, J.W. (1971b). Counterintuitive behavior of social systems. *Technology Review* 73: 52–68.

Gare, A. (2023). Was Günter Grass's rat right? Should terrestrial life welcome the end of humans? *Borderless Philosophy* 6: 32–76.

Gyllenhammer, P. (1977). *People at Work*. Addison-Wesley.

Habermas, J. (1979). *Communication and the Evolution of Society*. Heinemann.

Hall, A.D. (1962). *A Methodology for Systems Engineering*. D. Van Nostrand Co.

Harnden, R.J. (1989). Outside and then: an interpretive approach to the VSM. In: *The Viable System Model* (eds R. Espejo and R.J. Harnden), pp. 383–404. Wiley.

Haskins, C. (Ed.) (2021). *Systems Engineering for Sustainable Development Goals*. MDPI.

IIill, P. (1971). *Towards a New Philosophy of Management*. Gower Press.

Hoffman, B.G. (2017). *Red Teaming*. Piatkus.

House of Commons Report. (2021). Report of the Health and Social Care and Science and Technology Committees to the UK House of Commons, 'Coronavirus; lessons learned to date'. 21 September.

Hoverstadt, P. (2008). *The Fractal Organization: Creating Sustainable Organizations with the Viable System Model*. Wiley.

Hutcheson, M., Morton, A. and Blair, S. (2023). Critical systems heuristics: a systematic review. *Systemic Practice and Action Research*. https://doi.org/10.1007/s11213-023-09665-9

INCOSE. (2021). *Systems Engineering: Vision 2035*. INCOSE.

Jackson, M.C. (1987). Present positions and future prospects in management science. *Omega* 15: 455–466.

Jackson, M.C. (1991). *Systems Methodology for the Management Sciences*. Plenum.

Jackson, M.C. (1997). Pluralism in systems thinking and practice. In: *Multimethodology* (eds J. Mingers and A. Gill), pp. 347–378. Wiley.

Jackson, M.C. (2000). *Systems Approaches to Management*. Kluwer/Plenum.

Jackson, M.C. (2003). *Systems Thinking: Creative Holism for Managers*. Wiley.

Jackson, M.C. (2019). *Critical Systems Thinking and the Management of Complexity*. Wiley.

Jackson, M.C., Johnston, N. and Seddon, J. (2008). Evaluating systems thinking in housing. *Journal of the Operational Research Society* 59: 186–197.

Kaminski, I. (2023). Growing number of countries consider making ecocide a crime. *The Guardian*. 26 August.

Kay, J. and King, M. (2020). *Radical Uncertainty: Decision-Making for an Unknowable Future*. Bridge Street Press.

Keats, J. (1899). *The Complete Poetical Works and Letters of John Keats*. Houghton, Mifflin and Company.

Keats' Kingdom website. (2021). Negative capability. http://www.keatsian.co.uk/negative-capability.php.

Kiss, I. and Tomlinson, R. (1984). Introduction. In: *Rethinking the Process of Operational Research and Systems Analysis* (eds R. Tomlinson and I. Kiss), pp. xi–xiii. Pergamon Press.

Lane, D. (2000). Should system dynamics be described as a 'hard' or 'deterministic' systems approach. *Systems Research and Behavioral Science* 17: 3–22.

Lane, D.C. (2008). The emergence and use of diagramming in system dynamics: a critical account. *Systems Research and Behavioral Science* 25: 3–23.

Lane, D. (2022). Fons et origo: reflections on the 60th anniversary of *Industrial Dynamics*. *System Dynamics Review* 38: 292–324. https://doi.org/10.1002/sdr.1717.

Laouris, Y. and Dye, K. (2023). Multi-stakeholder structured dialogues: five generations of evolution of dialogic design. *Systems Research and Behavioral Science*. https://doi.org/10.1002/sres.2971.

Lewis, E. and Stephens, A. (2022). A responsible approach to intersectionality. *Integration and Implementation Insights*, 29 November.

Liew, J. (2023). English cricket's reign of shame exposed with devastating admission of guilt. *The Guardian*, 27 June.

Malczynski, L.A. and Lane, D.C. (2023). Sublime reason: when Isaac Asimov met Jay Forrester. *System Dynamics Review* 39: 64–79. https://doi.org/10.1002/sdr.1720.

Martins, J.M., Pathmanathan, I., Tan, D.T., Lim, S.C. and Allotey, P. (Eds) (2021). *Systems Thinking Analyses for Health Policy and Systems Development: A Malaysian Case Study*. Cambridge University Press.

Mason, R.O. and Mitroff, I.I. (1981). *Challenging Strategic Planning Assumptions: Theory, Cases and Techniques*. Wiley.

Mazzucato, M. (2021). *Mission Economy: A Moonshot Guide to Changing Capitalism*. Allen Lane.

McKenna, P. (2022). Critical systems thinking for the design and improvement of complex social service program outcomes. M.Phil. thesis. Queensland University of Technology.

McKenna, P. (2024). The strengths and weaknesses of program logic from a critical systems thinking perspective: evidence from a study of the emergency relief program in Australia. *Systems Research and Behavioral Science*, forthcoming.

Meadows, D.H. (2008). *Thinking in Systems*. Chelsea Green Publishing.

Meadows, D.H., Meadows, D.L., Randers, J. and Behrens, W.W. (1972). *The Limits to Growth*. Universe Books.

Medina, E. (2014). *Cybernetic Revolutionaries: Technology and Politics in Allende's Chile*. MIT Press.

Midgley, G. (1990). Creative methodology design. *Systemist* 12: 108–113.

Midgley, G. (2000). *Systemic Intervention: Philosophy, Methodology, and Practice*. Kluwer/Plenum.

Miller, J.G. (1978). *Living Systems*. McGraw-Hill.

Mingers, J. (2014). *Systems Thinking, Critical Realism and Philosophy*. Routledge, Kindle edition.

Mingers, J. and Brocklesby, J. (1997). Multimethodology: towards a framework for mixing methodologies. *Omega* 25: 489–509.

Morin, E. (2006). Restricted Complexity, General Complexity. Presented at the Colloquium 'Intelligence de la complexité: épistémologie et pragmatique', Cerisy-La-Salle, France, June 26th, 2005. Translated from French by Carlos Gershenson.

Morozov, E. (2023). The Santiago Boys: 9-episode podcast. Chora Media.

Munro, E. (2010). *The Munro Review of Child Protection Part 1: A Systems Analysis*. TSO.

Nonaka, I. and Takeuchi, H. (1995). *The Knowledge Creating Company: How Japanese Companies Create the Dynamics of Innovation*. Oxford University Press.

Pepper, S.C. (1942). *World Hypotheses*. University of California Press.

Pérez Rios, J. (2012). *Design and Diagnosis for Sustainable Organizations*. Springer.

Pfiffner, M. (2022). *The Neurology of Business: Implementing the Viable System Model*. Springer, Kindle edition.

Pickering, A. (2010). *The Cybernetic Brain: Sketches of Another Future*. University of Chicago Press, Kindle edition.

Potts, M.W., Sartor, P.A., Johnson, A. and Bullock, S. (2020). Assaying the importance of system complexity for the systems engineering community. *Systems Engineering*. https://doi.org/10.1002/sys.21550.

Raworth, K. (2023). Economist Kate Raworth chooses the environmental scientist 'Dana' Meadows'. BBC Audio, 22 August.

Ray, L. (2004). Pragmatism and critical theory. *European Journal of Social Theory* 7: 307–321.

Reeves, M. and Fuller, J. (2021). *The Imagination Machine: How to Spark New Ideas and Create Your Company's Future*. Harvard Business Review Press.

Reeves, M., Boulenger, A. and Job, A. (2023). Making corporate change work: lessons from superprojects. BCG Henderson Institute, March 15.

Rescher, N. (1977). *Methodological Pragmatism: A Systems-Theoretic Approach to the Theory of Knowledge*. Basil Blackwell.

Robinson, K.S. (2015). *The Complete Mars Trilogy: Red Mars, Green Mars, Blue Mars*. Harper Voyager, Kindle edition.

Rodenas, M.A. and Jackson, M.C. (2021). Lessons for systems engineering from the Segura River reclamation project: a critical systems thinking analysis. *Systems Research and Behavioral Science* 38: 368–376. https://doi.org/10.1002/sres.2789.

Rosenhead, J. and Mingers, J. (Eds) (2001). *Rational Analysis for a Problematic World Revisited*. Wiley.

Rouwette, E.A.J.A. (2022). System dynamics and power. Conference paper. https://www.researchgate.net/publication/364308965.

Royal Academy of Engineering, Royal College of Physicians and Academy of Medical Sciences. (2017). *Engineering Better Care: A Systems Approach to Health and Care Design and Continuous Improvement*. Royal Academy of Engineering.

Schumacher, E.F. (1973). *Small is Beautiful: A Study of Economics as if People Mattered*. Blond and Briggs Ltd.

Seddon, J. (2005). *Freedom from Command and Control*. Vanguard Press.

Seddon, J. (2019). *Beyond Command and Control*. Mayfield Press.

Shafak, E. (2023). In the battle to save the world's forests, women are leading the resistance. *The Guardian*, 26 August.

Sillitto, H. (2012). Integrating systems science, systems thinking, and systems engineering: understanding the differences and exploiting synergies. INCOSE International symposium, July.

Stephens, A. (2013). *Ecofeminism and Systems Thinking*. Routledge, Kindle edition.

Stephens, A., Lewis, E.D. and Shravanti, R. (2018). Towards an inclusive systemic evaluation for the SDGs: Gender equality, Environments and Marginalized voices (GEMS). *Evaluation*. https://doi.org/10.1177/1356389018766093.

Stephens, A., Taket, A. and Gagliano, M. (2019). Ecological justice for nature in CST. *Systems Research and Behavioral Science* 36: 3–19.

Sterman, J.D. (2000). *Business Dynamics: Systems Thinking and Modeling for a Complex World*. Irwin/McGraw-Hill.

Sterman, J.D. (2002). System Dynamics: Systems Thinking and Modeling for a Complex World. MIT Engineering Systems Division, Working Paper Series, ESD-WP-2003-01.13.

Sterman, J.D. (2003). Learning in and about complex systems. In: *Systems Thinking*, vol. 3 (ed. G. Midgley), pp. 330–364. Sage.

Sweeney, B. (2017). *Lean – Quickstart Guide*, 2e. Clydebank Business.

Thompson, K.M. and Tebbens, R.D.T. (2008). Using system dynamics to develop policies that matter: global management of poliomyelitis and beyond. *System Dynamics Review* 24: 433–449.

UK Government. (2022). Government to use vaccine taskforce model to tackle health challenges. Press Release, 28 November.

Ulrich, W. (1983). *Critical Heuristics of Social Planning*. Haupt.

Wallis, N. (2022). *The Great Post Office Scandal: The Fight to Expose a Multimillion Pound IT Disaster Which Put Innocent People in Jail*. Bath Publishing.

Walton, M. (1994). *The Deming Management Method*. Management Books 2000 Ltd.

Williams, B. and Hummelbrunner, R. (2010). *Systems Concepts in Action: A Practitioner's Toolkit*. Stanford University Press.

Zokaei, K., Seddon, J. and O'Donovan, B. (Eds) (2011). *Systems Thinking: From Heresy to Practice*. Palgrave Macmillan.

7

Critical Systems Practice 3 – *Intervene* Flexibly

> *The test of a first-rate intelligence is the ability to hold two opposed ideas in the mind at the same time, and still retain the ability to function.*
>
> (Fitzgerald, 1936)

7.1 Introduction

This chapter discusses *Intervene*, the third stage of Critical Systems Practice (CSP). It considers how best to execute a multimethodological intervention in accordance with the agreement reached about which systems approaches are best suited to addressing the primary issues of interest. The discussion starts with a reminder of where we are in the *EPIC* cycle and the need to remain flexible during *Intervene*. The process of conducting *Intervene*, being true to its pluralist intent while also respecting situational constraints, is examined. Examples are provided which illustrate the *Intervene* process and highlight the need for flexibility. The potential theoretical problem that 'paradigm incommensurability' poses to multimethodological practice is examined. CSP's adoption of pragmatism as an underpinning philosophy provides the way forward.

7.2 *Intervene* – Preliminaries

I have emphasised the need to adhere to the philosophy and principles of CST at each stage of a CSP intervention. The main problem at the *Intervene* stage is to remain true to CST's commitment to systemic pluralism. *Intervene* is guided but not determined by the nature of the primary and secondary issues surfaced by *Explore* and the appropriate intervention strategy agreed on during *Produce*. It is

Critical Systems Thinking: A Practitioner's Guide, First Edition. Michael C. Jackson.
© 2024 John Wiley & Sons, Inc. Published 2024 by John Wiley & Sons, Inc.

Intervene itself that will give rise to the greatest learning about which systems approaches are most useful and what improvements are possible in the situation of interest. As learning accumulates and the context changes, as will inevitably transpire, *Intervene* will need to register what is happening and adjust accordingly. To respond successfully and avoid closure of possibilities, it needs access to the full range of systemic perspectives and systems methodologies. This continued requirement for systemic pluralism during *Intervene* is met by taking action based on frequent revisiting of the *Explore* and *Produce* stages.

7.3   *Intervene* – Process

We have passed through the *Explore* and *Produce* stages. The intervention is planned and scheduled. The action can start. Figure 7.1 reminds us of where *Intervene* sits in the *EPIC* process and of the elements involved. They are now briefly discussed. The examples provided in Section 7.4 put meat on these bones.

7.3.1   Use Systems Methodologies, Models and Methods Flexibly

Intervene begins when we have one or two systems methodologies chosen because of their ability to address the greatest number of primary issues. These will provide an initial steer to the intervention. Appropriate models and methods from the systems field, or elsewhere, will also have been identified with a view to customising the methodology or methodologies for the context. The intervention can begin according to the recommendations offered by those methodologies and the requirements of the models and methods. The outline of the different methodologies and the references given in Chapter 6, as well as the details in Jackson (2019), will provide the necessary guidance.

7.3.2   Stay Alert to the Evolving Situation (Revisit Stage 1)

During an intervention, the *Explore* stage needs revisiting on a regular basis to see what has changed. This may reveal, for example, that issues previously regarded as 'secondary' have become more urgent as the situation has developed, perhaps in response to the impact of the intervention itself.

7.3.3   Stay Flexible About Appropriate Methodologies, Models and Methods (Revisit Stage 2)

If returning to *Explore* reveals the need for a significant reorientation of the intervention, then a revisiting of *Produce* is called for. This may indicate the need for a change in the leading systems methodology or methodologies. The key to success

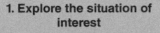

1. Explore the situation of interest

- View it from five systemic perspectives
- Identify primary and secondary issues

2. Produce an intervention strategy

- Appreciate the variety of systems approaches
- Choose appropriate systems methodologies
- Choose appropriate systems models and methods
- Structure, schedule and set objectives for the intervention

3. Intervene flexibly

- Use systems methodologies, models and methods flexibly
- Stay alert to the evolving situation (revisit Stage 1)
- Stay flexible about appropriate methodologies, models and methods (revisit Stage 2)

4. Check on progress

- Evaluate the improvements achieved
- Reflect on the learning gained about the systems approaches used
- Discuss and agree next steps

Figure 7.1 The four *EPIC* stages of Critical Systems Practice.

with CSP is to embed flexibility into the process of conducting the intervention. This applies to the choice of systems methodologies and to the models and methods employed in support.

Regular, rapid iteration back through *Explore* and *Produce* is the sensible route to protecting methodology, model and method diversity. If we are explicit about the reasons for the initial choice of methodology or methodologies and are ready to switch, then that initial choice will not impose limitations in the long term. It will not keep us from introducing alternative methodologies based on different systemic perspectives as required.

7.4   *Intervene* – Examples

These examples are drawn from different time periods and different authors and do not necessarily reflect CSP as currently articulated. However, they are all multimethodological and/or multimethod interventions. There is a particular focus on the important issue of what might generate a switch in methodology once an intervention has begun. Gerald Midgley (personal communication) suggested to me that this can occur because of the natural progression of an intervention, be provoked by something significant happening which requires a change in focus, or result from the drastic action necessary to save a project from collapse. I follow this idea in ordering the examples.

The first example concerns the creation of a new business school at the University of Hull in the United Kingdom. This has been detailed elsewhere as an application of CSP (Jackson, 2019). I refer to it again because it offers a classic example of different methodologies being used during *Intervene* due to the natural progression of the project. Briefly, Hull University Business School (HUBS) was founded in 1999 and, by 2011, had gained accreditation from the three major business school accrediting bodies – placing it in the top 1% of business schools worldwide. I was Dean during those 12 years and often used CSP, in its Mode 2 guise, to inform thought and practice. I believe that this contributed significantly to the success of HUBS. In this example, the primary issues identified for immediate attention, in 1999, were derived from the mechanical and organismic systemic perspectives.

The business school needed a goal and the resources to pursue that goal. The initial goal was to gain accreditation from the three main business school accrediting bodies. An engineering approach was taken to get the necessary resources to achieve this. Student numbers had to grow, and this required streamlining recruitment processes at all levels. Greater numbers were managed efficiently by instigating a common first year for undergraduate degrees, sharing modules across postgraduate programs and establishing a staff workload model.

HUBS needed to survive and thrive in a competitive environment. It helped to conceive of it as an organism learning its way to becoming a top-rated business school. Using the Viable System Model (VSM) ensured that HUBS identified the primary activities that it wanted to direct to the market and structured itself around those activities, providing them with managerial attention and appropriate support. The VSM also focused minds on how HUBS could secure sufficient autonomy to become a viable system itself while continuing to be a part of its host university. Because of the distinct features of the business school environment, it needed to have dedicated marketing, alumni, administrative, finance, human resource management and quality functions. Figure 7.2 shows a VSM diagram of the structural arrangements adopted by HUBS in its early days. These changed over time as the business school and its environment co-evolved.

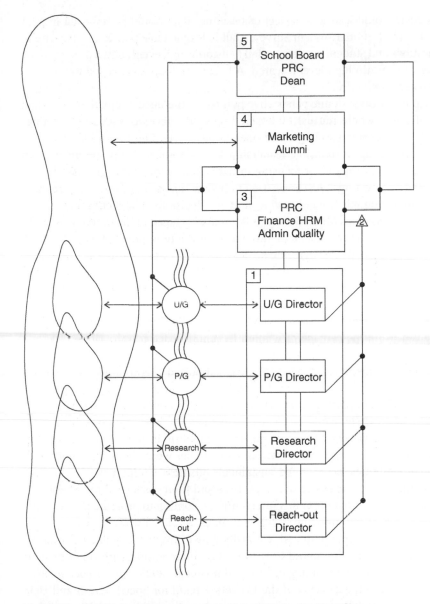

Figure 7.2 Hull University Business School modelled using the VSM.

As the intervention progressed, other systemic perspectives brought to attention significant issues and different systems methodologies achieved prominence.

The interrelationships perspective meant a close eye was kept on the possible unintended consequences of initiatives. For example, it became apparent that a need generated by the 'Research Excellence Framework', to recruit high-performing researchers, could lead to a neglect of teaching. This would be reflected in poor results in the National Student Survey, a fall in league table position, a decrease in applications and student numbers, a fall in income and, eventually, a decline in the capacity to sustain high-level research. A balancing loop was needed to reinforce good teaching practice.

The purposeful systemic perspective pointed to the need to create fora, formal and informal, where mutual understanding could develop. Frequent meetings were held to develop strategic and operational plans. The vision of a business school promoting 'responsible leadership for a complex world' emerged as an Idealized Design capable of focusing initiative and effort. Strategic Assumption Surfacing and Testing (SAST) was used to review the assumptions we were making about stakeholders when taking strategic decisions. I was conscious of the stages of Soft Systems Methodology (SSM) while engaged in the everyday practice of reviewing the current state of the 'mess', developing possible ways forward, discussing what to do and agreeing on changes which were feasible and desirable. Sometimes aspects of SSM were used more explicitly to structure debate around issues of importance in HUBS. Figure 7.3 is an example of a Rich Picture employed as part of an exercise to explore the strategic positioning of the business school.

The societal/environmental perspective frequently came to the fore. Attention was given to the percentage of women in senior posts, to minority ethnic and Lesbian, Gay, Bisexual, Transgender + (LGBT+) issues and to preventing an academic/administrative divide. This lens supported the argument for concessions on admissions requirements for local students suffering disadvantage. It led to a successful campaign to ensure that the coffee outlet in HUBS was 'fair trade'. HUBS was an early signatory to the 'Principles for Responsible Management Education' and was one of the first business schools to introduce an undergraduate module on business ethics. Environmental issues were highlighted, and many degree programmes incorporated 'sustainable business' components.

In summary, all five systemic perspectives and their associated methodologies were used in combination in this intervention – coming to prominence, receding in importance and resurfacing at different times. But all, always, kept alive.

In a second example, Rajneesh Chowdhury, working with 'holistic flexibility' (his own brand of CSP), chose CSH to lead an intervention with other systems methods brought in later in support (Chowdhury et al., 2023). The project involved work to improve the capacity of the Universal Team for Social Action and Help (UTSAH), a child protection non-governmental organisation (NGO) based in India. The purpose of UTSAH was to translate government policy on child protection down to the grassroots level in its locality by preventing and responding to violence, exploitation and abuse against children. An initial exploration of the operating environment revealed that UTSAH would need a multitude of stakeholders to work together if improvement was to be realised. These stakeholders

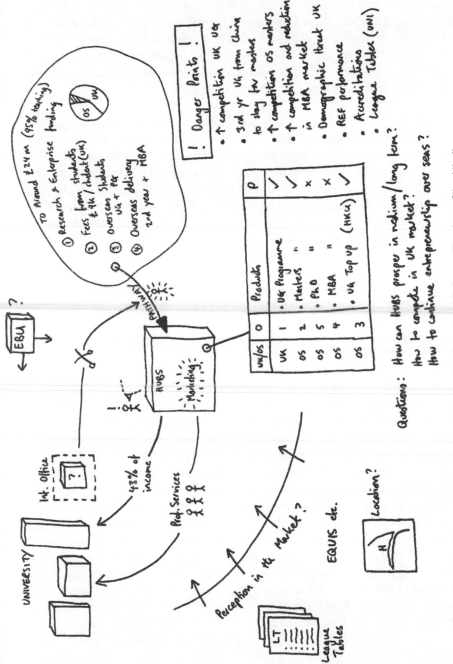

Figure 7.3 A Rich Picture to help explore the strategic positioning of HUBS. *Source:* Thanks to Giles Hindle.

were diverse in their beliefs, in their assumptions about who should be involved in decision-making around child protection and in the power they could exercise. Everything pointed to CSH as a good initial choice of methodology; it would help unfold different viewpoints, aid understanding of tensions and give an equal voice to less-powerful stakeholders. Moving ahead with the methodology, the 12 'boundary questions' were used to structure interviews with UTSAH staff and external stakeholders. In the words of Chowdhury et al.:

> Insights generated from the boundary questions were consolidated, and a convergence workshop was facilitated by the consultant with the UTSAH programme team. Apart from deliberating on the insights, the workshop was intended to prioritize the programme areas and arrive at the design for the future roadmap, and it was realized that, to achieve these ends, CSH needed to be complemented with other methods. To provide a more action-oriented focus, two systems methods were employed: CATWOE and an issue rating matrix. (Chowdhury et al., 2023)

In essence, following the success of the CSH work, the project could be reconceived as a systematic endeavour to specify a roadmap for improvement that took account of the issues seen as most significant by the stakeholders. CATWOE, from SSM, and an adaptation of 'assumption rating', from SAST, were employed as methods to drive this forward. It is not unusual for a soft or emancipatory methodology to achieve sufficient mutual understanding among participants to permit a shift to a more goal-directed approach. Regular revisiting of the *Explore* stage remains necessary to check that continued reliance on the alignment of purposes is justifiable.

Another intervention by Chowdhury in the UK National Health Service employed the VSM, SSM and SAST sequentially. The project illustrated the importance of continually returning to 'problem-structuring' (what I call *Explore*), throughout *Intervene*, to reorientate problem-solving as necessary. Problem-structuring 'needs to flow through an intervention as an iterative process [and] not be regarded as a one-time activity' (Chowdhury, 2021).

Alvaro Carrizosa's three-year involvement with Kingston Gas Turbines, helping with their ambitious 'double the business' strategy, demanded extreme responsiveness to changing business and environmental circumstances as the project progressed (Carrizosa, 2002; Jackson, 2019). Frequent changes of dominant systems methodology were necessary. A vast array of models, methods, tools and techniques were utilised. Those derived from the systems tradition, such as Rich Pictures, metaphors, Root Definitions, Purposeful Activity Models, the VSM and System Dynamics models, were happily mixed with many from outside.

In my 12-year engagement as chair of trustees and trustee with Hull and East Yorkshire Children's University (HEYCU), it has been natural to occasionally use systems methodologies to support planning and decision-making. As HEYCU grew significantly in size, SAST was employed to challenge and rethink the existing strategy in light of new opportunities. As the charity took on new tasks, especially with children-in-care, and spread its geographical reach to East Yorkshire, the VSM was used to help with two restructuring exercises which ensured a better matching of organisational and environmental variety.

Gerald Midgley provided three examples of projects where something significant happened which provoked a change in orientation. In all cases, CSP enabled the necessary shift in focus.

The first of these was a project concerned with the housing needs of older people (Midgley et al., 1998). In this case, the change in orientation was necessary because the original remit was untenable. Social Services Departments in the United Kingdom are legally obliged to seek the views of their clients with a view to improving service provision. This requires that they gather relevant information and the initial remit of the project was

> ... to discover how information from assessment of individual older people applying for housing services could most effectively be aggregated and used in the development of housing policy. (Midgley et al., 1998, p. 471)

Once this was completed, it was envisaged that the project would move on to designing improvements to the information provision. Interviewing stakeholders was going to be important, and the systems team were worried that the views of service users might be drowned out by the dominant professional discourse. From a CSH perspective, therefore, it was essential to ensure that older people were fully involved and heard. The interviews revealed that simply addressing the issue of information provision would be drawing the boundaries of the study too narrowly. It would fail to address many of the concerns, including a mismatch between what older people requested in assessments and what was provided, and problems arising from multi-agency working. A way forward had to be found which would address these broader issues. Fortunately, it was possible to agree with the sponsors a changed remit and extended boundaries for the project. Three workshops were held in which stakeholders were asked to come up with their view of the desired properties of an 'ideal' housing system. The methods employed to help guide their thinking were the Idealized Design stage of Interactive Planning (IP) and the 12 questions from CSH. There was substantial agreement among the three lists of desired properties. This made it possible to start supporting managers in the design of a way of multi-agency working that would facilitate progress towards achieving the 'ideal' housing system. The VSM was employed as a guide for this design because it suggests how the efforts of multiple agencies can be coordinated in a non-hierarchical manner and what information flows are necessary.

The second project was with a food production company in the Niger Delta region of Nigeria (Ufoa et al., 2018). It saw a change in focus because a significant ethical issue came to the fore. The company was intent on using a 'lean' approach, from the engineering systems tradition, to tackle issues of waste minimisation and the possible reuse of waste products. This approach would ensure that these were dealt with efficiently to the satisfaction of stakeholders closely involved with the company. There were, however, other stakeholders who were unlikely to be given consideration under the rationale of lean thinking, in particular the local community, who were suffering from the effects of the waste, including livestock waste dumped close to where they lived. They saw the company's actions as 'reckless', as causing an appalling stench and as posing a potential public health hazard. Fortunately, the company, responding to external pressure, was amenable to taking a different approach to the waste issues that would recognise the concerns of a wider range of stakeholders. Following a CSH logic, interviews were held to capture the community's and the company's perspectives. These were followed by workshops, in which Rich Pictures, CATWOE and Purposeful Activity Models were used to reveal the complexity of the situation and to express the multiple perspectives that were relevant to it. The company embraced the new approach, which they could see complemented the original lean thinking. Ufoa et al. (2018) commented on the circumstances that made the change in orientation possible: Essentially, the company was willing to listen to and engage with a wider range of stakeholders. In the current CSP language, exploring the situation through the societal/environmental systemic perspective revealed that an 'emancipation through discursive rationality' approach was worth trying. There will be occasions, revisiting *Explore*, when the ethical sensibilities of a systems team are offended and nothing can be done. The organisation will not change its practices. A shift to an 'emancipation as liberation' stance is called for. As Churchman (1970) argued, a professional systems practitioner must always consider whether it is desirable to help certain organisations to commit suicide.

The third example, in this class, was a green innovation project concerned with developing a technology for the recovery of valuable metals from steel slag (Gregory et al., 2020). A site of interest was a former steelworks in the Northeast of England. Initially, the intention was to hold a workshop to surface stakeholder opinion on the technology itself. As it turned out, it became clear that the recovery of rare metals was unlikely, in this instance, to be commercially viable. The workshop was reframed as a community-based event with the expanded aim of looking for future possible uses for the whole site, and various options were surfaced and explored. CST had, in any case, made it clear that the issues around the technology could not be separated from strategic issues concerning the future of the site itself. The transition to an approach that recognised the importance of social desirability, alongside technical feasibility and economic viability, was therefore natural and necessary.

We turn to examples where changes in direction were essential to prevent interventions from collapsing. The project mentioned in Chapter 6, with North Yorkshire Police, was a salutary case. It began with an organismic orientation, promoted by the VSM, designed to introduce more local autonomy for divisions and ensure greater flexibility. The imminent risk of failure led the systems team to urgently embrace a purposeful perspective, employing SSM. It became clear that there was no cultural appreciation of how decentralisation could work in a county police force, and that it was changing perceptions that should have had priority.

Another intervention, in which Gerald Midgley was involved, faced 'existential threats' which demanded changes of emphasis, departing from the original proposal, to avoid failure. It was an action research project to investigate the issue of young people (under 16) living on the streets in central Manchester and to identify suitable responses (Boyd et al., 2004). There were difficulties in working with and involving vulnerable young people who needed space and encouragement to express their opinions properly. The agencies involved had conflicting viewpoints and some – the Police, Social Services and the Education Department – might feel threatened by what surfaced. Various systems methodologies and methods were employed, but it was more the ability of the systems team, helped by CST, to continuously reflect on and address issues of marginalisation, power and participation, that enabled the project to survive and deliver some useful outcomes.

There are many more examples of multimethodology and multimethod interventions to be found in Jackson (1991, 2000, 2003, 2019), Flood and Jackson (1991), Flood (1995, 1999), Midgley (2000) and Chowdhury (2019, 2024).

We can turn our attention to a particular theoretical issue that is seen by some to compromise multimethodological interventions.

7.5   *Intervene* – Issues

A frequent theoretical objection raised against those who want to adopt a multi-methodological approach is the argument from 'paradigm incommensurability'. This originates from the work of Kuhn (1970) and was extended to organisational analysis by Burrell and Morgan (1979). Proponents of paradigm incommensurability regard it as impossible to employ systems methodologies owing allegiance to different paradigms in a complementary manner because this would require standing 'above' the paradigms. In Chapter 3 we saw that, in its early days, CST did indeed fall foul of this argument, seeking to be a 'metaparadigm'. A possible way forward presented itself in the form of 'discordant pluralism'. CST was seen as a framework that encouraged 'reflective conversation' between paradigms rather than claiming to stand in a superior position above them. Adopting discordant pluralism allowed CSP to sidestep the paradigm incommensurability argument.

It did, however, leave it bereft of theoretical support and opened the door to relativism. Pragmatism, as was argued in Chapter 3, provides both a coherent philosophy for CST and a way of judging the endeavours of CSP. Systemic perspectives, unlike paradigms, do not compete for one ontological truth. They offer various 'adequate' ways of seeing the world which link to systems methodologies – alternative ways of engaging with the world which, according to pragmatism, can be evaluated on the basis of whether they 'pay' in life. The paradigm incommensurability argument becomes irrelevant, and, at the same time, relativism is avoided.

Possible cognitive, cultural and societal constraints on multimethodological practice, and issues concerning cost and time commitments, are considered in Chapter 9.

7.6 Conclusion

We have outlined *Intervene* – the CSP approach to multimethodological practice. A formal description of this type can make it seem as though the process must be led by experts and followed to the letter. It is therefore worth stressing, in conclusion, that *Intervene* should always privilege the experience of those working in the context, with their knowledge of its history, culture and politics. ST has discredited itself in the past when it has claimed that it can replace local knowledge and experience with systemic prowess. For example, when it has asked those on the ground to address their problems using single, inflexible systems methodologies or tried to force-fit their problems into a limited range of 'systems archetypes'. CSP practitioners work together with decision-makers, employing systemic perspectives, systems methodologies, models and methods, to help them think insightfully about complexity and to enable them to bring about improvement in the situations they face.

References

Boyd, A., Brown, M. and Midgley, G. (2004). Systemic intervention for community OR: developing services with young people (under 16) living on the streets. In: *Community Operational Research: OR and Systems Thinking for Community Development* (eds G. Midgley and A.E. Ochoa-Arias), pp. 203–252. Kluwer.

Burrell, G. and Morgan, G. (1979). *Sociological Paradigms and Organizational Analysis*. London: Heinemann.

Carrizosa, A. (2002). Platforms for Critical Systems Practice. PhD thesis. University of Lincoln.

Chowdhury, R. (2019). *Systems Thinking for Management Consultants: Introducing Holistic Flexibility*. Springer.

Chowdhury, R. (2021). Applying VSM, SSM, and SAST for problem-structuring and problem-solving in health systems. *Systemist* 42 (2): 1–48.

Chowdhury, R. (2024). *Holistic Flexibility for Systems Thinking and Practice*. Routledge.

Chowdhury, R., Gregory, A. and Queah, M. (2023). Creative and flexible deployment of systems methodologies for child rights and child protection through holistic flexibility. *Systems Research and Behavioral Science*. https://doi.org/10.1002/sres.2955.

Churchman, C.W. (1970). Operations research as a profession. *Management Science* 17: B37–B53.

Fitzgerald, F.S. (1936). The crack-up. *Esquire*, February. www.classic.esquire.com.

Flood, R.L. (1995). *Solving Problem Solving*. Wiley.

Flood, R.L. (1999). *Rethinking the Fifth Discipline: Learning Within the Unknowable*. Routledge.

Flood, R.L. and Jackson, M.C. (1991). *Creative Problem Solving: Total Systems Intervention*. Wiley.

Gregory, A., Atkins, J., Midgley, G. and Hodgson, A. (2020). Stakeholder identification and engagement in problem structuring interventions. *European Journal of Operational Research* 283: 321–340.

Jackson, M.C. (1991). *Systems Methodology for the Management Sciences*. Plenum.

Jackson, M.C. (2000). *Systems Approaches to Management*. New York: Kluwer/Plenum.

Jackson, M.C. (2003). *Systems Thinking: Creative Holism for Managers*. Chichester: Wiley.

Jackson, M.C. (2019). *Critical Systems Thinking and the Management of Complexity*. Wiley.

Kuhn, T.S. (1970). *The Structure of Scientific Revolutions*, 2e. University of Chicago Press.

Midgley, G. (2000). *Systemic Intervention: Philosophy, Methodology, and Practice*. Kluwer/Plenum.

Midgley, G., Munlo, I. and Brown, M. (1998). The theory and practice of boundary critique: developing housing services for older people. *Journal of the Operational Research Society* 49: 467–478.

Ufoa D., Papadopoulos, T. and Midgley, G. (2018). Systemic lean intervention: enhancing lean with community operational research. *European Journal of Operational Research* 268: 1134–1148.

8

Critical Systems Practice 4 – *Check* on Progress

There are no whole truths; all truths are half-truths. It is trying to treat them as whole truths that plays the devil.

(Whitehead, 1956)

8.1 Introduction

This chapter discusses *Check*, the fourth stage of Critical Systems Practice (CSP). CSP does not expect in one intervention to bring about comprehensive and sustainable improvement. Ideally, it should be run as a continuous process which identifies and manages new issues as they arise. However, changing priorities, time and/or financial constraints, or just a wish to know what has been achieved so far, will at some point call a halt to a specific intervention. *Check* will then assume centre stage. An effective way of evaluating interventions in complex situations is necessary. A brief argument that this must be systems-based is provided before three alternative forms of systemic evaluation are presented and assessed. These are the use of 'single systems methodologies', the 'systems concepts' approach and a proposal based on Critical Systems Thinking (CST). The latter, it is argued, rests on firmer foundations and offers more complete guidelines for evaluations in complex situations. Also important in *Check* is to harness the learning gained during the intervention by reflecting on CST and CSP, and the systems approaches used. Finally, *Check* asks decision-makers and other stakeholders to use the results of the evaluation to initiate a discussion on the next steps. Examples are provided of the ways in which *Check* can be employed, and some concerns with this model of evaluation are discussed.

Critical Systems Thinking: A Practitioner's Guide, First Edition. Michael C. Jackson.
© 2024 John Wiley & Sons, Inc. Published 2024 by John Wiley & Sons, Inc.

8.2 *Check* – Preliminaries

The only contentious element of *Check*, I imagine, is the way it seeks to 'evaluate the improvements achieved' (see Figure 8.1). It is this to which the 'preliminaries' section is devoted. I give it space because, as we shall see, it relates directly to how best to use Systems Thinking (ST) in practice.

A fundamental commitment of CST is to bring about improvement in the world. To ensure this is honoured, a CSP intervention must be evaluated in terms of the

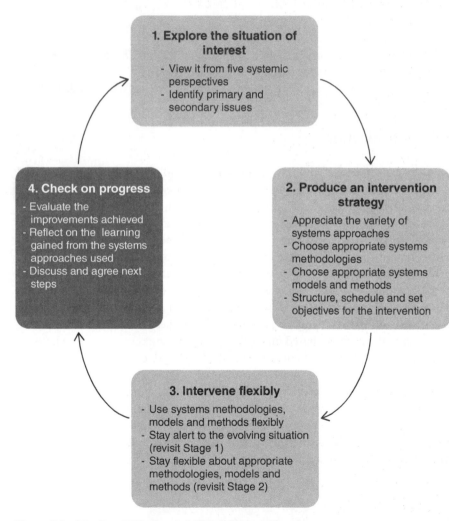

Figure 8.1 The four *EPIC* stages of Critical Systems Practice.

benefits, or otherwise, that its use brings to decision-makers and other stakehold-ers. Evaluation is defined by the American Evaluation Association (AEA) as '... a systematic process to determine merit, worth, value or significance' (AEA, 2022). Sounds simple. However, as it has sought to extend its practice, the professional evaluation community has come up against the same problems of the VUCA world (volatility, uncertainty, complexity and ambiguity) that ST has been seeking to address. It has been discovered that 'systematic' approaches are inappropriate in the face of multiple causalities, non-linearity, dynamic change, a pluralism of perspectives and the need to consider issues of inequality, sustainability and envi-ronmental impact. As Reynolds et al. put it:

> Problems of conventional evaluation models can be understood as an impoverished 'conversation' between realities (of non-linearity, indetermi-nate attributes, and ever-changing context), and models of evaluating such realities. (Reynolds et al., 2016, p. 662)

This has led many working in evaluation to embrace systems and complexity thinking to improve their models (Gates et al., 2021). Indeed, Imam et al. (2006) argued that the development of the evaluation field mirrors that of the systems field. Patton has been a strong and influential advocate for ST in the global eval-uation community. Thinking systemically is a guiding proposition in his principles-focused evaluation (Patton, 2018) and central to what he calls 'Blue Marble' evaluation (Patton, 2020). He wants evaluation to be developmental and to play an active role in helping to address the complex issues that confront the world today:

> Incorporating the Blue Marble perspective means looking beyond nation-state boundaries and across sector and issue silos to connect the global and the local, connect the human and ecological, and connect evaluative think-ing and methods with those trying to bring about global systems transfor-mation. (Patton, 2020, p. 1)

In the same vein, Schwandt and Gates (2021) sought to rethink the nature of evaluation for a world of 'wicked problems', arguing that evaluation should be seen as a process of 'developing' value rather than, in the traditional manner, 'determining' value. This requires a 'value-critical' stance that encourages learn-ing among all stakeholders and is best supported, they argued, by systems think-ing and complexity science (STCS).

In formulating an appropriate evaluation approach for CSP, we now review how systems thinkers have sought to contribute to evaluation theory and practice. They have done so in three ways: By demonstrating the value of 'single systems methodologies', by formulating a 'systems concepts' approach and by advancing a proposal based on CST.

8.2.1 Systemic Evaluation: The Single Systems Methodology Approach

It was the publication of the 'expert anthology', *Systems Concepts in Evaluation* (Williams and Imam, 2006), that gave impetus to the single systems methodology approach. The anthology was the product of debates between evaluation and systems practitioners, primarily at AEA meetings. In the anthology, System Dynamics (SD) (Burke), cybernetic (Fitch), soft systems (Attenborough; Tay, Bobby and Lim), Critical Systems Heuristics (CSH) (Reynolds) and complexity-based approaches (Eoyang) to evaluation were presented. Since that time, numerous papers have appeared suggesting how single systems methodologies and methods can contribute to enhancing evaluation work. Williams (2019) picked out the Viable System Model (VSM) and CSH as providing particularly useful sets of evaluation questions. The collectively authored paper 'Towards Systemic Evaluation' (Reynolds et al., 2016) has Marra urging evaluators to adopt a complexity framework and Gates arguing for CSH and Boundary Critique as means of attending to the interests of the marginalised in evaluation practice. Gates (2018) developed the case for CSH in another paper, seeing it as enabling evaluators to be '… critically reflective about valuing'. Schwandt (2015) and Schwandt and Gates (2021) further pressed the case for CSH and Boundary Critique, seeing them as providing a means of reflecting on the professional ethics of evaluators and as offering primary methodological support for their 'value-critical' approach to evaluation. De Souza (2022) offered a 'critical realist' approach to ST in evaluation which, she suggested, enables account to be taken of the causal effects of the social context on an evaluand. Stephens et al. have produced an evaluation guide for the UN Women Independent Evaluation Office which champions inclusive systemic evaluation in support of the UN's Sustainable Development Agenda. It

> … brings together transdisciplinary evaluation methods, re-thinks systemic evaluation methodology and introduces the Gender equality, Environments and Marginalized voices (GEMS) framework. (Stephens et al., 2018, p. 220)

This is an impressive body of work which has established that there are single systems methodologies that can contribute to evaluations conducted for a variety of specific purposes, for example, to assess whether the voices of the marginalised have been heard. But single methodologies reflect partial worldviews. We should not mistake any half-truth for the whole truth. If the aim is to evaluate a multi-methodological intervention using CSP and to bring about improvement in the context of 'general complexity', the evaluation must draw upon the range of systemic perspectives and itself be multimethodological. We must make the best of all the 'adequate' half-truths we possess.

8.2.2 Systemic Evaluation: The Systems Concepts Approach

The 'systems concepts' approach is the most influential in the evaluation community. Bob Williams sees it as a way of offering useful ST guidance to evaluators who might otherwise be alienated by the existence of multiple systems methodologies and methods:

> One way around this conundrum is to identify some concepts and ideas underpinning the majority of systems approaches in a way that can be linked to existing evaluation methodologies and methods. In effect, allowing evaluation to become more systemic without having to adopt, accommodate and learn specific systems methods. (Williams, 2019, p. 7)

The three 'systems concepts' first identified by Imam et al. (2006), as essential for evaluators, were 'entangled systems', 'perspectives' and 'boundaries'. In Williams (2019), these concepts or 'principles' remained unchanged – 'understand interrelationships', 'engage with perspectives' and 'reflect on boundaries'.

The 'systems concepts' approach espoused by Williams has been endorsed by many others interested in applying ST to evaluation. Hummelbrunner (see Reynolds et al., 2016) sees the concepts of 'interrelationships', 'perspectives' and 'boundaries' as constituting the essence of the systems approach. Schmidt-Abbey et al. (2020) regard 'interrelationships', 'multiple perspectives' and 'boundaries' as the three elements of ST that 'are particularly key for evaluation'. Patton (2020) sees ST as a 'guiding principle' of his developmental evaluation and associates this with 'understanding interrelationships', 'engaging with contrasting perspectives', 'reflecting ethically on boundaries' and 'dynamics'. The Systems in Evaluation Topical Interest Group of the AEA (SETIG, 2018) issued a report setting out four principles for effective use of ST in evaluation – 'interrelationships', 'perspectives', 'boundaries' and 'dynamics'.

A critic might wonder why these three or four systems concepts are more important for evaluators than, say, Checkland's (1981) 'two pairs of ideas which are the core of systems thinking: emergence and hierarchy, communication and control'. They would find no convincing explanation. They are not representative of all aspects of ST. The critic might then point out that, anyway, the meaning of concepts such as interrelationships, perspectives and boundaries is contested – i.e., they are interpreted differently in different systems traditions. For example, to a champion of the VSM, interrelationships refers to the connections between vital sub-systems, and of the system with its environment; to the user of Soft Systems

Methodology (SSM), it is the interrelationships between different worldviews that matter. The concept of boundary defines, for a SD practitioner, the variables that must be included in a model to ensure a reasonable representation of actual system behaviour; to an advocate of CSH, a boundary emerges from the facts and values driving a systems design. The SETIG document acknowledges the problem:

> The principles presented here will inevitably be interpreted differently when understood using different definitions of the core concepts. (SETIG, 2018, p. 7)

But it fails to recognise how damning this is for the systems concepts approach it recommends. Miller does:

> Yes, there are broad, shared similarities among various schools of [systems] thought ... but at the razor's edge of practice, the differences in concepts, methods, and practice can be stark ... As Jay Wright Forrester, the founder of system dynamics wisely observed in a 1992 interview, it is not enough to engage in an undisciplined use of select system concepts (e.g., boundaries, perspectives, and relationships) if the goal is to understand complex problems and engage in innovative social problem solving. (Miller, 2016, pp. 267–268)

The 'systems concepts' approach relies on the belief that the words we use (e.g., interrelationships, perspectives and boundaries) have a definite meaning independent of the 'language games' in which they are employed. Since what is known as 'the linguistic turn' in Western philosophy, this position is regarded as untenable by almost all philosophers. Instead, as Peirce argues, the 'signs' we use in language must be understood as part of the broader conceptual schemes in which they are embedded. Gallie, explaining Peirce's 'semiology', states:

> The belief ... that a sign can stand in a simple two term relationship, called its meaning, to its object, is thus seen to rest on a radical misconception of the kind of thing a sign is and of the way in which it functions. The truth is that a sign can function only as an element in a working system of signs. (Gallie, quoted in Bernstein, 2010, pp. 44–45)

Edmonds and Eidinow explain 'the linguistic turn' in terms of Wittgenstein's later philosophy:

> Moreover, if we examine how language is actually used, we will notice something else: that most terms have not just one use but a multiplicity of

uses, and that these various applications do not necessarily have a single component in common. Wittgenstein gave the example of the term 'game'. There are all sorts of games – patience, chess, badminton, Australian-rules football, kids playing catch. There are competitive games, cooperative games, team games, individual games, games of skill, games of luck, games with balls and games with cards. Question: what is it that unites all the games? Answer: nothing. There is no essence of 'game'. (Edmonds and Eidinow, 2001, pp. 180–181)

Systems concepts are understood and used in radically different ways. Consequently, it is always necessary to relate the concepts to systemic perspectives to give them precise meanings and grasp their usefulness. As Pepper (1942) had it: 'Concepts which have lost contact with their root metaphors are empty abstractions'. Attempts to 'simplify' ST by focussing on 'shared' concepts are flawed. Following Pepper's line of thought, proceeding this way is like Tolstoy's approach to finding the 'true religion':

> His means of obtaining this 'true religion' in conformity with 'reason and human knowledge', it soon appears, is to find out what beliefs are held in common by all religions after 'distortions' have been cleared away. Such a method is excellently calculated to sterilize the facts. Even if this method were properly used, it is clear the result could not be an induction from the facts concerned, but only from beliefs about the facts ... Tolstoy's 'true religion' is a little nest of hypostatizations, concepts subtly claiming cognitive value because of their very emptiness. (Pepper, 1942, pp. 124–127)

If systems concepts have a multiplicity of meanings, they will be interpreted differently by people working in evaluation just as they are by the different systems traditions. Concepts that are little more than empty abstractions, when detached from the systemic perspectives that give them meaning, are not going to be powerful enough to steer users in the direction of non-linear, non-mechanistic, engaged forms of evaluation. Their very emptiness makes them non-challenging.

Recently, the 'systems concepts' approach has been questioned from within the evaluation community itself. Walton et al. (2021) offer a comprehensive critique. In their view, it can offer a useful doorway into ST but, as a long-term strategy, it is weak. Evaluators can gain greater value by 'more deeply applying theory, methodologies, or approaches'. An analysis of the literature suggests that using STCS methodologies better equips evaluators to reflect on the strengths and weaknesses of alternative approaches, including their underpinning theory, match and refine methods for specific needs and engage in methodological innovation. The potential of STCS-informed evaluation can only be realised with

> ... deeper engagement with more detailed methods and associated theory underpinning different systems and complexity traditions and approaches. Such deeper engagement will support theory scaffolding, building upon understanding of systems with topic-specific theory. Deeper engagement will also support the refinement of evaluation theory associated with STCS use within evaluation .... In our view, this signifies a depth of engagement with a systems theory and methodology and an integration of this into the core evaluative process. (Walton et al., 2021, p. 167)

This is exactly what the CST approach to systemic evaluation offers.

8.2.3 Systemic Evaluation: The Critical Systems Thinking Approach

As mentioned in Section 3.5, CST follows Churchman and Ackoff's conception that improvement is about the progress of humankind in pursuit of the 'ideal'. Evaluation must then check whether progress is being made towards the various aspects of the ideal. The CST embodiment of this idea was developed by researchers at the Centre for Systems Studies, University of Hull. A paper written by Jackson and Medjedoub in 1988 set the scene by identifying three major types of evaluation approach based on their theoretical roots – 'goal-based', 'organismic' and 'multiple-actor' – and matching them to different contexts using Jackson and Keys' (1984) System of Systems Methodologies (SOSM). This work was carried forward by Amanda Gregory in a project, sponsored by the Leverhulme Trust, on the evaluation of Councils for Voluntary Service (Gregory, 1995). The first paper from the research (Gregory and Jackson, 1992a) again sought to tackle the confusion caused by a multiplicity of evaluation approaches, identifying four types. It went on to suggest a contingency approach which linked the four types to different contexts. A follow-up (Gregory and Jackson, 1992b) presented an analysis of the theoretical underpinnings of the four forms of evaluation and set out a system of evaluation methodologies again linked to the circumstances in which they might be used. This, and another paper by Gregory (1997), highlighted the need to give more attention in evaluation practice to identifying whether some stakeholders were disadvantaged by the intervention. It should be noted that all this work favoured a 'formative' or 'developmental' style of evaluation rather than a 'summative' or 'determining' approach.

In a later paper stemming from the Leverhulme project, Gregory (1996) took another crucial step in the development of the CST approach to systemic

evaluation by moving on from contingency thinking. Relating the four paradigms in evaluation theory to developments in organisation theory, she suggested that for much of their history, they have remained in 'isolation', warring
with one another. Using the thinking behind the SOSM, and Flood and Jackson's
(1991) Total Systems Intervention, she argued in favour of using them in a complementary way. Dismissive of attempts to 'integrate' the different approaches,
Gregory preferred 'multidimensional evaluation' where methodologies are used
together in parallel, engaging with one another through 'reflective conversation'. This allows for a more rounded evaluation and protects the different contributions the four paradigms can offer according to their distinctive theoretical
underpinnings:

> In this paper the practice of integration was assessed and it was concluded
> that whilst an integration might be achievable in practice, this should
> not be seen as a theoretical integration but more of a means of enabling
> the use of the methodologies in parallel through 'reflective conversation'.
> (Gregory, 1996, p. 306)

The foundations were in place that would enable CSP to incorporate a fully
'developmental' and multimethodological approach to evaluation into its practice.
We can turn to the details of the *Check* phase of CSP.

8.3   *Check* – Process

Check requires participants in CSP to evaluate the improvements achieved, reflect
on the learning gained and discuss and agree on the next steps. Figure 8.1 reminds
us of the elements of *Check* and where it sits in the *EPIC* process.

8.3.1   Evaluate the Improvements Achieved

Since the five 'systemic perspectives' all offer valuable ways of viewing the world
and promote useful ways of acting to improve it, a multiperspectival and multimethodological approach to evaluation is also essential. It is necessary to ensure
that the concerns of all five systemic perspectives are registered in any evaluation
and that their related methodologies are employed, if necessary, to conduct a thorough appraisal. An intervention may appear successful viewed through one systemic perspective but, looked at through alternative lenses, might show no
benefits or even seem to have made things worse. For example, an intervention
designed to improve efficiency might make an organisation less responsive to its
environment from the organismic perspective. One designed to make a system

more responsive to its environment might make things worse, from the purposeful systemic perspective, if the changes provoke conflict because they are poorly communicated and forced through. From the societal/environmental perspective, Freire and Macedo's (1987) claim that an adult literacy program in Guinea-Bissau was a success because it raised people's awareness of their position in society might seem impressive. It will ring hollow from the mechanical systemic perspective because the intervention failed to meet targets in terms of the numbers taught to read and write.

A successful CSP intervention will want to see improvement from all five perspectives. Over the long term, an intervention should score well on improving efficiency and efficacy (according to the mechanical perspective); awareness of interconnections and unintended consequences (according to the interrelationships perspective); promoting viability and resilience (according to the organismic perspective); attention to stakeholder purposes (according to the purposeful perspective); championing empowerment, emancipation and the natural environment (according to the societal/environmental perspective). I have suggested (Jackson, 2019) that a bar chart be constructed at the beginning of an intervention showing the current state of a situation of interest according to indicators reflecting the different systemic perspectives. As the process of change proceeds, the bar chart can be updated with estimates of how things are going according to the different criteria. At any time during an intervention or at the end of a particular project, an assessment can be made of how things stand in terms of all the criteria. Primitive, but the extent and nature of the trade-offs would provoke constant discussion and possibly a rethinking of dominant methodology or methodologies.

That CST encourages *Check* to employ the five systemic perspectives in any evaluation provides it with advantages compared to the other two systemic evaluation approaches. In any detailed evaluation, *Check* can also employ the systems methodologies related to those perspectives to provide an appropriate toolbox of evaluative approaches and questions suitable for the context. The use of single systems methodologies in evaluation has generated considerable learning, and this can be drawn upon to inform *Check* at this point. It is also worth considering, as we shall see, how CSP and the systems concepts approach might be reconciled to achieve a 'golden mean' of evaluation theory and practice.

8.3.2   Reflect on the Learning Gained About the Systems Approaches Used

CSP, as explained in Section 3.5, is used in the 'action research' mode. The *Check* stage should, therefore, contribute not only to evaluating any improvement in the situation of concern but also to improving the means of bringing about improvement. Any use of CSP is, in principle, capable of yielding learning about the systemic perspectives, the multimethodology and the individual systems approaches employed, as well as about the system of interest. To make this possible, the action researcher needs to be clear up-front about the present state of knowledge and seize the learning opportunities provided by an intervention. Checkland and Holwell (1998) set out what is needed. Figure 8.2 shows the cycle of action research as they prescribe it. The action researcher first seeks out a situation of concern that can yield learning relevant to their research themes. They then negotiate entry into that area of concern (A), declaring in advance the framework of ideas (F) and methodology (M) they will use in trying to bring about improvements. They take part in action in the situation and reflect on what happens using F and M. This yields findings that are relevant to F, M and A, and some new research themes. In action research, no two situations are ever the same, so the results cannot be justified based on the scientific criterion of repeatability. However, Checkland and Holwell argue, rigour can be introduced by declaring the F and M in advance and keeping careful records of what exactly occurs in A. The outcomes can then be related back to and described in terms of the F and M. This

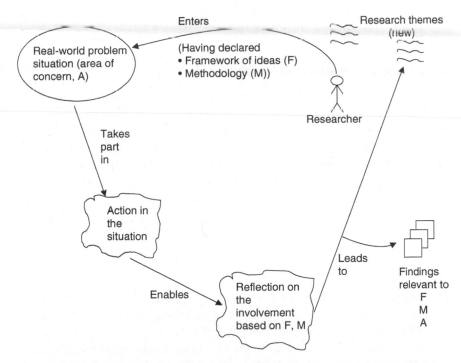

Figure 8.2   The cycle of action research. *Source:* From Checkland and Holwell, 1998, reproduced by permission of John Wiley.

allows the *recoverability* of the whole research story by someone standing outside the process and enables coherent debate about what happened and why.

Throughout their history, CST and CSP have been used to try to improve 'areas of concern'. This 'action in the situation' produced learning about F that saw the abandonment of the original metaparadigm orientation, the reconstitution of CST around discursive pluralism and then the rebuild that placed pragmatism at the heart of the 'framework of ideas' (see Chapter 3). The same engagement saw learning about M which produced the refinements leading from Total Systems Intervention to early versions of CSP, and to CSP as now conceptualised (see Chapter 4). The improvements made to CST and CSP as a result have enhanced their ability to understand, intervene and improve areas of concern. The operation of this cycle of action research, the findings and their impact on the development of CST and CSP are fully documented in Jackson (2019), and so this research is *recoverable* in Checkland and Holwell's terms.

Most participants in a CSP intervention will not be interested in such formal research. Nevertheless, they should reflect on what they have learned. Exposure to the range of systemic perspectives and methodologies will have enhanced their cognitive flexibility – an attribute essential for working with multidimensional complexity. It is important that the learning is carried forward in future work.

8.3.3   Discuss and Agree Next Steps

The priorities of the decision-makers and other stakeholders will determine what happens when an intervention ends. If there is satisfaction that the initial objectives have been met on schedule, then agreement might be reached on another CSP project. The results of the evaluation, perhaps displayed on a bar chart, will suggest where future efforts should concentrate, for example, what other systems methodologies can usefully be brought into play. The aim of a prolonged CSP intervention is to achieve and demonstrate improvement viewed from the range of systemic perspectives.

8.4   *Check* – Examples

The standard way of doing *Check* is to use it to measure progress in an ongoing intervention or to evaluate the results when an intervention ends. In the case of Hull University Business School (HUBS), outlined in the previous chapter, all five systemic perspectives were in continuous use. Initiatives to improve the system of interest were constantly evaluated to see what impact they were having on efficiency, efficacy, viability, resilience, effectiveness, serving stakeholder purposes, mutual understanding, empowerment, emancipation and sustainability. A check was kept on whether any unintended consequences of the initiatives could be predicted or discerned. Occasionally, this type of informal approach turned into more rigorous evaluations using methodologies such as the VSM and CSH. Towards the end of my time as Dean, the research activity of HUBS came under scrutiny. It was apparent that an earlier attempt to create transdisciplinary research centres, focussed on significant external issues, had failed. The disciplinary groups had reasserted themselves, and apart from in the Centre for Systems Studies and the Logistics Institute, research was largely isolated from its environment (or, at least, the non-academic parts of the environment). Another initiative was launched. All existing groups were abolished with a view to starting from scratch, and considerable encouragement was given to new transdisciplinary centres. There were no Research Excellence Framework assessment deadlines looming, so chaos could reign for a while, hopefully allowing new groups to self-organise. The research function could then be redesigned using the VSM as a guide. I was soon to leave, and the initiative failed. No new groups became established and, yet again, old disciplinary allegiances came to the fore. Looking back from the comfort of retirement and foregrounding *Check*, I recognise that the initiative was bound to fail unless accompanied by a redirection of resources using an engineering approach and a cultural shift accomplished by working with SSM.

Check can also be used to suggest how change initiatives could have been carried out better. This example draws on the work of Luis Sambo (2009), former World Health Organization (WHO) Regional Director for Africa, looking at how a large-scale health intervention in which he was involved could have been better managed if it had adopted CSP. The problem context was the health system in an African country with a population of around nine million. Economic performance was poor, and poverty was rising. Health indicators were deteriorating due to a lack of money, human resource issues and a dearth of vital medicines and other health technologies. A new government undertook reform, but twelve years after this initiative, major problems remained. Reflecting on what had gone wrong, with the benefit of his PhD work on CST, Sambo concluded that those responsible for the reform were ill-equipped to understand and react to the dynamic interconnectedness of the situation they faced. The only theoretical and methodological assistance available drew upon a 'positivist' understanding of health systems – in other words, a mechanical systemic perspective. If it had been possible to view the context with the help of other relevant systemic perspectives and to employ a variety of systems methodologies, aware of their different strengths and weaknesses, then the chances of overall improvement would have been higher. In Sambo's view, a flexible and informed combination of the VSM, SSM and CSH was required to provide support in pursuit of the reform goals. The VSM could have helped manage structural issues of centralisation and decentralisation, resilience, coordination and control. SSM could have been used to enhance mutual understanding among stakeholders and produce a coalition in favour of change. In this respect, three 'conceptual models' are suggested that would have guided more productive discussions about how to integrate the various health-related programmes. The use of CSH would have provided a constant check on whether the interests of all parties affected by the reforms were being considered and whether the outcomes led to improved health for all citizens. Understanding and use of theoretical and methodological pluralism, Sambo concluded, could have helped embed the reform agenda and yielded significantly better results.

The issue of preparedness for health emergencies looms large in the aftermath of recent epidemics. The example of COVID-19, used in Section 5.4 to illustrate *Explore*, also demonstrates how *Check* could be employed to evaluate the ability of a health system to cope with future crises. Using the systemic perspectives focuses attention on different aspects of preparedness. Does the health system have plans, the necessary resources and efficient processes in place? Have vital interrelationships, for example, between hospitals and the care sector, been considered? Is the health system agile enough to cope and are responsibilities delegated to the appropriate levels? Is there trust among the stakeholders and a sufficient alignment of purposes? Has the specific impact on minority and marginalised groups been examined?

A variant on this theme is to use *Check* to evaluate whether a field of research can adequately support practitioners in the face of the complexity arising in their area of concern. Papers by Jackson and Sambo (2020) and Sambo and Jackson (2021) consider the theoretical and methodological capacity of current Health Systems Research (HSR) to enable health practitioners to understand and meet the challenges posed by emergencies such as the 2014 Ebola epidemic. Luis Sambo was responsible for coordinating the local response to the Ebola outbreak on behalf of the WHO. We found that HSR has a limited appreciation of ST, and this hinders its theoretical awareness and its ability to improve practice. Three issues stood out. First, a mismatch between how health 'systems' are conceptualised and how they are addressed. They are seen as 'complex adaptive systems', but a 'restricted complexity' rather than a 'general complexity' approach is advocated. Second, a failure to embrace the full range of systems theories and methodologies. Overwhelmingly, HSR favours SD at the expense of other systems methodologies. Using only the SD lens to view health systems and address their issues ignores the opportunities provided by other possible ways of seeing and intervening. For example, reflecting on whether VSM principles of viability and resilience have been respected in health system design; viewing the issues as being about multiple stakeholders with different perspectives that must be reconciled; or considering that the system's purposes might be distorted to serve powerful groups. Third, a failure to consider how systems methodologies might be used in combination to tackle the multidimensional character of public health emergencies, as exemplified in the Ebola epidemic. The discussion that does exist about using them in combination is superficial and ignores the decades of work that have gone into developing multimethodological practice in CST. *Check* demonstrates that HSR needs empowering by CST and CSP if it is to successfully engage with the interacting technical, organisational, social, political and economic forces at play in emergencies such as the 2014 Ebola epidemic (Sambo and Jackson, 2021).

CST has been using *Check* throughout its history to interrogate other sub-disciplines of management science, seeking to expose shortcomings and suggest what is needed to make them more effective in their domains of practice. Examples are Total Quality Management (Flood, 1993), Evaluation (Gregory, 1996), Information Systems (Jackson, 1992), Knowledge Management (Jackson, 2005), Logistics (Mears-Young and Jackson, 1997) and Project Management (Jackson, 2019).

Finally, Peter Wandwesi, Head of the UN Independent System-Wide Evaluation Mechanism (UNISWEM), has identified CSP as the ideal instrument for the form of 'meta-evaluation' promoted by Scriven (Wandwesi, 2022). Meta-evaluation is defined as the 'evaluation of evaluations' and seeks to judge the strengths and weaknesses of a given evaluation. The role of CSP is to gauge the comprehensiveness of an evaluation by using the systemic perspectives, and its thoroughness by using systems methodologies. Applying *Check* to the 'Joint Evaluation of the Role and Contribution of the United Nations System in the Republic of South Africa' (UNDP, 2009), for example, reveals the limited range of evaluation criteria used, with organismic, purposeful and societal/environmental concerns receiving insufficient coverage from a CSP perspective.

8.5 *Check* – Issues

In discussing the issues that arise with the CST approach to evaluation, I am aided by the considered response from Michael Quinn Patton (2023) to my journal article on *Check* (Jackson, 2023a). Before setting out my reply, it is necessary to say that I agree with him completely that systemic evaluation should be non-sequential, iterative, useful, developmental and engaged and that it finds philosophical justification in pragmatism. The CST approach meets all these criteria. On some points, however, we differ (Jackson, 2023b).

Patton suggests that, by giving space to the mechanical systemic perspective, CSP encourages the failed linear, logic-based model of evaluation. This is a strange point. I do think it is important in any evaluation to give thought to whether the chosen goals are being achieved efficiently. Nothing wrong with that, surely, when CSP also highlights four other systemic lenses – interrelationships, organismic, purposeful and societal-environmental – and promotes them as equally valid. Becoming comfortable viewing the world through these alternative perspectives provides the evaluator with an understanding of the limitations of mechanistic thinking. Its importance continues to be recognised, but it can no longer pose a danger by claiming to have the whole truth.

Patton argues that the CSP approach to evaluation is too complicated and demanding to respond to the contingencies of most evaluation situations, for example, constraints imposed by time and resources. I am clear that it represents an 'ideal type' that will require adjusting in any situation in which it is used. In effect, CSP seeks to provide a 'maximum specification' for systemic evaluation drawing upon my understanding of ST as it currently exists. Employing systemic perspectives that have served the human species well, it asks questions about whether an intervention has efficiently achieved its goals; whether it has considered the wide range of factors impacting the situation and the possible consequences of any intervention; if it has ensured that the system of concern is more adaptive and resilient than before; if there is increased mutual understanding among stakeholders; and whether it has involved the disadvantaged and improved their lot. This may be a 'maximum specification', but it corresponds to what the Organization for Economic Cooperation and Development (OECD) is calling for when it insists on six 'evaluation criteria' ('relevance', 'coherence', 'effectiveness', 'efficiency', 'impact' and 'sustainability') complemented by a 'human rights and gender equality lens' (OECD, 2021). CSP provides methodologies to guide and implement evaluations relevant to these different criteria. These methodologies can, in turn, easily be employed to derive the comprehensive range of evaluation questions the OECD criteria demand.

Patton is in favour of the 'systems concepts' approach to systemic evaluation. He sees these concepts (perspectives, interrelationships, boundaries, dynamics) as 'sensitizing'; as providing a 'minimum specification' that opens the door to systemic evaluation for people who are not systems specialists. For him, they play this role well because they are easily understood. In my view, they have multiple meanings but are likely to be interpreted and used according to the dictates of the dominant mechanical perspective. The traditional systems engineer, for example, will have no trouble understanding them in terms of a mechanistic mindset and incorporating them into a linear methodology. I agree that we must start somewhere in challenging traditional forms of evaluation, but we also need to provide some clear direction. Concepts which are little more than empty abstractions when detached from the traditions that give them meaning are not going to be powerful enough to steer users in the direction of non-linear, non-mechanistic, engaged forms of evaluation. Providing 'minimum specifications' for systemic evaluation is insufficient.

Between the 'maximum specification' of CST and the 'minimum specification' of the 'systems concepts' approach will lie the 'golden mean' in any actual case of systemic evaluation. However, I make no apologies for insisting that CSP offers a more ambitious use of ST and provides a necessary standard against which any actual systemic evaluation can be measured to determine where it falls short because it is compromised in some way.

8.6 Conclusion

Just one reflection to conclude this part of the book on CSP. The approach is iterative, and in a prolonged intervention, there is little difference between the *Explore* and *Check* phases. Even in writing this linear account of CSP, I have struggled to separate them. In an actual CSP intervention, all four phases bleed into one another, occupying the mind simultaneously. The systemic perspectives and the systems methodologies share an intimate relationship. Understanding the varied perspectives allows the different methodologies to be used to their best advantage. Using any one methodology in practice then reinforces the value of its linked perspective. Using the set of methodologies demonstrates the value of working flexibly with different worldviews.

References

AEA. (2022). *What Is Evaluation?* https://www.eval.org.

Bernstein, R.J. (2010). *The Pragmatic Turn*. Polity.

Checkland, P.B. (1981). *Systems Thinking, Systems Practice*. Wiley.

Checkland, P.B. and Holwell, S. (1998). *Information, Systems and Information Systems*. Wiley.

De Souza, D.E. (2022). A critical realist approach to systems thinking in evaluation. *Evaluation*. https://doi.org/10.1177/13563890211064639.

Edmonds, D. and Eidinow, J. (2001). *Wittgenstein's Poker*. Faber and Faber.

Flood, R.L. (1993). *Beyond TQM*. Wiley.

Flood, R.L. and Jackson, M.C. (1991). *Creative Problem Solving: Total Systems Intervention*. Wiley.

Freire, P. and Macedo, C. (1987). *Literacy: Reading the Word and the World*. Bergin & Harvey.

Gates, E.F. (2018). Toward valuing with critical systems heuristics. *American Journal of Evaluation* 39: 201–220.

Gates, E.F., Walton, M., Vidueira, P. and McNall, M. (2021). Introducing systems- and complexity-informed evaluation. *New Directions for Evaluation* 170: 13–25.

Gregory, A.J. (1995). Organizational Evaluation: A Complementarist Approach. PhD thesis. University of Hull.

Gregory, A.J. (1996). The road to integration: reflections on the development of organizational evaluation theory and practice. *Omega* 24: 295–307.

Gregory, A.J. (1997). Evaluation practice and the tricky issue of coercive contexts. *Systems Practice* 10: 589–609.

Gregory, A.J. and Jackson, M.C. (1992a). Evaluating organizations: a systems and contingency approach. *Systems Practice* 5: 37–60.

Gregory, A.J. and Jackson, M.C. (1992b). Evaluation methodologies: a system for use. *Journal of the Operational Research Society* 43: 19–28.

Imam, I., LaGoy, A. and Williams, B. (2006). Introduction. In: *Systems Concepts in Evaluation: An Expert Anthology* (eds B. Williams and I. Imam), pp. 3–10. American Evaluation Association.

Jackson, M.C. (1992). An integrated programme for critical thinking in information systems research. *Journal of Information Systems* 2: 83–95.

Jackson, M.C. (2005). Reflections on knowledge management from a critical systems perspective. *Knowledge Management Research and Practice* 3: 187–196.

Jackson, M.C. (2019). *Critical Systems Thinking and the Management of Complexity*. Wiley.

Jackson, M.C. (2023a). Critical systems practice 4: *Check* – evaluating and reflecting on a multimethodological intervention, *Systems Research and Behavioral Science* 40: 617–632. https://doi.org/10.1002/sres.2912.

Jackson, M.C. (2023b). In search of a golden mean for systemic evaluation: a response to Michael Quinn Patton. *Systems Research and Behavioral Science* 40: 636–638.

Jackson, M.C. and Keys, P. (1984). Towards a system of systems methodologies. *Journal of the Operational Research Society* 35: 473–486.

Jackson, M.C. and Medjedoub, S. (1988). Designing evaluation systems: theoretical groundings and a practical intervention. In: *Cybernetics and Systems'88* (ed. R. Trappl), pp. 165–171. Kluwer.

Jackson, M.C. and Sambo, L. (2020). Health systems research and critical systems thinking: the case for partnership. *Systems Research and Behavioral Science* 37: 3–22.

Mears-Young, B. and Jackson, M.C. (1997). Integrated logistics – call in the revolutionaries! *Omega* 25: 605–618.

Miller, R.L. (2016). On messes, systems thinking, and evaluation: a response to Patton. *American Journal of Evaluation* 37: 266–269.

OECD. (2021). *Applying Evaluation Criteria Thoughtfully*. OECD.

Patton, M.Q. (2018). *Principles-focused Evaluation: The Guide*. The Guilford Press.

Patton, M.Q. (2020). *Blue Marble Evaluation: Premises and Principles*. The Guilford Press.

Patton, M.Q. (2023). Letter to the editor, *Systems Research and Behavioral Science* 40: 633–635.

Pepper, S.C. (1942). *World Hypotheses*. Berkeley and Los Angeles: University of California Press.

Reynolds, M., Gates, E., Hummelbrunner, R., Marra, M. and Williams, B. (2016). Towards systemic evaluation. *Systems Research and Behavioral Science* 33: 662–673.

Sambo, L. (2009). Health Systems Thinking: The Need for a More Critical Approach. PhD thesis. University of Hull.

Sambo, L. and Jackson, M.C. (2021). Empowering health systems research to engage with technical, organizational, social and economic forces: lessons from the 2014 Ebola epidemic. *Systems Research and Behavioral Science* 38: 307–320.

Schmidt-Abbey, B., Reynolds, M. and Ison, R. (2020). Towards systemic evaluation in turbulent times – second-order practice shift. *Evaluation* 26: 205–226.

Schwandt, T.A. (2015). Reconstructing professional ethics and responsibility: implications of critical systems thinking. *Evaluation* 21: 462–466.

Schwandt, T.A. and Gates, E.F. (2021). *Evaluating and Valuing in Social Research*. The Guildford Press.

SETIG. (2018). *Principles for Effective Use of Systems Thinking in Evaluation*. American Evaluation Association.

Stephens, A., Lewis, E.D. and Reddy, S. (2018). Towards an inclusive systemic evaluation for the SDGs: gender equality, environments and marginalized voices (GEMSs). *Evaluation* 24: 220–236.

UNDP Independent Evaluation Office. (2009). *Joint Evaluation of the Role and Contribution of the United Nations System in the Republic of South Africa*. UNDP.

Walton, M., Gates, E.F. and Vidueira, P. (2021). Insights and future directions for systems and complexity-informed evaluation. *New Directions for Evaluation* 170: 159–171.

Wandwesi, P. (2022). The case for enhancing the quality of primary evaluations through metaevaluation in developing country contexts. *Africanus: Journal of Development Studies*. https://doi.org/10.25159/2663-6522/5708.

Whitehead, A.N. (1956). *Dialogues of Alfred North Whitehead*. Mentor.

Williams, B. (2019). *Systemic Evaluation Design: A Workbook*, 2e. https://gumroad.com/evaldesign.

Williams, B. and Imam, I. (Eds) (2006). *Systems Concepts in Evaluation: An Expert Anthology*. American Evaluation Association.

Part 3

Towards a Systems Thinking World

Since synergy is the only word in our language meaning behavior of wholes unpredicted by behavior of parts, it is clear that society does not think there are behaviors of whole systems unpredicted by their separate parts.
(Buckminster Fuller, R., 1969, *Operating Manual for Spaceship Earth*. Lars Muller Publishers)

9

Critical Systems Leadership: Overcoming the Implementation Barriers

A leader is best when people barely know he exists, when his work is done, his aim fulfilled, they will say: we did it ourselves.

(Lao Tzu, c. 400 BCE)

9.1 Introduction

The need for Systems Thinking (ST) as an essential aid in managing apparently intractable situations of concern is increasingly recognised. The chapter begins by providing examples of the call for ST from institutions of all types – international, governmental, public sector, private, charitable and professional. Documented cases of the successful use of ST to bring about improvement are less common. ST is not realising its potential to enhance decision-making because there are barriers to its widespread acceptance. The way ST is presented and perceived, as well as various cultural and societal constraints, hinder it from becoming an established mode of thinking and acting. Various means of overcoming these barriers are suggested. As an example, universities must act to close the capability gap between the demand for more systems thinkers and the paucity of supply. The final section of the chapter builds on previous discussions of Critical Systems Thinking (CST) and Critical Systems Practice (CSP) to suggest the type of leadership approach necessary if systems thinkers are to flourish in the current environment and advance the cause of ST. The characteristics of Critical Systems Leadership (CSL) are outlined. These consist of certain attributes the leadership team should possess, a flexible mindset that embraces the various 'systemic perspectives' and an understanding of when to employ the related systems methodologies.

Critical Systems Thinking: A Practitioner's Guide, First Edition. Michael C. Jackson.
© 2024 John Wiley & Sons, Inc. Published 2024 by John Wiley & Sons, Inc.

9.2   The Growing Interest in Systems Thinking

We restrict this discussion on the growing interest in ST to a few examples, primarily derived from international institutions, the UK Government, businesses and project management.

The United Nations Development Programme (UNDP, 2021), the Organization for Economic Cooperation and Development (OECD, 2020) and the World Health Organization (WHO), through the Alliance for Health Policy and Systems Research (AHPSR, 2019), are three international bodies promoting the use of ST. The UNDP, for example, in its Strategic Plan for 2022–2025, argued that the only way the United Nation's Strategic Development Goals (SDGs) can be achieved is by delivering integrated solutions through a systems approach that addresses their points of connection:

> COVID-19 reminded the world that development challenges are dynamic, interconnected puzzles of multidimensional risk that require systemic solutions. (UNDP, 2021, p. 3)

The endorsement of ST, from these and other international institutions, is greatly welcomed. It should, however, be noted that most of the supporting documents adopt a 'restricted complexity' perspective and prioritise a modelling approach to 'complex adaptive systems'. In the OECD report, it is 'next-generation systems analysis models' that are apparently up to the job. The work of the AHPSR, as we saw in the previous chapter, is being held back by an attachment to System Dynamics (SD) as its preferred systems methodology (Jackson and Sambo, 2020).

The spread of interest in ST in UK Government circles is impressive. Sir Patrick Vallance, as Head of UK Government Science and Engineering, launched three documents designed 'to act as a springboard into ST for civil servants', stating that:

> It is vital that Civil Servants are able to confidently and effectively engage with the complexity and uncertainty inherent in the problems we tackle in Government. Systems thinking approaches allow us to understand the full impact of interventions across department and policy area boundaries – ultimately leading to better solutions. (Vallance, 2022, p. 2)

The first of these resources, *The Civil Servant's Systems Thinking Journey* (GO-Science, 2022a), briefly describes ST and suggests that it should be 'weaved … throughout the policy design process'. The second, *An Introductory Systems Thinking Toolkit for Civil Servants* (GO-Science, 2022b), aims to introduce ST tools and relate them to the stages of the policy cycle – confirm the goal, understand the system, co-design and test and implement, monitor and evaluate. The third, a *Systems Thinking Case Study Bank* (2022c), provides 14 case studies of ST being used by civil and public servants. The three documents are complemented by a *Systems Leadership Guide* produced by the Department for Business, Energy and Industrial Strategy (BEIS, 2023).

It is emphasised in the documents that what is offered is a 'starting point' from which civil servants can begin their ST journey and that, if certain tools are highlighted, it is because they have 'relevance and accessibility to civil servants' and 'align to demanding time scales' (GO-Science, 2022b). The 'tools' that receive the most attention are derived from SD. An excellent Causal Loop Diagram, highlighting interactions of importance in the roll-out of electric vehicles (built to inform the Net-Zero Strategy), finds itself cited in three of the four documents. There are frequent references to 'understanding the system', 'revealing structures', 'identifying structural causes', 'identifying system archetypes' and 'identifying appropriate leverage points'. These make sense from an SD perspective but not from the point of view of other systems methodologies. The emphasis on SD is no doubt a result of the ease with which its methods can be incorporated into the four policy design stages. In other words, it is the least challenging of the systems methodologies, requiring no great shift in mindset. The danger is that these tools are likely to be absorbed into the existing ways of thinking of civil servants. The documents acknowledge other 'powerful systems thinking techniques' (Viable System Model [VSM], Soft Systems Methodology [SSM], Critical Systems Heuristics [CSH] and CST) that do require a significant shift in mindset – an embrace of alternative 'systemic perspectives' – but there is only brief mention of these in the Appendix of the *Toolkit*. They must be given more attention in promised future versions of the documents.

Three further reports championing ST from UK Government sources should be mentioned. Firstly, a 'Niteworks' White Paper, *Holistic Complex System Intervention Evaluation – Understanding the Nature of Defence Capability* (Jordan and Wilkinson, 2017), sets out an approach with many similarities to CSP in the way it advocates coping with uncertainty. A shift in mindset from reductionism to 'holistic critical thinking' is seen as necessary. This entails 'a multimethod approach ... exploratory and pragmatic', involving 'multiple investigations to explore multiple alternatives'. Secondly, the Department for Environment, Food and Rural Affairs (DEFRA) has issued a document on *Integrating a systems approach into DEFRA* (DEFRA, 2022). This finds value in both 'people-focused' systems approaches, such as SSM and CSH, and 'model-focused' approaches involving systems mapping and recommends 'mixing methods from across the systems field and beyond'. Thirdly, a learning resource for 'Systems Thinking and Practice' compiled for the Foreign, Commonwealth & Development Office (FCDO) draws on the GO-Science *Toolkit* and a wide range of other ST and complexity theory sources. It identifies 'three key aspects of systems thinking' (the usual suspects – relationships, perspectives and boundaries), offers useful reflections on embedding ST into FCDO business processes and how to overcome institutional barriers to ST, and provides some case study material (Woodhill and Millican, 2023).

The level of interest in ST in the UK civil service is indicated by the fact that, as of December 2023, there were over 700 members of the Systems Thinking in Government (STIG) interest group.

Two examples now of business thinking that promotes ST and CSP. Bart Madden, former managing director of Credit Suisse HOLT, offered a 'pragmatic theory of the firm' which treats it as a holistic system. For Madden, a firm's purpose should consist of 'four mutually reinforcing goals':

- Communicate a *vision* that can inspire employees 'to work for a firm committed to behaving ethically and making the world a better place'
- *Survive and prosper* 'through continual gains in efficiency and sustained innovation'
- 'Work continuously to *sustain win-win relationships* with all the firm's stakeholders'
- Take care of *future generations* by embracing 'a genuine commitment to the sustainability of the environment'

(Madden, 2020, pp. 26–27; italics in the original)

Success in achieving this fourfold purpose depends on a firm nurturing its 'knowledge building' proficiency. This, in turn, requires staff at all levels to cultivate a holistic understanding of complexity, embrace experimentation and challenge deeply held assumptions that the firm holds about itself. All this, as Madden made clear, is deeply rooted in ST. He quoted Paul Polman, the former CEO of Unilever:

I truly believe that future leaders will be systems thinkers. It is inconceivable that anyone will successfully steer companies, or countries, through our volatile world without understanding the inter-dependencies between the systems on which we depend. (Polman, quoted in Madden, 2023)

In Madden's (2023) view, 'as managers rise in the corporate hierarchy, the more important becomes their systems-thinking skill'. His multidimensional view of purpose, with four aspects that must be pursued simultaneously and balanced, is of course resonant of CSP, of which he is an enthusiastic supporter.

John Montgomery and Mark Van Clieaf's book on how companies can transition to net-zero business models and play a role in creating a net-zero economy is also consistent with the logic of CSP. Different domains of ST are seen as necessary at different levels:

> ... transition to a net zero economy requires leadership with three distinct domains of systems thinking: operational, business systems, and global systems. (Montgomery and Van Clieaf, 2023, p. 237)

The operational level covers eco-efficiency processes – for example, replacing a fleet with electric delivery vans – and requires relatively simple systems skills. At the business systems level, there is greater complexity and more sophisticated ST is necessary, for example, to design new business models. The global systems level, covering industry-wide and economy-wide systems and ecosystems, is still more complex and requires an ST competence capable of facilitating the emergence of new shared norms and values. The authors call for a shift to stakeholder capitalism, paying proper attention to the interdependency of people and planet, and favourably cite Kate Raworth's 'doughnut economics' in which the pursuit of various requirements for human well-being are prioritised within the constraints of the planet's boundaries.

Turning to project management, CST was a key input into the original International Centre for Complex Project Management's (ICCPM) *Competency Standards* (ICCPM, 2012). A later ICCPM roundtable meeting on 'harnessing emergence in complex projects' upheld the importance of this mode of thinking. A pragmatic approach to project management is recommended:

> Consequently, worldview is that lens through which we view, interpret and understand our world. Importantly, worldview is best understood as an epistemological artifact with associated ontological assumption, rather than as an ontological mirror of reality. (ICCPM, 2020)

This approach can be translated into practice by employing a multiparadigmatic appreciation of projects and appropriate ST capabilities. The latest ICCPM 'Complex Project Leadership Competency Standards', authorised by the Australian Department of Defence, reinforce this orientation. They recommend 'a pragmatic complexity lens' capable of dealing with projects of different degrees of complexity. This requires going beyond classical approaches while encompassing them. Five 'units of complexity' competence are prescribed: 'drive systemic thinking and action', 'focus strategically on delivering project outcomes', 'engage collaboratively with stakeholders', 'exercise contextual leadership awareness' and 'apply system governance and delivery assurance' (ICCPM, 2023).

The clamour for ST, and sometimes CST, also emanates from UK local government (Hobbs, 2019); public sector organisations such as the UK National Health Service (NHS, 2017); charities such as Oxfam and the Lankelly Chase Foundation; the UK Institution of Civil Engineers (ICE, 2020,2022); the Institution of Chemical Engineers (IChemE, 2021); consultancy (Chowdhury, 2019; Deloitte, 2023; Ramaswamy et al., 2023); logistics and supply chain management (Wilden et al., 2023); and many other places. Unfortunately, increasing advocacy has not been matched with action on any scale. ST has yet to realise its potential as a significant aid to decision-makers grappling with complex situations of interest. It is rather, as Nguyen et al. showed in the case of public policy:

> ... that there is growing interest in how ST concepts and tools can aid decision- and policy-making in the government and public sector. However, public policy has yet to exploit the full potential of ST and its full range of methods. (Nguyen et al., 2023a)

And, as El-Jardali et al., suggested, in the health domain:

> Our study showed that while there is general interest and acknowledgment of the relevance and value of ST for health systems research and policy-making, experience in applying it has been limited in the EMR [Eastern Mediterranean Area]. (El-Jardali et al., 2014)

It is incumbent on the systems community, having generated such interest in ST, to go further and help ensure that it is translated into practice. In the next section, the discussion turns to how ST can achieve its full potential by overcoming the various hurdles that stand in the way of implementation.

9.3 Overcoming the Barriers to Implementation

Many of the barriers limiting the implementation of ST are common across different areas of practice. I will, therefore, draw on a range of literature in teasing out some general points. The following account relies on the Canadian Academy of Health Sciences and the Academy of Medical Sciences (CAHS & AMS) report (2021), El-Jardali et al. (2014), Haynes et al. (2020), Nguyen et al. (2023a, 2023b), Nolan-McSweeney et al. (2023), Palmer and Cavicchi (2023), Ramaswamy, et al. (2023), WHO (2012, 2022) and Woodhill and Millican (2023). The barriers arise from misconceptions about ST, from problems with the presentation of ST and from contextual factors. They are discussed below together with ideas about how they can be overcome.

9.3.1 Misconceptions About Systems Thinking

ST is seen by many as technically difficult, time-consuming and costly. This is sometimes true when ST proceeds from a 'restricted complexity' position and aims for a comprehensive model of a system which can be used for the purposes of prediction and control. It is a misconception when a 'general complexity' approach is taken and systems thinkers work alongside decision-makers to explore a situation of interest and use systems methodologies, on a trial-and-error basis, aware of their strengths and limitations. There are still likely to be disruptions to usual work routines, difficulties in getting people in the room at the same time and ensuring marginalised stakeholders have a voice. But the benefits, compared to the costs, should be palpable as the intervention proceeds.

CSP is designed to help make the best use of limited resources. Not everything is complex, and CSP leads decision-makers to relatively simple engineering solutions if these are appropriate. In the face of complexity, it steers those involved to concentrate their efforts in the best places and, if corners must be cut, to make sensible choices. Occasionally, when things remain stable long enough, the costs of employing experts to build complex mathematical models will be justified.

9.3.2 Problems with Systems Thinking

A WHO document warns that:

> ... it can be difficult to enter into and navigate the nebulous concept of systems thinking without guidance, and even more challenging to choose the right approach. (WHO, 2022, Preface)

A report from the CAHS & AMS asserts that:

> Barriers to the wider adoption of systems-based approaches include academic literature and terminology that can be hard to navigate, creating a perception that systems-based approaches are too difficult to apply. (CAHS & AMS, 2021)

ST can seem dense and complex, and systems thinkers are sometimes more interested in academic and theoretical matters than practical applications. They can come across as 'evangelical researchers' who alienate decision-makers by engaging them in 'painful discussions' (Haynes et al., 2020). This is exacerbated because the systems movement is made up of sub-communities, each arguing for their own favoured approach while dismissing others.

The systems community needs to simplify ST without distorting it to the extent that the benefits it can bring are lost. Two ways of achieving this are currently on the table. The first argues that there are four building blocks that underpin all of ST – 'distinctions', 'systems', 'relationships' and 'perspectives' (DSRP) (Cabrera et al., 2015; and forthcoming). This, of course, is a variant of the 'systems concepts' approach discussed in Chapter 8. To remind the reader of the distortion involved, it is enough to repeat that these concepts exclude much of the systems tradition of work, and that

> ... there are certainly common concepts used in many of the systems paradigms represented in the literature [but] as soon as we dig beneath the surface the meanings of these concepts are inevitably contested, or what is left unsaid by focusing only on a limited set of words becomes too important to ignore. (Midgley, 2006, p. 12)

The second approach is the one proposed in this book. In my view, CSP, with its five 'adequate' systemic perspectives and aligned systems methodologies, does justice to the full range of what ST has to offer, with minimum distortion, and enables an informed choice to be made of the appropriate systems approaches to use in an intervention, capitalising on their different strengths. CSP answers the call of Nguyen et al. to address the shortcomings currently obstructing the implementation of ST in public policy:

> As there are a variety of ST tools and each tool serves a different purpose, users need to deploy them with intentionality and discernment as part of best practice ... In addition, those with more experience with ST may wish to combine this approach with other systems approaches and realise the potential of such mixed methods. Combining methods may help tackle complex problems that would be difficult to address with a single tool. (Nguyen et al., 2023a, p. 16)

Further, CSP meets the demand that applied ST 'should be more explicitly theorised' (Kwamie et al., 2021) by relating the systems methodologies to 'world hypotheses' in philosophy and to social theory.

CSP can contribute to overcoming other issues frequently associated with the application of ST. John Mingers and John Brocklesby (1997) questioned whether ST demands too much cognitive flexibility from humans when it requires interventions using multiple methodologies. Whatever the difficulties involved, a way forward must be found. As Kay and King (2020) argued, to deal with 'radical uncertainty', decision-makers need to be equipped with a range of 'narratives' drawing on different schools of thought. They can then select one that provides insight into their context while keeping others alive in their minds. This demands they hold different narratives in their heads at the same time. Consciously echoing F. Scott Fitzgerald, they submit that

> ... the mark of the first-rate decision-maker confronted by radical uncertainty is to organise action around a reference narrative while still being open to both the possibility that the narrative is false and that alternative narratives might be relevant. (Kay and King, 2020, loc. 4280)

That is exactly what CSP helps to facilitate. There are other helpful suggestions. Midgley (2000) advances a 'model of learning' that, over time, leads systems practitioners to develop their appreciation of different methodologies and methods. The use of multidisciplinary teams, and/or groups consisting of different psychological and personality types, is frequently recommended. Sagasti and Mitroff (1973), for example, considered two kinds of 'conceptualizers': the *diverger* and the *converger*. They concluded that:

> The skills and traits of the diverger type would be most valuable in the conceptualization phase. At this stage, it becomes important to develop several alternative conceptualizations of a problem. (Sagasti and Mitroff, 1973, p. 703)

Convergers are seen as more valuable in the 'modeling and model solving phases'.

The CSP approach sees systems thinkers as enablers, contributing to decisions, rather than as experts armed with a knowledge of general systems laws and, therefore, capable of making decisions. ST is not a panacea, and systems researchers need to be patient when their recommendations are not immediately adopted and implemented. They should acknowledge 'competing policy priorities, decision-making styles and political constraints' (Lin et al., 2021). They should recognise the complexities of the

> ... larger universe in which the policy-maker operates and the externalities that must be factored into the difficult exercise of crafting policy. (WHO, 2012, p. 13)

The ideal scenario for successful praxis is an early engagement of systems thinkers with decision-makers and a partnership throughout the project. Haynes et al. (2020) have shown how a successful collaboration was forged within the Australian Prevention Partnership Centre that enabled ST to be put into policy action. There had to be close engagement between researchers and policymakers during the research process, a feeling generated that knowledge was being co-produced and an 'emphasis on applied mutual learning targeting priorities in policy-makers' own jurisdictions'. CSP's issue-focused, action-research orientation encourages close collaboration between researchers and decision-makers, with both taking responsibility for the outcomes.

ST must be able to demonstrate its value to decision-makers. This argument has been rehearsed many times in health systems research (HSR). Margaret Chan, former Director General of the WHO, wrote:

> In the absence of sound evidence, we will have no good way to compel efficient investments in health systems. (Chan, quoted in WHO, 2012, p. 3)

Others who have endorsed this view (El-Jardali et al., 2014; CAHS and AMS, 2021; Kwamie et al., 2021) have insisted on the need for a strong evidence base showing how ST is done in practice, the benefits it brings and its cost. Lamont (2021) called for 'compelling stories which embrace systems thinking without losing clarity and impact'.

One issue that needs resolving is the type of evidence that is appropriate. The traditional 'scientific' approach operates well when cause and effect are easy to identify. It is impossible to apply in the face of multiple causality, non-linearity, dynamic change and a pluralism of perspectives. It has been argued that HSR

> ... must not judge itself by the standards that biomedical research, clinical research or traditional public health research have set. It has to develop its own standards for evaluating 'evidence', assembling 'knowledge' and translating it into recommendations that decision-makers and researchers in the health system can comprehend, trust and implement. (WHO, 2012, p. 15).

And regarding public policy:

> Research and implementation must ... consider a multi-dimensional evaluation of the quality and efficacy of ST implementation. This requires the development of a guiding evaluation framework that captures different perspectives of a successful ST application ... . (Nguyen et al., 2023a, p. 16)

ST must develop an approach to evaluation appropriate to the complex situations of concern which it seeks to improve. It should work with 'multiple measures of change and impact' which are 'meaningful to different stakeholders' (Lamont, 2021). I like to think that the *Check* phase of CSP, described in Chapter 8, points the way forward.

9.3.3 Contextual Factors

There are significant cultural, organisational, political and educational barriers to overcome in making progress towards a world in which ST achieves proper recognition.

A huge cultural obstacle is the mechanistic worldview which, as we saw in Chapter 1, came to dominate Western philosophy and science in the seventeenth century. Alternative ways of thinking and relating to the world – other systemic perspectives – were marginalised. The drive for prediction and control which was set in train seems, if anything, to be accelerating. As Arran Gare (2023) says, we have become willing slaves of our own technologies, even as they lead us 'on a trajectory to global ecological destruction'. Things have become so bad, he suggests, that we should ask ourselves if 'humans as a species are so fundamentally flawed that terrestrial life would be better off without them'. Gare sees hope. Humans can reflect on the thinking that has brought about the current situation and are capable of transforming the dynamic to which it gave rise. If we can reconnect with the ambitions of the Radical Enlightenment, then a different future can be envisaged.

The dominant strands of ST are a product of the West. The belief that they can be directly translated into action in other cultures is a continuation of colonialism. It is hardly surprising that it is met by incomprehension and resistance. As Abraar Karan said:

> If you are from a high-income country working in a low-income setting, and you don't think and rethink about this topic [the colonial mindset] often, there is a good chance you are contributing to the problem. (Karan, 2019)

Yunkaporta reflected on the ways professionals educated in the Western tradition seek to engage with Indigenous communities. They *direct* them on what to do based on their expert knowledge; *reflect* on why this doesn't work; *connect* with the people to see why; and finally learn to *respect* the community they have ruined: 'They cry as they say farewell and return to the city, calling, "Thank you, I have learnt so much from you!"' (Mumma Doris, quoted in Yunkaporta, 2019). Systems thinkers should put *respect* first when they approach those they seek to advise. CSP is a product of the West and must try hard not to be part of the problem. It suggests (see Chapter 4) that pragmatism provides a philosophical space where Western, Eastern, Indigenous and other systems traditions can meet on an equal footing and develop a productive dialogue.

The great majority of organisations remain in thrall to the dictates of 'scientific management'. They are hierarchical, operate along command-and-control lines, are divided into functional departments and exhibit bureaucratic administrative structures. These characteristics make them antithetical to ST, as Network Rail found out:

> However, the interviews with rail leaders suggest that such an integrative approach [as ST] is difficult in practice because of the hierarchical nature of the organisation(s) involved and the tendency to focus on technical 'silos' rather than across disciplines, functions, and layers. (Nolan-McSweeney et al., 2023, p. 12)

Network Rail, through a 'Systems Thinking Team Partnership', is seeking to use ST to transform its operations and to extend the approach throughout the rail industry. However, in a safety-critical industry, with local subcultures resistant to change, it is proving difficult to shift to a decentralised structure encouraging of local autonomy, get cooperation across traditional boundaries and beat bureaucracy. It is never easy anywhere, given the prevalence of traditional management thinking. Woodhill and Millican, in a document prepared for UKaid, outlined some useful steps that can be taken by senior management:

- Regularly acknowledge systems thinking and practice as important
- Develop practical mechanisms for integrating ST into organisational functions
- Develop and value a culture of organisational learning
- Invest in intra-disciplinary and multi-stakeholder processes
- Make the ability to lead systems approaches to change an explicit part of job descriptions and performance appraisal
- Invest in the capacity of staff to think and act systemically
- Support the development of systems thinking and practice capabilities in partner organisations

(Woodhill and Millican, 2023)

In the policy arena, it is particularly tricky to sustain support for ST given competing political interests and constantly changing priorities. Nguyen et al. (2023a) called for political endorsement and the establishment of a central entity at government level to promote implementation of ST in public policy in the UK. Kwamie et al. (2021) argued for greater government investment and institutional incentives 'to augment the capacities and practice of systems thinking in policymaking' in public health. The need for political endorsement for ST is even more necessary because it is 'outside the mainstream' (CAHS and AMS, 2021) and disadvantaged by established funding mechanisms. In health research, for example, governments pay much greater attention to what they see as fundamental science than to Health Policy and Systems Research (HPSR). As Lin et al. (2021) lamented, 'randomized controlled trials are touted as the gold standard ... there is a strong lobby ... for everything to be measured through causal models using statistics'. This is the case even though it is well recognised that there must be strong health systems in place to deliver the benefits that clinical and biomedical research can provide, for example, vaccines (Bennett et al., 2018). An additional element is that donors and bodies such as the World Bank (Van Olmen et al., 2012) prefer interventions where results come quickly and can be measured. They are inclined to support 'specific time-bound development assistance projects, which may help build some capacity for HPSR but are not sustainable investments' (Lin et al., 2021). With HPSR, the capacity to look beyond apparent 'quick fixes' is important. Systemic transformation can be a long-term endeavour. Rutter et al. summarise the challenge well:

> Instead of asking whether an intervention works to fix a problem, researchers should aim to identify if and how it contributes to reshaping a system in favourable ways ... Achievement of this kind of shift ... will require substantial changes to the ways in which research is funded and conducted, academic work is valued, and policy is formulated. Unless the wider scientific community engages appropriately and meaningfully with these complex realities, many major public health challenges, from emerging infections to non-communicable diseases, will remain intractable. Oversimplification of these problems to fit inappropriate models of research and practice dooms such research and policy implementation to repeated failure. (Rutter et al., 2017)

The literature on how knowledge and implementation of ST can be spread is replete with demands for more education and training in the field to build capacity. Universities should be central to meeting these demands, but they remain wedded to traditional disciplines. There are exceptions. The University of St. Gallen, in Switzerland, has been an influential provider of 'cybersystemic education' for over 50 years (Schwaninger, 2022). SE is strong in many universities. SD research and teaching at the Massachusetts Institute of Technology is world-renowned. However, contemplating the broad-based training necessary to produce 'systems architects' capable of addressing today's 'wicked problems', Geoff Mulgan is not wrong when he concluded that

> ... work in universities is organised in its own silos which means that even the language used in this paper means very different things, typically, to engineers, policy analysts and computer scientists. As a result there is no obvious centre in any university that is yet able to do the kind of systems analysis and design proposed here. (Mulgan, 2023, p. 25)

Universities have little incentive for engaging in transdisciplinary research relevant to addressing 'wicked problems' of real-world concern. As Madden (2023) noted, teaching ST requires cross-faculty, multidisciplinary collaboration, and faculties rarely collaborate. Paths to academic promotion and funding mechanisms support the status quo. Attempts to confound these barriers in the past have failed. Nelson states, of the demise of the Berkeley Bubble:

> System thinking often gave rise to animus in established disciplines and traditional professions. Academic pressure increased to reinforce traditional silos of knowledge ... there were few places – valences – for the heirs of the Berkeley Bubble in traditional academic, business, or governmental programs. There were few career-friendly environments or spaces for systemic polymaths .... (Nelson, 2022, p. 9)

One systemic polymath, Russ Ackoff, did succeed in founding a programme in Social Systems Sciences at The Wharton School, University of Pennsylvania, in 1980. As Rita McGrath, the last PhD student ever to graduate from it, writes:

> His program was a bit of an anomaly, even at the time. Wildly popular with Wharton's MBA students, it had an uneasy relationship with the more conventional academic activities of the school. In the Center's heyday, "Triple S" students did action research with companies, while their peers did statistical analysis of large data sets. His students were interested in ideas that cut across intellectual boundaries. They were pragmatic; some observers thought that this left them without sufficient academic rigor. Eventually, because of this uneasy fit, Russ left the university ... (McGrath, 2009, pp. 1–2)

In the UK, the kind of ST presented in this book has failed to establish itself in the most prestigious universities and barely hangs on in a few isolated outposts. Elsewhere, a few brave experiments are taking place, for example, at The University of Maine, in the US (Hart and Silka, 2021); La Universidad de Ibagué, Colombia, led by its rector, Alfonso Reyes (López-Garay and López, 2023); and The Australian National University (ANU), which

> ... is introducing a universal undergraduate requirement that responds to decades long calls for universities to take seriously the development of expertise in the transdisciplinary problem solving required to address the major challenges facing society. (Bammer et al., 2023, Abstract)

To enable ST to realise its potential, many more dedicated systems programmes are needed. Students enrolled on courses related to medicine, public health, engineering, etc., should be exposed to ST as part of the core curriculum. Government pressure and support will be necessary to make these things happen. Significant ST experience does exist in consultancies and non-governmental organisations, but this can only be accessed, if at all, through the 'grey literature' (CAHS and AMS, 2021). Communities of practice should be established which bring together academic and non-academic systems thinkers and practitioners. It is encouraging that a Systems Thinking Working Group (STWG) has been established between the Government Office for Science (GO-Science) and the UK professional body for systems thinkers, Systems and Complexity in Organisation (SCiO), to further promote the use of ST in the UK Government.

9.4 Critical Systems Leadership

Making the best use of what ST has to offer and overcoming the barriers that prevent it from realising its potential will require *systems leadership*. Systems leadership is essential in the face of the most complex, multidimensional challenges:

> The 2030 Sustainable Development Agenda includes 17 interrelated Sustainable Development Goals (SDGs), each representing complex systems – such as climate, food, health, cities – with myriad stakeholders. Achieving progress on this agenda requires a departure from traditional top-down, hierarchical and linear approaches to implementing change. Instead, it requires innovative and adaptive approaches that engage broad networks of diverse stakeholders to advance progress toward a shared vision for systemic change. This approach is called Systems Leadership. (Dreier et al., 2019, p. 4)

A burgeoning literature has appeared in recent years seeking to describe exactly what systems leadership is, for example, Ghate et al. (2013); NHS Leadership Academy (2017); Senge et al. (2015); Dreier et al. (2019); Rosenhead et al. (2019); Begg (2020); Bigland et al. (2020); Bolden (2020); Hobbs and Midgley (2020); and O'Donnell (2023). These accounts have much in common. As characterised by Ghates et al., systems leadership is seen as possessing two key attributes:

> Firstly, that it is a **collective form of leadership** ... the concerted effort of many people working together at different places in the system and at different levels, rather than of single leaders acting unilaterally. Secondly, systems leadership crosses boundaries, both physical and virtual, existing simultaneously in multiple dimensions. It therefore extends individual

leaders well beyond the usual limits of their formal responsibilities and authority. (Ghate et al., 2013, p. 5; emphasis in the original)

The literature also recognises that systems leadership requires an understanding of 'how systems work'. Here, however, it is weak, failing to take advantage of what is available in the wider ST tradition.

Critical Systems Leadership (CSL) seeks to bring together the attributes of systems leadership as set out in the current literature, with the range of ST perspectives about 'how systems work' and the related systems methodologies offering guidance on how to improve them. It seeks to suggest how leaders, equipped with an understanding of CST and CSP, and acting in situations where there is a relatively favourable alignment of contextual factors, can best secure the implementation of desirable changes to a system of interest. It links three essential components of systems leadership: appropriate attributes, appropriate mindset and appropriate methodological competence.

9.4.1 Attributes of Critical Systems Leadership

Looking at the literature, it is possible to discern a set of 'attributes' required to effect systems leadership. The seven attributes noted here have been distilled from the systems leadership literature referenced previously (strong in this respect) and two UK Government publications (Institute for Apprenticeships, 2022; BEIS, 2023). They express a requirement for:

9.4.1.1 Collective Leadership and Collaboration

Collective leadership rather than 'heroic leadership' by a single individual or agency is necessary because wicked problems cross boundaries and involve many stakeholders. Systems leaders question the 'command and control' mentality and see themselves as nurturing and enabling the leadership capabilities of others (the essence of the Lao Tzu quote that heads this chapter). Systems leadership can emerge from many places. Systems leaders pursue collaborative rather than hierarchical decision-making when the circumstances call for it. Patience, resilience and the ability to remain calm under pressure are essential.

9.4.1.2 Communication of a Vision and Open Dialogue

Systems leaders should co-develop and communicate a positive vision of a desirable future that engages their fellow stakeholders. Open dialogue is essential to build trust and ensure a shared vision and values. Maintaining momentum for systemic change demands a sustained effort that involves stakeholders in meaningful conversation, reflection and learning. Softer skills are to the fore – advocacy, shaping, influencing, enabling, consensus building and helping others live with uncertainty.

9.4.1.3 Co-creation

Making systems change is seen as a collective enterprise. Stakeholder identification and engagement is essential (Gregory et al., 2020). Systems leaders are tasked with assembling and gaining commitment to change from a diverse array of stakeholders ranging across traditional organisational boundaries. They galvanise a coalition of willing stakeholders by promoting shared values and empowering, rather than directing, them to co-create a desirable future.

9.4.1.4 Attention to Managing the Collaboration

Systems leaders need to ensure well-managed multi-stakeholder governance and coordination arrangements are in place to effectively harness the contributions of diverse stakeholders with distributed tasks and responsibilities. These must be flexible because systems leaders must ensure a balance between the direction and cohesion necessary to get things done and the decentralisation that is essential to respond to localised circumstances. Disagreements are inevitable and can be a source of constructive challenge, but they should not be allowed to descend into open conflict (Bigland et al., 2020).

9.4.1.5 An Open Approach to Learning

Systems leaders are open minded and question their own assumptions. They ask relevant questions rather than provide ready-made solutions. They are good at listening, encourage challenge and seek partners they can learn from. They entertain alternatives and balance the evidence. Systems leaders can cope with complexity and uncertainty and embrace 'strategies that are emergent, adaptive and flexible, because complex systems are always changing' (Dreier et al., 2019). They recognise that continuing to develop themselves is a crucial element in leading systemic change.

9.4.1.6 An Ethical Orientation

The values most closely associated with systems leaders are honesty, integrity, transparency, humility, authenticity, compassion, understanding and self-awareness. Systems leaders are committed to the public good rather than their own objectives. They are willing to share power, resources and the credit for any success. They accept a moral responsibility to ensure equity and seek to encourage excluded groups to become involved in and contribute to decision-making.

9.4.1.7 Promotion of Appropriate Evaluation

Systems leaders should ensure that positive progress is maintained towards shared goals by monitoring and evaluating progress in a manner that takes complexity and continuous change into account and recognises that improvement is a long-term endeavour.

9.4.2 Mindset for Critical Systems Leadership

The systems leadership literature suggests that a shift in mindset is required to recognise the importance of and act in accordance with the attributes mentioned. It is, however, vague about the nature of the necessary systems mindset. This is described, variously, as 'seeing the larger system' (Senge et al., 2015), understanding 'how the system works' (Dreier et al., 2019) or viewing organisations as 'composed of interrelated parts' that must be 'joined up' into 'a greater whole' (Hobbs and Midgley, 2020). Cultivating this systems mindset is seen to be about appreciating a particular set of systems concepts or employing a more systemic 'lens'. From a CSP perspective, neither option is satisfactory. The usual systems concepts recommended – interrelationships, perspectives and boundaries (O'Donnell, 2023) – fail to do justice to the richness of ST and, because they can mean such different things, will likely be interpreted according to an existing worldview rather than push leaders to adopt a radically different one. The usual 'lens' offered to move decision-makers beyond mechanistic thinking is the interrelationships perspective, which is seen as activated through the tools of SD (Dreier et al., 2019). Another often-proffered lens is the 'living systems' as favoured, for example, by Bolden (2020). Both are useful but also limited in what they can reveal.

As detailed in Chapter 5, CSP employs five 'adequate' systemic perspectives to explore situations of interest. These five are 'experiential gestalts' with a long historical provenance. Each sheds light on some things and hides others. They act as critics of one another. The CSL mindset required, in a VUCA context, consists of being able to see the world through the mechanical, interrelationships, organismic, purposeful and societal/environmental perspectives. This demands considerable cognitive flexibility. It is a challenge but one that can be clearly articulated and to which systems leaders can aspire.

9.4.3 Methodological Competence for Critical Systems Leadership

As Hobbs and Midgley noted,

> ... the true power of systems thinking comes from exploring the unique context at hand and designing a bespoke programme that draws on the best of many approaches. (Hobbs and Midgley, 2020, p. 1)

The use of the five systemic perspectives opens the door to the use of the full range of systems methodologies. The five types of methodology described in Chapter 6 can translate the five constituent elements of the systems mindset into action to bring about improvement in a situation of interest. With CSL, a flexible systems mindset (based on the five perspectives) and the use of the related systems methodologies reinforce one another. Being able to see the world through each perspective provides an appreciation of what its related methodology or methodologies are seeking to achieve and how they should be properly used. It eliminates, for example, slipping into using the VSM according to the logic of the mechanical systemic perspective. The use of a methodology buttresses the practitioner's understanding of the value of its underpinning systemic perspective.

CSL requires that the various systems methodologies, models and methods be used in an informed manner according to context. It sees the type of leadership necessary as primarily determined by the choice of methodology or methodologies. There is, therefore, no one correct leadership approach. The appropriate approach to use is always situational. Further, any situation of interest is likely to contain some problems that are easy to deal with, some issues that are complicated, and some 'messes' that are complex. It will also be constantly changing. Different leadership approaches will be called upon in the same project and will need adjusting during an intervention. In these respects, CSL is at one with the recommendations on leadership flowing from the *Cynefin* framework (Snowden and Boone, 2007). The appropriate form of leadership should reflect the context in which the leader is embedded, its multidimensional nature and its dynamism. The big difference between *Cynefin* and CSL is that the former seeks to use complexity science to provide an ontological basis for decision-making while CSL champions a pragmatic, epistemological approach.

CSL does not require leaders to possess the knowledge and ability to use all the systems methodologies. Expertise can be called upon as necessary. What is needed is an awareness of the existence of the different types of methodology and what they are capable of. This is easily gained through the understanding provided by CSP. CSL can then provide leaders with the capability to deliver on the four promises Bolden (2020) associated with systems leadership – effectiveness, efficiency, engagement and equity. CSL does ask systems practitioners to be humbler, to accept that their favoured approach does not have all the answers and that they should call on others if their expertise is more relevant to the situation at hand.

9.5 Conclusion

It is reasonable to ask how much formal power is needed to be a successful systems leader. Does it demand a position high up in the hierarchy of an organisation? I would argue that, though it is usually more difficult, systems leadership can be exercised without formal power and from any level in a hierarchy. Gregory and Atkins (2022) offered insight on this contention when they asked how Greta Thunberg and other young people have been able to assume such prominent roles in leading the climate change agenda. They argued that from a systemic perspective, which sees leadership as emergent, many of the situations we face lend themselves to the sort of leadership that young people can provide. They are issue-based, cross traditional institutional boundaries, require novel responses and demand the kind of collaboration and acting together easily facilitated using new technologies. In the words of Dom Jaramillo:

> We decided we had to do something because we are in a climate emergency ... We are not the leaders of the future. We are the leaders of today. (Jaramillo, quoted in Gregory and Atkins, 2022, p. 182)

Tentatively, Gregory and Atkins suggested that the commitments of CST can provide useful principles of 'good' leadership for young leaders and that CSP and its associated methodologies can be of service to them 'when addressing wicked issues within their own contexts'. I hope they are right and that young leaders will take up the banner of CSL.

References

AHPSR. (2019). Website accessed 29/5/2019.

Bammer, G., Browne, C.A., Ballard, C., et al. (2023). Setting parameters for developing undergraduate expertise in transdisciplinary problem solving at a university-wide scale: a case study. *Humanities & Social Sciences Communications.* https://doi.org/10.1057/s41599-023-01709-8.

Begg, H. (2020). *Systems Leadership Rapid Review.* National Leadership Centre.

BEIS. (2023). *Systems Leadership Guide: How to Be a Systems Leader.* BEIS.

Bennett, S., Frenk, J. and Mills, A. (2018). The evolution of the field of health policy and systems research and outstanding challenges. *Health Research Policy and Systems* 16: 43. https://doi.org/10.1186/s12961-018-0317-x.

Bigland, C., Evans, D., Bolden, R. and Rae, M. (2020). Systems leadership in practice: thematic insights from three public health case studies. *BMC Public Health* 20: 1735. https://doi.org/10.1186/s12889-020-09641-1.

Bolden, R. (2020). *Systems Leadership: Pitfalls and Possibilities.* National Leadership Centre.

Cabrera, D., Cabrera, L. and Powers, E. (2015). A unifying theory of systems thinking with psychosocial applications. *Systems Research and Behavioral Science* 32: 534–545.

Cabrera, D., Cabrera, L. and Midgley, G. (forthcoming). The four waves of systems thinking. In: *Routledge Handbook of Systems Thinking* (eds D. Cabrera, L. Cabrera, and G. Midgley). Routledge.

CAHS & AMS. (2021). *Systems-based Approaches in Public Health: Where Next?* Canadian Academy of Public Health and The Academy of Medical Sciences.

Chowdhury, R. (2019). *Systems Thinking for Management Consultants: Introducing Holistic Flexibility*. Springer.

DEFRA. (2022). *Integrating a Systems Approach into DEFRA*. DEFRA.

Deloitte. (2023). *Architecting Giga Projects*. Deloitte, February.

Dreier, L., Nabarro, D. and Nelson, J. (2019). *Systems Leadership for Sustainable Development: Strategies for Achieving Systemic Change*. Harvard Kennedy School.

El-Jardali, F., Adam, T., Ataya, N., Jamal, D. and Jaafar, M. (2014). Constraints to applying systems thinking concepts in health systems: a regional perspective from surveying stakeholders in Eastern Mediterranean countries. *International Journal of Health Policy and Management* 3: 399–407.

Gare, A. (2023). Was Günter Grass's rat right? Should terrestrial life welcome the end of humans? *Borderless Philosophy* 6: 32–76.

Ghate, D., Lewis, J. and Welbourne, D. (2013). Systems Leadership: Exceptional Leadership for Exceptional Times. Synthesis Paper.

GO-Science. (2022a). *The Civil Servant's Systems Thinking Journey*. GO-Science.

GO-Science. (2022b). *An Introductory Systems Thinking Toolkit for Civil Servants*. GO-Science.

GO-Science. (2022c). *Systems Thinking Case Study Bank*. GO-Science.

Gregory, A.J. and Atkins, J.P. (2022). Green shoots: emergent systemic leadership and critical systems practice. In: *Rethinking Leadership for a Green World* (ed. A. Taylor), pp. 176–189. Routledge.

Gregory, A.J., Atkins, J.P., Midgley, G., et al. (2020). Stakeholder identification and engagement in problem structuring interventions. *European Journal of Operational Research* 283: 321–340.

Hart, D.D. and Silka, L. (2021). What's required for universities to address complex societal challenges? *Integration and Implementation Insights*, 11 May.

Haynes, A., Garvey, K., Davidson, S. and Milat, A. (2020). What can policy-makers get out of systems thinking?: policy partner's experiences of a systems-focused research collaboration in preventative health. *International Journal of Health Policy Management* 9: 65–76.

Hobbs, C. (2019). *Systemic Leadership for Local Governance*. Palgrave MacMillan.

Hobbs, C. and Midgley, G. (2020). *How Systems Thinking Enhances Systems Leadership*. National Leadership Centre.

ICCPM. (2012). *Complex Project Manager Competency Standards, Version 4.1*. ICCPM.

ICCPM. (2020). *Harnessing Emergence in Complex Projects*. ICCPM.

ICCPM. (2023). *Complex Project Leadership Competency Standards*. ICCPM.

ICE. (2020). *A Systems Approach to Infrastructure Delivery*. ICE Knowledge.

ICE. (2022). *A Systems Approach to Infrastructure Delivery – Putting the Principles into Practice*. ICE Knowledge.

IChemE. (2021). Make systems thinking education mandatory. IChemE, 12 March.

Institute for Apprenticeships. (2022). The Systemic Skillset. Systems Thinking Practitioner.

Jackson, M.C. and Sambo, L.G. (2020). Health systems research and critical systems thinking: the case for partnership. *Systems Research and Behavioral Science* 37: 3–22.

Jordan, C. and Wilkinson, M. (2017). Holistic Complex System Intervention Evaluation – Understanding the Nature of Defence Capability. Niteworks White Paper.

Karan, A. (2019). Opinion: it's time to end the colonial mindset in global health. *Goats and Soda*, 30 December.

Kay, J. and King, M. (2020). *Radical Uncertainty: Decision-Making for an Unknowable Future*. The Bridge Street Press, Kindle edition.

Kwamie, A., Ha, S. and Ghaffar, A. (2021). Applied systems thinking: unlocking theory, evidence and practice for health policy and systems research. *Health Policy and Planning*. https://doi.org/10.1093/heapol/czab062.

Lamont, T. (2021). But does it work? Evidence, policy-making and systems thinking. *International Journal of Health Policy Management* 10: 287–289.

Lao Tzu. (c400 BCE). *Tao Te Ching*. Penguin.

Lin, V., Ghaffar, A., Khor, S.K. and Reddy, K.S. (2021). Strengthening health systems globally: a lingering challenge of funding. *Public Health Research and Practice*. https://doi.org/10.17061/phrp3142115.

López-Garay, H. and López, J.J.G. (2023). The current crisis of higher education and the *necessary university project* (NUP): a case study in evolutionary systems design. *Cybernetics and Systems*. https://doi.org/10.1080/01969722.2023.2175151.

Madden, B.J. (2020). *Value Creation Principles: The Pragmatic Theory of the Firm Begins with Purpose and Ends with Sustainable Capitalism*. Wiley.

Madden, B.J. (2023). Understanding the benefits of capitalism through the lens of a new theory of the firm. *Capitalism and Society* 17: Article 2. https://ssrn.com/abstract=4489645.

McGrath, R. (2009). Remembering Russ Ackoff. *Harvard Business Review*. November 17.

Midgley, G. (2000). *Systemic Intervention: Philosophy, Methodology, and Practice*. Kluwer/Plenum.

Midgley, G. (2006). Systems thinking for evaluation. In: *Systems Concepts in Evaluation: An Expert Anthology* (eds B. Williams and I. Imam), pp. 11–34. American Evaluation Association.

Mingers, J. and Brocklesby, J. (1997). Multimethodology: towards a framework for mixing methodologies. *Omega* 25: 489–509.

Montgomery, J. and Van Clieaf, M. (2023). *Net Zero Business Models: Winning in the Global Net Zero Economy*. Wiley, Kindle edition.

Mulgan, G. (2023). Thinking Systems: How the Systems we Depend on Can Be Helped to Think and to Serve us Better. STEaPP Working Paper Series 1. Department of Science, Technology, Engineering and Public Policy. UCL.

Nelson, H. G. (2022). Systemic design as born from the Berkeley Bubble. *Contexts – The Journal of Systemic Design* 1. https://doi.org/10.58279/v1001.

Nguyen, L-K-N., Kumar, C., Jiang, B. and Zimmermann, N. (2023a). Implementation of systems thinking in public policy: a systematic review. *Systems*. https://doi.org./10.3390/systems11020064.

Nguyen, L-K-N., Kumar, C., Bisaro, S.M., et al. (2023b). Civil servant and expert perspectives on drivers, values, challenges and successes in adopting systems thinking in policy-making. *Systems*. https://doi.org/10.3390/systems11040193.

NHS Leadership Academy. (2017). *Developing Systems Leadership: Interventions, Options and Opportunities*. NHS Leadership Academy.

Nolan-McSweeney, M., Ryan, B. and Cobb, S. (2023). Interviews with rail industry leaders about systems thinking in the management of organisational change and risk management. *Safety Science*. https://doi.org/10.1016/j.ssci.2023.106168.

O'Donnell, J. (2023). *Developing a Systems Thinking Lens for Collective Leadership*. Collective leadership for Scotland.

OECD. (2020). *Systemic Thinking for Policy Making*. OECD *iLibrary*.

Palmer, E. and Cavicchi, B. (2023). Systems based Methods for Research & Innovation Policy. R&I Working Paper 2023/05. European Union.

Ramaswamy, S., Reeves, M. and Job, A. (2023). Thriving in an Interconnected World: The Systems of Business. BCG Henderson Institute, 24 August.

Rosenhead, J., Franco, L.A., Grint, K. and Friedland, B. (2019). Complexity theory and leadership practice: a review, a critique, and some recommendations. *The Leadership Quarterly*. https://doi.org/10.1016/j.leaqua.2019.07.002.

Rutter, H., Savona, N., Gionti, K., et al. (2017). The need for a complex systems model of evidence for public health. *The Lancet* 390 (10112): 2602–2604. https://doi.org/10.1016/S0140-6736(17)31267-9.

Sagasti, F.R and Mitroff, I.I. (1973). Operations research from the viewpoint of general systems theory. *Omega* 1: 695–709.

Schwaninger, M. (2022). Cybersystemic education: enabling society for a better future. www.emeraldinsight.com/0368-492X.htm.

Senge, P., Hamilton, H. and Kania, J. (2015). The Dawn of System Leadership. Stanford Social Innovation Review.

Snowden, D.J. and Boone, M.E. (2007). A leader's framework for decision making. *Harvard Business Review* November: 69–76.

UNDP. (2021). *UNDP Strategic Plan, 2022–2025*. United Nations.

Vallance, P. (2022). *In: An Introductory Systems Thinking Toolkit for Civil Servants*. GO-Science.

Van Olmen, J., Marchal, B., Hill, P.S., et al. (2012). Health systems frameworks in their political context: framing divergent agendas. *BMC Public Health*. https://doi.org/10.1186/1471-2458-12-774.

WHO. (2012). *Changing Mindsets: Strategy on Health Policy and Systems Research*. WHO.

WHO. (2022). *Systems Thinking for Noncommunicable Disease Prevention Policy: Guidance to Bring Systems Approaches into Practice*. WHO European Region.

Wilden, D., Hopkins, J. and Sadler, I. (2023). Towards the coalescence of systems thinking and supply chain management – a conceptual framework utilizing critical systems practice for intervention. Unpublished paper.

Woodhill, J. and Millican, J. (2023). *Learning Resource: Systems Thinking and Practice*. UKaid.

Yunkaporta, T. (2019). *Sandtalk*. Text Publishing.

Conclusion

The hour is very late, and the choice of good and evil knocks at our door.

(Wiener, 1954)

Señor, señor
Can you tell me where we're headin'?
Lincoln County Road or Armageddon?
Seems like I been down this way before
Is there any truth in that, señor?

(Dylan, 1978)

The tale is told. It is a story of a world of increasing multidimensional complexity. The wicked problems this throws up at the global level are mind-boggling. For example, an Oxfam report reveals that:

> The richest 1% of humanity is responsible for more carbon emissions than the poorest 66%, with dire consequences for vulnerable communities and global efforts to tackle the climate emergency .... (Watts, 2023)

How do you start to untangle that? But it is not just at the global level. As we have seen, leaders of institutions and organisations of all types, and at all levels, are having to find ways of coping (or not) with multidimensional complexity.

Some believe that Artificial Intelligence (AI) will help us find a way through. Charles Foster got it right when he was asked about this possibility and replied: 'I find it difficult to understand how the primary product of the problem can be the solution' (Foster, 2022). A change in our way of thinking is necessary before we can be sure AI becomes a useful servant rather than a dangerous master.

The change in thinking necessary is to complement mechanism with Systems Thinking (ST). Mechanism, with the traditional scientific method as its most

Critical Systems Thinking: A Practitioner's Guide, First Edition. Michael C. Jackson.
© 2024 John Wiley & Sons, Inc. Published 2024 by John Wiley & Sons, Inc.

powerful weapon, has brought significant benefits but has invaded domains of thought and practice where it has no place. It is now the source of many of the wicked problems that endanger humanity. Critical Systems Thinking (CST), by opening minds to other ways of seeing and acting, can help us throw off the 'mind-forg'd manacles' identified by Blake (1794) more than two centuries ago. Further, Critical Systems Practice (CSP), guiding the informed use of systems methodologies, puts in the hands of decision-makers the means of shaping a more 'balanced' future. It just requires courageous systems leadership with the right attributes, flexibility of mindset and an appreciation of what the different methodologies have to offer.

As I have insisted throughout the book, ST is not a panacea and cannot supply all the answers. Some will be disappointed with this. ST can, however, supply policymakers and decision-makers with the enhanced imaginative capability and some powerful methodologies that can help them do better when confronted with the many significant issues where traditional science has little to offer. That is contribution enough. I have tried to bring together, order, summarise and make accessible what the broad ST tradition of work has been able to produce that can help in this respect.

It is now over to you, dear reader. ST has been good to me ever since I began to worry what interconnections were being missed when studying 'regional geography' at school. It led me to Marxism as an initial schema for organising my understanding of what was going on in society. It has provided me with a research career and helped me to whatever success I have enjoyed at work or in consultancy. But this is my last book. Writing about ST does not make you a systems person. In fact, while showing you what you should become, it can detract from you getting there. This passage from Charles Darwin is apposite:

> My mind seems to have become a kind of machine for grinding general laws out of large collections of fact, but why this should have caused the atrophy of that part of the brain ... on which the higher tastes depend, I cannot conceive ... The loss of these tastes is a loss of happiness, and may possibly be injurious to the intellect, and more probably to the moral character, by enfeebling the emotional part of our nature. (Darwin, quoted in Schumacher, 1973, p. 77)

The effort involved in writing a book like this is huge. It prevents you from developing your mind in other ways, from cultivating those relationships that make you human, and from communing with the natural world and feeling at home in the universe. On those things I shall now focus my attention. If I succeed, you won't hear from me again.

On the other hand, if I fail, then there is always the task of working out what ST can learn from Spinoza, the philosopher who got most things right, and how ST can further enhance his thinking ...

References

Blake, W. (1794). London. In: *The Complete Poems* (ed. A. Ostriker, 1977). Penguin Classics.

Dylan, B. (1978). Señor (Tales of Yankee Power). Columbia Records.

Foster, C. (2022). Helen Bond in conversation with Charles Foster. YouTube.

Schumacher, E.F. (1973). *Small is Beautiful: A Study of Economics as if People Mattered*. Blond & Briggs Ltd.

Watts, J. (2023). Richest 1% account for more carbon emissions than poorest 66%, report says. *Guardian*, 20 November.

Wiener, N. (1954). *The Human Use of Human Beings: Cybernetics and Society*. Eyre and Spottiswoode.

Index